The Miracle Ship

The Extraordinary Story of a Modern-Day Disciple

by

Brian O'Hare

From Conversations with John Gillespie

Edited by
Veronica Castle

Published by
Crimson Cloak Publishing

ISBN 13: 978-1-68160-025-3
ISBN 10: 1-68160-025-0

"We know that you are a teacher who comes from God; for no one could perform the signs you do unless God were with him." [John3:2]

The scriptural quotations used in this book are taken from the Christian Community Bible (Catholic Pastoral Edition) or from the Collins Liturgical Sunday and Weekday Missals.

Table of Contents

INTRODUCTION

When I first met John Gillespie, his reputation had preceded him. I was not quite sure what to expect, perhaps someone tall, imposing, wearing a black suit, someone other-worldly and ethereal. Instead, and I know he won't take it amiss when I say this, I found a very ordinary man in his early fifties, medium height and build, jeans, open-necked shirt, hair going slightly grey, little to distinguish him in a crowd. He was extremely unaffected, chatty, constantly laughing.

As I got to know him, however, I began to learn that here was a man characterised by a fierce determination, a trait not immediately discernible on early casual acquaintance. He is possessed, too, of a strong sense of vocation, so caught up in bringing Jesus and His healing to people that he can see himself as little more than a simple conduit between God and the petitioner seeking help. And it was in this utter lack of a sense of self that I found a man with a profound and abiding faith in God and an unassailable belief in Jesus' power to heal.

Yet nothing about this plain-speaking man cries out, or even whispers, that he was destined to live a most extraordinary ministry. He is an ordinary man, a farmer's son. He was born into a pious, hard-working family who lived generally frugal lives. Wealth was never a possibility for them nor, indeed, was it ever an aspiration. John has inherited and continues to live this essentially Christian ethic of working to earn what his family needs and seeking nothing more than that.

John is not a seventh son of a seventh son. He claims no mystic connections to the universe or to exotic foreign cults. As Shakespeare once said, “Such men are dangerous.” Initially he was reluctant to undertake the ministry Jesus had planned for him. John had his own plans for his life. He was eventually to experience a conversion, however, a life-changing decision to live his life as Jesus wanted him to live it, not as he wanted to live it himself. He became a man who, as Pope Benedict XVI once said about his own ordination to the priesthood, “… has been touched by the mission of Christ and was privileged to carry his presence to the people.”

There is little to find in John’s humble background that could have presaged his miraculous ability to bring healing to thousands. And yet, is that so strange? Peter Seewald, in his book on Benedict XVI, says that “…real ‘personalities’ are to be recognised, not in magnificence, but in humility.” John’s humility is utterly genuine and unaffected. He is not aware of it. It is not a state he strives for. It just is. He feels no sense of personal achievement at the strange healings that are accomplished through his hands because, as he says simply, “I don’t do anything! Jesus does it!”

During our occasional brief meetings, John would tell me amazing stories. I found them fascinating and I was delighted when he asked me to write his story. When he began to tell me the personal details of his early life, however, about the sufferings he endured for years, about his intense, argumentative, sometimes belligerent relationship with a silent, strangely unresponsive God, about the powerful faith that never allowed that relationship to wane, I began to fear that I could not do his story justice. The strength of his belief, his single-minded determination to meet, as he says, his "violent state with violent prayer," his innate conviction of Jesus' desire to heal all of His people, left me humbled. Only once before (and that's a story written elsewhere) have I encountered such determined belief, such ineffable patience in the face of extreme adversity, such hope where no hope seemed to have any right to exist.

Fortunately my fears of inadequacy do not matter. John's personal story is so astonishing, the simple facts of the extraordinary healings are so complete in themselves, that their telling requires no great literary skill. The pages that follow are testament to that.

Brian O'Hare

FOREWORD

There is the story of the young monk who went to his Abbot. He said to him, “Father Abbot, we are encouraged to die to ourselves. What does this mean?”

A brother in the monastery had recently died and the Abbot told the young monk to go and stand at his grave. He was to praise Brother Facius out loud and shout out all the good points and then come back to the Abbot.

“Well? Did Brother Facius say anything?”

“Not a word,” replied the monk.

“Then go again to the grave and call aloud all his vices and faults.”

The monk returned. “Not a word came from the grave,” he told the Abbot.

“Now, here is the message,” replied the Abbot. “From Brother Facius you will learn what dying to self means. Neither flattery nor abuse moved him for he is dead. The one who is dead to self will hear neither praise nor criticism. His self-consciousness, his personal feelings, will be lost in the service of his Master.”

I think this story sums up my experience of John Gillespie. I have only met him a few times but my spirit has always been quickened in John’s presence. As I prayed with John that day [See Prologue] I would have experienced yieldedness in him. There is a kindred spirit in a person who has been baptised in the Holy Spirit. But with John that day my own spirit was high and, behold, I met this humble man who I knew was wide open and receptive to God's gifts.

I sensed that John had discovered God's highest purpose for him and that was to be transformed into the image of Jesus as Healer and Deliverer. As soon as you yield, God begins to work not only in you but also through you. With John on that Alleluia day I was aware that the Holy Spirit was upon me. There is never a lack when the unction of the Spirit is upon you. I had a feeling of abundance in the prayer over John and his wife. I felt the Lord saying, "The harvest is already here." I looked around for an image to convey the feeling.

The image of a ship came into view in my spirit. I surrendered and ceased my own thoughts: 'Not I but Christ!' But I had to wait on the Lord as there is no good speaking unless I speak from the heart. Nothing in the world glorifies God so much as the simple rest of faith in God's Word. Then words came in torrents.

John exemplifies faith. God has a measure of power for you which cannot be exhausted and faith enables you to claim the blessings. We have a miracle-working God. John has that measure of brokenness which enables him to claim again and again this mighty power. John exhibits that holy boldness by standing on what the Word says. He knows that the Holy Spirit comes in increasing power in many ways on a continuous basis.

The miracle of John Gillespie for me is not his works which I honour and for which I give God thanks. No, the miracle for me is John's gift of faith. The great disaster in the world is unbelief. As you read this book, you will see that it was not easy for John. At times, as the author says, he was in a "mental tug of war". He was rejoicing in the hard corner like a punch-drunk boxer who could only find solace on his knees. John teaches us to get our eyes off the conditions and circumstances and glue our eyes to the person of Jesus. This book could change your life as John's life becomes a window through which we see God at work. I would like to give John a holy hug!

John's prayer for us would be that of St. Paul:

'... that Christ may dwell in your hearts through faith that you, being grounded in love, may have power to comprehend with all the saints what is the breadth and length and depth and height, and to know the love of Christ which surpasses knowledge, that you may be filled with all the fullness of God.'

Ephesians 3:17

Fr. Ronnie Mitchell SMM, [Provincial]
Southampton.

NOTICE: All spellings in this book are the UK version. We decided not to change them to the US versions because the author and the priest, as well as most, if not all, of the people in the stories are also from there.

PROLOGUE

The Prophecies [February 1998]

Father Ronnie Mitchell was tired. It had been a long week. But he allowed himself a quiet inner smile. It had also been a good week. And now he was back home in Belfast. As an 'occasional' spiritual director to the Holy Trinity Prayer Group in Belfast he liked to say Mass for them from time to time and to pray with them. He had been energised by their faith and fervour but he was now feeling the strain from the past week. He had just completed conducting his fourth retreat in succession and he was feeling the need of time for himself, for a few days of quiet prayer and reflection to recharge his spiritual batteries.

Father Ronnie, tall, slim, dark hair going grey, was a gentle, humble man, with a calm and pleasant demeanour. He was a popular choice for conducting retreats. His ministry was spreading, enkindled by the holiness of his prayer, stimulated by the clarity with which he taught and explained the scriptures, and anointed by his gift for occasional prophecies which were widely recognised as authentic. He was standing in the church hall, just a few yards from the chapel, chatting with a lady from the group. Little knots of people stood in various parts of the hall. The lady smiled as she left him and the priest inclined his head in acknowledgement. Quite a number from the seminar group had come to him for a blessing on this occasion. He looked around to see if there was anyone else. His eye caught a married couple that he knew, a somewhat stocky man in his forties and his pretty blond wife. The priest smiled a greeting and waved them over to him, intending to pray over them as he had done on a number of occasions before.

He held his hands above the couple and bowed his head to pray the blessing. As he prayed, he was suddenly conscious of a familiar inflow of the Spirit, a precursor to a prophetic vision. It was not something that happened often, but it happened often enough to make him aware that he had been given the Holy Spirit's gift of prophesy. When the gift manifested itself, it usually meant that something significant was about to be said. As always, he was deeply moved and grateful for such a moment. He looked up and stared at the man who was standing there, quiet, unassuming, unaware.

The couple earnestly returned his gaze and the priest began to speak, arms still outstretched. "The Lord is very much with you two … I see you standing at the altar on your wedding day. Jesus is standing before you, beside the priest. As you make your vows, Jesus takes a ring off His own finger and puts it in both of your hands. Jesus is taking a cloth from around His waist and wrapping it around both of your hands. He is speaking. *You are to pray constantly together and always say the Rosary. I am with you today and I will be with you always. This cloth will bind you always together, here on this earth and forever in eternity*."

The couple stood utterly still, listening intently, waiting to hear more. "I see a large party, a celebration. There is a huge birthday cake, many candles lit upon it. You are to celebrate every birthday in your family, every anniversary, and everything the Lord is doing in your lives. And you are to pray for all married couples and, when either of you need to see Jesus, you are to look into each other's eyes."

Father Ronnie's head lifted but his eyes remained closed. "I see water … a harbour. There is a large ship coming in, low in the water … very low. It is so full of cargo that it can barely stay afloat. There is a figure standing at the helm. It's Jesus. You two are standing on the dock and He is staring directly at you. He has so much love for you. There is a name on the prow of the ship. I can't read it … but it's coming closer. I sense that the ship is sinking under the weight of the Lord's love. He has so much love for His people and He is bringing gifts … so many gifts." He paused again. "I see the letters … the name of the ship. It's called The … Mir … a … The Miracle Ship. This ship is full of miracles. It is laden down with thousands upon thousands of miracles for His people. God is bringing you a miraculous healing ministry. The distribution of the miracles in the ship depends upon you. Only you can deliver these gifts. He wants you to accept this calling. There will be thousands of miracles worked through your hands and the Lord wants you to record them and write them down in a book. It will go down in history and pass from generation to generation."

He paused briefly and then said, "You will find yourself in constant battle with Satan and his demons. He will try many deceits and tricks to stop you, but you are not to worry. You will always have the power of Jesus by your side. And He will show you where the demons lurk, what evil work they are attempting to do, the havoc they are determined to wreak. You will face many trials because of them, but do not fear. Jesus will give you the power to oppose them and to scatter them in his name."

The priest turned to the woman to say, "This is a work that needs two people. You are to be with your husband as his help and support as he heals God's people."

Father Ronnie fell silent. The visions had ended. He smiled at the couple, his hands held in front of him, slightly apart now. He put a hand on the man's shoulder and said quietly, "The Lord assures you that you need never have any fear about your needs or the needs of your family. Just listen to the Lord's direction. He will always provide you with whatever you or your family needs."

Again, that strange expression on the man's face. What he had just heard was monumental and yet …The priest looked directly into the man's eyes and said, "You are not happy about this, are you?"

The man shrugged and said simply, "If it's what the Lord wants."

The priest nodded and smiled, almost amused. "I don't believe you will have any real choice. Jesus can be very persuasive."

PART ONE: JOHN

Chapter One

Grieving

The boy stood at the edge of the lake, his hands in his pockets, his eyes fixed on the ruffled surface. He absently scuffed a stone from the soft ground with the toe of his boot and kicked it into the water. He lifted his head and stared vacantly at the green, uncultivated landscape that surrounded him. His gaze traversed the fields and farms that clustered in the distance on other heights beyond the hills that girdled the lakes. The wind was strong and cold. Grey, menacing rain clouds hung low on the hills but their dark threat was less oppressive than the onus of impending responsibility that was weighing heavily on the boy's slight, sixteen-year-old shoulders.

John Gillespie may have been looking at the magnificent Donegal scenery but he was not seeing it. At least, not in this present dimension. He was seeing it in another time, when the sky was a clear blue, when the clouds were white, when the surfaces of the lakes were a shimmering, glassy green. He was looking at his father, Paddy, with his weather-beaten face, his silvery hair, his ready smile, standing in his waders a few yards into the lake. He watched his father cast his fly-line as far as he could throw it while regaling a much younger John with stories of other times. He watched the younger John who could not take his eyes from his father's face, as he listened in childish adoration to the tales.

Tears began to fill John's eyes. He brushed them away angrily and stepped away from the edge of the lake. His beloved father had been buried a few days before and John still felt the loss deeply. But he was not about to cry. He walked towards the hills, his head down again, favouring his right leg. It had started giving him pain almost at the time his father had died.

Memories continued to flood his mind. Life on the small farm where he had grown up had not been easy and Paddy, with his wife, Mary, had to work hard to provide for their five children. John's thoughts flashed briefly to Seamus, who should have been a sixth, but he had died a few weeks after he had been born. He experienced a familiar regret and wondered, as he had done so often before, what Seamus would have been like had he lived.

Paddy augmented the farm's meagre income by working also as a stone-mason and a carpenter. Given the demands of this additional work, he was not often in the home yet John had a million memories of him eating with them in the kitchen, praying with them in the evenings, playing with them on sunny afternoons, telling them stories. John remembered, too, his father's wisdom, the sage advice that he gave his son while they went on walks or fished in the lakes, advice on how to live in honesty and fairness, on helping those who were in greater need than themselves. John remembered his father's powerful faith, his constancy in prayer, and the intense honesty that interfused all of his dealings with his neighbours.

What has been laid down as foundation will last a lifetime. The foundation of faith John received at his father's side was to expand and grow far beyond anything his father could ever have imagined. In the last two years of his life, John learned much from his father that was to stay with him all his life. He could still hear his father's calm yet arresting voice as he offered to John simple but essential directives for living. "By doing ill-will to neighbours and falling-out over land and property, we only draw ill-will to our own doors … and we might well have terrible trouble getting away from it." Paddy Gillespie was very sensitive to the working of the Holy Spirit and had a great gift of insight.

But he was not always so serious, so introspective. On this day, at this moment, John was remembering his father, the musician and singer, the man who played his fiddle with such energy and verve. He replayed bitter-sweet memories of the great times he shared with his father, visiting neighbours' houses in the evenings ('céili-ing', in the local terminology), watching with pride as his father regaled the assembled neighbours with music and songs and stories. He remembered the craic (conversations and laughter), the card-games in the winter-time, and the houses where there was always a 'seannachi' to tell strange and dramatic stories. Paddy Gillespie was a man who loved company and who was equally loved, a man for whom everyone made a space when he entered a room. John looked at the sky and muttered fiercely, "I would never swap the sixteen years I had with you, Dad, for sixty years with any other father."

John shook his head and blinked some incipient tears from his eyes. He bent forward to seize a tuft of grass as leverage to pull himself over a small but steep ledge in the hillside. His right leg simply would not hold his weight properly any more. As he stood erect on top of the mound, a sharp wind tore at him but the boy was impervious to it.

From this vantage point he surveyed the landscape once again.

Glencolmcille was situated on a peninsula in south-west Donegal. It was wild, rugged, but it had its own harsh magnificence. A long valley gouged through the centre of the peninsula, while the Atlantic Ocean, often white and furious, surrounded it on three sides. He could see the family farm now on a high hillside and, in the distance, the village of Cashel … well, the locals called it a village. It was only a small cluster of houses, a couple of convenience stores, and three public-houses. Their farm was somewhat isolated on that hillside but there were other farms only a mile or two away in any direction and the family was never lost for friends and company.

Few of the families in this district were any better off than the Gillespies. This backwater of Donegal did not have the standard of living experienced in the large towns. But the people here helped each other. Families would always help other families in times of need. If John's family had no milk, they could always be sure of getting some from a neighbour. And if a neighbour lacked something the Gillespies had, he only had to ask. Everybody shared what they had with everyone else. It was a wonderfully tight-knit and Christian community

John loved this land. How could he else? It was in his heart, it was in his bones, it was in his very blood. He had never left it and never wanted to. He loved the people. They reflected the land they lived on, rough, strong, hardy, but always good-natured and kind. As a child John played with the children of neighbouring farms, as well as with his own brothers and sisters. Now he would join their fathers on the bogs, in the fields, and at the gathering in of the corn. And he loved the bogs. He loved to walk in them and he loved to work on them. He had begun cutting peat with the other farmers at the age of fourteen despite some legal niceties that had not quite reached the ken of the hard-working farmers and their families

His father, too, had loved this place. It was a hard life, but it was peaceful and slow-moving. Stress was unknown. John loved the calmness and the stillness. On the little mound, he turned, slowly, a hundred and eighty degrees to view again the lakes below him. Another world. Such peace. No intrusion from modernity or progress, no cars, no buses, no lorries, no buildings or commerce, a world that had not changed in a hundred years. Here there were no sounds save the sounds of nature, the song of the birds, the bleating of lambs in the summer, the buzzing of insects. It was a wonderland where John often went to fish with his friends, with his father, and often alone … just to think, to absorb, or simply to be.

As his thoughts returned to his father, John's heart was wrenched again and another wave of grief coursed through him. As if to escape the sudden heartache, he jumped down from the mound and grimaced as he landed awkwardly, causing pain to shoot through his right leg and hip. He stopped for a moment, bent over, his hands on his knees. His lips were pulled tight as he waited, breathing noisily through his nose, until the pain diminished … the pain that was the secondary cause for that morning's introspection.

Devastated though he was by his father's passing, John suffered additional hurt from the extent of his mother's grief and vowed to keep his own heartache to himself. She was feeling enough heartache without him adding to it. She tried not to let her children see how wounded she was, how hard she found it to keep going. From time to time she would speak to one of the older children about her sadness and the loneliness she was feeling at her husband's passing.

Nonetheless, she was a strong woman and kept forcing herself to be cheerful for the younger children.

Still, John pursed his lips, she would now need help. She had five children to rear but all that the family owned was the small bit of land, a few cows, and the annual crop of wheat. Her husband's death had robbed the family of their breadwinner and of the extra income that had been provided by his carpentry and stone-masonry. John's older brother, Pat, had already applied for, and secured, a job in a local factory, so that would definitely help. But there was still the farm to be looked after, wheat to be brought in – with a scythe, they were too poor to afford any form of mechanisation – peat to be cut from the bog, cows to be fed and milked, byres to be kept clean. Mary, the oldest, would be helping in the house, cleaning, cooking, doing the many chores that followed inevitably from the frenetic living of five growing children. Anne was still at school and Michael was still only a wee slip of a lad. It would be years before he would be any use for anything. Clearly John would have to take over the running of the farm. Again he shook his head in frustration. But what about his leg and his hip!

He was not going to pain his mother by adding his sadness to hers. But neither was he going to cause her any additional concern by telling her about the pain is his leg. Only recently had he become aware of this pain but he was not the type of person who would complain of minor ailments or seek to bother others with his problems. But he was worried about it. The pains were definitely getting worse. He was already doing very heavy work, man's work, lifting hundredweights of fodder, with only his own strong back and arms, digging, scything, labouring for long hours that would that would be unheard of in the modern era of working time directives and legislation. If the pain continued to increase, could he still look after the farm?

Chapter Two

Suffering

John's concern about his ailing hip was justified. As the days after his father's death merged into weeks, John was increasingly victim to pain that now radiated out from his hip, down through his thigh into his knee. He found himself constantly limping and knew, without advice from any doctor, that something was seriously wrong. He continued to try to hide his suffering from his mother but inevitably she noticed his limp. From time to time she would remark, "You're limping, John. Is there something wrong with your leg?"

And John would reply, affecting nonchalance, "No, there's nothing wrong." But to keep her from worrying, he would add, "I get the feeling sometimes that this leg is weaker than the other one. Maybe that's what's making me limp and me not even aware of it." And he would walk calmly from the kitchen, implying that he had not a care in the world. But even though he did not look back, he could feel his mother's hard stare following him. How much longer could he maintain the pretence?

A year passed. John still maintained his heavy work schedule but the hip and the leg were causing him great suffering which he found increasingly difficult to bear. By the time his seventeenth birthday had passed, in the winter of 1973, his mother and his older sister were convinced that there was indeed something seriously wrong with John and they began to urge him to see a doctor or a specialist. But John refused to do so. He chose instead to go to England for the winter to try to earn some money working on building sites. It was a hard time for him, away from home, lonely, in constant pain. But he ignored all of these sufferings, worked harder than anyone else on the site, and saved every penny he could to bring home with him in the spring.

In the early summer of 1974, he was back again cutting peat from the bogs and running the farm. It was heavy work, work without respite and, despite his determination, he was finding it very difficult to cope with. In his eighteenth year he was finally forced to admit to his mother that he was in constant pain. Distressed by her anxiety, he finally agreed to see a doctor. The doctor could make no definitive diagnosis but he did arrange for John's hip and leg to be x-rayed. The radiologist was baffled by what he saw on the film but knew it was a serious defect. He advised John to see a specialist and promised to arrange something for him.

In a few weeks, John received a letter informing him that a bone-specialist from Galway would be visiting Ballyshannon Hospital the following week and that he had agreed to see John and discuss his problem with him. John went alone to the appointment and found himself sitting in front of an office table, listening to a grey-haired, consultant-surgeon. The consultant had John's x-ray in his hand and he was staring at it intently, his lips pursed but moving, as if he was trying to find some way to transmit bad news in the best light possible. In fact, it quickly transpired that he was not at all concerned about 'the best light possible' and was, if anything, very direct.

"I have to tell you, John," he began, looking at the youth over the top of his gold-rimmed glasses, "I have seldom seen anything as bad as this. It's a very rare condition … only happens in one out of every thousand live births." He paused, and his empty hand began gesturing towards the x-ray as he prepared to launch into the technicalities of what he was looking at. "It's called 'developmental dysplasia', usually referred to as DDH. And I have to tell you that you're very unfortunate here. It's a multifactorial trait, a kind of genetic birth defect that occurs nine times more often in females than in males. You, unfortunately, are one of those one-in-ten-thousand males." He shook his head sympathetically and pointed to a vaguely grey patch on the x-ray. "I'll try to explain this in layman's terms that you'll understand. What you have here is your hip-joint." He pointed again. "This flattish bit here is supposed to be … ah … you'd probably best understand it as a 'socket'. Your femoral bone is supposed to fit into it and swivel around as your walk or bend or move about."

John nodded. He knew how a ball-and-socket joint was supposed to work. The doctor watched him for a minute and something like sympathy crossed his face. "The thing is, John, you have not one but two serious problems here." He pointed again. "See, here is the top of the femoral bone. That's supposed to be bulbous… rounded, you know, to slot into the socket and stay there." He spread his hands and shrugged apologetically. "But it isn't rounded, John. It just sort of peters out at the end." He turned to the x-ray again. "And here's the hip- socket." He looked up at John again and went on, "Except that it isn't … a socket, I mean. It's very shallow, almost flat. Even if you had a proper bulb on the end of your thigh bone, there's no real socket for it to slot properly into."

He spread his hands and sat back on his chair, holding up the x-ray to the light. "So you have this bone here grinding and moving around in this flat bit here and, indeed, frequently slipping right out of it. No wonder you are in such pain."

John had not interrupted the consultant, partly because he was anxious to learn what he could about his condition and partly because he did not feel that there was any point in talking unless he had something useful to say. But he now asked, "How do you fix this?"

The consultant shrugged again. "This is an extremely rare condition, John. To be honest, the time to treat it was when you were less than two years old. This is really serious and if you don't get something done about it, hip deformity and a permanent limp are inevitable. In fact, it's almost certain that you'll be crippled with osteoarthritis and in a wheel-chair before you're forty."

Again John asked the obvious question, "So what can I do to sort this out?"

The consultant was a kind man and was trying to be helpful but John had little problem recognising that the doctor was at a loss, that he had no real solution to offer. He did try to throw John a life-line, however. "I have a colleague down at Merlin Park Hospital in Galway who is a renowned bone-specialist. I've seen him do wonderful things. I'll show him your x-rays. Perhaps he might be able to design some sort of graft that he could attach to the socket and give the femoral bone more stability, hopefully stop it scraping and grinding around in there the way it's doing now."

John balked inwardly at the idea of an operation. He stood and thanked the doctor for seeing him and said that he would think about the suggestion to go to Merlin Park.

It was to be months, however, before he thought about it again. John had inherited his father's strong faith and his propensity to pray through tribulation. John believed passionately that if he prayed often enough and hard enough, Jesus would eventually heal him as He had healed the crippled men in the New Testament. He prayed continuously through the day, during his work, during quiet times in the evening, but the healing was not immediately forthcoming. Eventually, after several weeks, driven almost to distraction by the pain, he decided to contact the consultant again and ask for his help. After some correspondence back and forward, it was eventually agreed that John would be admitted to Merlin Park in Galway.

John, restless and uneasy, left his ward the evening before the operation was scheduled, and wandered around the hospital, attempting to while away some time. He was to learn later from his neighbour in the next bed, another young Donegal man who was also suffering from a bone disease, that while he was absent from the ward the two consultants had called in to speak to him.

"D'ye know what they wanted?" John asked.

"Well … they waited for you for a while and I heard them talking. There's something about your x-rays that they hadn't noticed before." He hesitated. "To tell you the truth, I get the impression they don't want to go ahead with your operation … but they'll be back in a while. You're to wait here till they come."

John was upset. Jesus had not directly intervened and cured him as he had hoped but he later came to believe that Jesus had decided to heal him through the intervention of human surgery. He had, therefore, begun to experience great hope that this operation was the answer to his prayer, that it would bring him the healing he had been desperately praying for. Hearing this disturbing news from his fellow-patient unsettled him and as he sat on the edge of his bed he prayed again to Jesus. "Lord, I need this operation. My family needs this operation. How can I work and help my mother and my brothers and sisters, if I have to go home with my leg like this? Lord, you're going to have to make these two guys do this operation."

He lay back on the bed, with his hands behind his head, staring at the ceiling. He was now steeling himself for an argument with the surgeons when they came back. The eighteen- year-old had convinced himself that this operation was part of God's plan, the answer to his desperate daily pleadings, and he was not prepared to allow these two surgeons to sabotage that, no matter how unwittingly.

By the time the surgeons returned John was in a stubborn, almost truculent mood. They were accompanied by a nurse who stood quietly to one side and took no part in the conversation. John listened to the consultants' explanations for abandoning the operation, explanations that were so filled with technical and incomprehensible medical terms that they only added to his frustration.

"I'm in severe pain with this," he argued in return. "I don't want to go back to a life of further pain, of uselessness to my family. I need this operation to heal me and I want it done in the morning as arranged."

The surgeons exchanged glances and stared again at the determined young man. Should they risk crippling him on the off-chance that the proposed graft might work? Already the senior surgeon was shaking his head, knowing that the risk was too great. "Why don't you go home for … say … six months and reflect on this? If by then you're still determined to go ahead, we'll review our plans and try something else."

But John was adamant. "What's the point in my going home to six months of pain that's only going to get worse? If you're going to do it, then you might as well do it now."

Again the surgeons attempted to remonstrate with him, using language that held no meaning for John and which, therefore, was incapable of convincing him to change his mind. John could sense that they were almost as recalcitrant as he was, so he tried a slightly different argument. "Why don't you open up the hip anyway and have a look at it. You might find something there that you can't see on the x-rays." John still believed that somehow Jesus would guide the hands and eyes of the surgeons and that, even at the eleventh hour, they would find the solution to his problem.

Seeing that the young man was going to brook no denial at this point, the surgeons eventually shrugged their shoulders and said, "Take tonight to think about this! We'll talk to you again in the morning."

A little while later, the nurse who had accompanied the surgeons on the ward visit, came back alone and spoke quietly to John. "John, it's not my place to say this, but you shouldn't really be trying to force those surgeons to do this operation. They know what they're doing and they absolutely do not want to do this … and, if you would take my advice, you'd be far better putting on your clothes this very minute and going off home."

John's face registered extreme disappointment. Something about the nurse's tone and expression had been far more convincing than the doctors' medical arguments. "But why do they not want to touch me?" he asked, hoping that she would be unable to answer.

But the nurse remained persuasive. "I know these surgeons and I have great respect for them. If they say the operation could go seriously wrong, there's every chance that it will …"

John stared at her in mute appeal but had no response to offer. The nurse sat on the side of the bed beside him, her hands joined in her lap. After a moment's silence, she said, "I know you've been saying your prayers …" In answer to John's puzzled stare, the nurse jerked her head towards the patient in the next bed and said, "Your man, Hugh, told me. But anyway, if you say your prayers, you don't know what the Lord'll do for you. And it might take years. But one thing I do know," She stared at him earnestly, "this operation is obviously very risky, with little chance of success."

John leaned forward, elbows on his knees, his head in his hands, totally deflated. The nurse put a hand on his shoulder and said earnestly, "John, do you really believe in God?"

John turned to look at her. "Of course, I do," he said. "I firmly believe in God."

"Well, then," the nurse replied, "here's something I want you to do. I want you to say a decade of the rosary before you go to sleep tonight and the first thought that's in your head when you wake up in the morning, go with that!" She rose from the bed and looked down at him. "It'll be either to go home or stay for the operation. But go with the message God sends you." She gave him a final brief nod and left the ward.

Unhappy, now, but somehow deeply influenced by the nurse, John did as she suggested and said a fervent decade of the rosary before he lay down to sleep. He might not have been familiar at that time with the concept of discernment through the guidance of the Holy Spirit but when he woke the following morning he knew immediately that he should not undergo the operation. And, to his surprise, despite the despair he was feeling at the pain he knew he would have to face again, he felt a quiet and peaceful certainty that this decision was the right one.

He chatted with Hugh about it while he was dressing to leave and the Donegal man handed him a small slip of paper and said, "Here's a wee prayer to St. Joseph that I've been saying for years. Say it faithfully every day and St. Joseph won't let you down." John thanked his new friend and left. He prayed the prayer with great devotion every day, sometimes several times a day, not knowing that one day that prayer would be a significant element in his life.

"St. Joseph, whose protection is so great, so strong, so prompt, before the Son of God I place in you all my interests and desires. Oh Joseph, I never weary of contemplating you and Jesus asleep in your arms. I dare not approach while He reposes near your heart. Press Him in my name and kiss His fine head for me and ask Him to return the kiss when I draw my dying breath. St. Joseph, Patron of the Dying, pray for me."

Chapter Three

Enduring

John's mother and older sister, Mary, were shocked when he arrived home from Galway without having undergone the operation. They were both women of strong faith and prayer but John's bizarre decision made no sense to them.

"You said a decade of the rosary and got a message that you shouldn't go ahead with the operation?" his mother asked. It was a question that dripped disbelief and dismay.

"A big decision like that?" his sister echoed. "That wasn't an awful lot of evidence to be going on for something that important."

His mother was close to crying. "And your leg … and the pain? Did you give any thought to them when you were … when you were getting these messages?"

John had, in fact, given thought to little else. His mind was filled with dread at the prospect of returning to a life of suffering-filled days, of agony-wracked nights. But regardless of his mother's dismay, no matter how heavy his heart, nothing could shake his conviction that the decision he had made, was made "… with the help of the Spirit."

When he had informed the surgeons the following morning that he had decided to take their advice to forego the operation, they told him that they believed he was making the right decision. The worst part of that interview for John, however, was the further advice they gave him. They told him never to work again, "… especially any form of physical work." This directive caused John great concern but he simply did not have the luxury to make that choice. Nothing had changed at home. Pat was still working in the factory trying to put food on the table. His mother and Mary were still looking after the house. The farm still had to be managed. Only he was there to do it. He was going to have to go straight back to work, however much damage that might do to his hip and leg.

Thus John returned to his farm chores, to days of heavy manual labour, with nothing changed. The femoral bone was now constantly moving in and out of its socket; he could hear it clicking each time it did so. And he could feel it (Ah, dear God, could he ever feel it!) as it ground and scraped its way back into the socket again. The imaginings that these sounds created only increased his worry and concern about what was happening to his hip, and added a measure of mental torment to the already excruciating physical pain.

And thus the eighteen-year-old youth, whose life should have had its share of fun and freedom as well as work, came home in the evenings, spent, exhausted, with pain and worry etched on his features. Try as he might, he could not hide his state from his mother.

"John," she would insist. "You're going to have to ease back. You can't keep up this pace. Why don't you get a job that doesn't involve so much physical labour, driving a van or a lorry or something??"

But John was stubborn, if that is a word that could be ascribed to him. He was something beyond stubborn. Nothing could hold him back from doing what he believed had to be done, not his suffering, not his mother's concern, not the doctors' strict injunction. Not only did he persist in undertaking a full workload each day with what in today's terms would be classified as 'severe disability', but he also sought and found a second job to supplement the family income, doing heavy labouring on a building site.

John was uncomfortably aware that the harder he worked, the more he was abusing his hip-joint. And the more the abuse, the greater became his suffering. Stubbornly, he let his mother see less and less of his pain. He never complained or even commented about his state. Equally stubbornly, he refused to take pain-killers or any of the other medications prescribed by his doctors. He ignored all blandishments from friends and family to abandon work and apply for a Disability Living Allowance. He was praying constantly, adamantly expecting God to cure this ailment. He was waiting, in strong and unshakeable faith, for the healing that he was sure, that he knew, would take place. And thus he worked on tirelessly, day after day, week after week, month after month, praying, waiting. As he was often to say many years later, "I just got on with it, dragging the leg after me."

Chapter Four

Marrying

John's life was not entirely without its moments of calm and pleasure, brief though they might have been. He still retained his friendships from his childhood and schooldays, and apart from the odd evening in one of the village pubs, the 'céili-ing' in neighbouring houses, there was the fishing in his beloved lakes. And, if his physical sufferings were to continue unabated, something new in his life was to give him a deal of quiet joy.

Donegal, in summer, is an attractive destination for tourists and holiday- makers. Many city people own a second house there or rent one for a few weeks of the summer. In the summer of 1975, one such family from Belfast, the Dowlings, came to spend a few weeks near Glencolmcille. John was working, with his customary diligence, on a building site quite near the Dowlings' chalet. He had not heard any footsteps approach as he was struggling to clear a trench for water-pipes but he did hear a soft, female voice say, "Excuse me."

John looked up and saw a pretty, blonde girl of about his own age, smiling down at him. Something about this girl, a complete stranger to him, affected him in a way no other girl ever had. His face betrayed no sign of this as he nodded easily to the girl and climbed out of the trench. "Hello," he said. "Can I help you?"

"Yes," the girl replied, continuing to smile. "My mother saw you digging here and sent me to ask if you know anything about the evening entertainments there might be about here … bingo, or something."

The girl's name was Christina, and over the next few days, she and her mother were to use John as an unofficial source for tourist information. John was delighted to help, and always looked forward to seeing Christina clambering over the rubble on the site to speak to him. Inevitably a friendship developed and, as Christina's holidays began to near their end, John plucked up the courage to invite her to one of the local dances. By that time, his femoral bone was jumping constantly in and out of its socket, and his knee was now under stress as well. Ligaments were stretching and tearing, small muscles were being pulled, as John put extra pressure on his knee to try to protect his hip. He was in terrible agony but he danced that night as if he was floating on air.

Christina eventually went back to her job as a Civil Servant in Belfast but they kept in touch and friendship blossomed into love. There were long separations but Christina did manage the occasional visit to Glencolmcille, staying now with John's family, while John, too, managed the occasional visit to Belfast.

Life in Glencolmcille is slow-moving. So, too, it seems, is romance. John's relationship with Christina grew deeper but it was to be five years after they met, an evening in August 1980 during a short holiday they were taking with John's sister in Ballybofey, an evening when they were taking a seemingly inauspicious stroll towards a small public-house in town, that he was finally to say, "We're going to get married … aren't we?"

Christina threw him a sideways glance. John's gaze was open, direct, honest, and he had a slight grin on his face. She now knew him so well. She knew that he "… was never one for frills" and she knew better than to expect any 'frills' now. Her own smile was understated, subtle, but it was there. She shrugged slightly and said, "Yes, we are."

John was twenty-five at that time. Christina had long known about his limp but it had never been a problem in their relationship. John had continued all during these years to pray unceasingly, with undiminished fervour, with unshakeable faith, that one day the Lord would heal him and that his hip and leg would return to normal. His prayers were unstructured, untutored, sometimes wild and aggressive, but always filled with faith and deep sincerity.

"Lord," he would pray, "how is this leg helping me to do your work and help your people? There are so many people out there who need work done for them. How is me bein' a cripple going to help these people, your people?"

John and Christina got married in a quiet ceremony on February 13th 1981, some six months after his (fairly prosaic) proposal. They rented a little house not far from the village of Cashel and they set up home there. Christina resigned from her job in Belfast but was able to get work in the Glenbay Hotel, first as a waitress and then as a fully trained bar-maid. Christina loved this job but had to leave it after six or seven months when she was pregnant with their first child, Helen.

John continued to do what he had always done, labouring long hours each day on building sites, doing occasional other odd jobs when he could get them. Now that he was a married man with responsibilities and a child on the way, he found himself under greater pressure than ever from friends and family, pleading with him to take more care of himself, to stop the heavy work and apply for a Disability Living Allowance and other family allowances. But John equally persistently ignored their advice and kept assuring them that "everything is going to be all right."

Chapter Five

Persisting

On the tenth of February, 1983, Christina gave birth to her first daughter, Helen. Tracey was to follow on the twenty-ninth of September, 1984. John was still working on building sites or on half-completed houses. His leg was growing continually weaker and was causing him pain that he could scarce endure. He prayed as assiduously as ever but his prayers had changed to a constant plea for the Lord to get him through each single day, to help him complete each specific task he was assigned to do, to make sure he got home without collapsing on the job.

But every night he continued to pray earnestly and endlessly, never losing belief that he would be healed when he awoke the following morning. He repeated constantly the Prayer to St. Joseph that had been given to him by his bed-neighbour, Hugh, at Merlin Park Hospital. He saw around him others who were suffering from cancer, who were hospitalised with serious illnesses, who were struck down with crippling debility, and none of them healed. Yet he never doubted. Despite all evidence to the contrary, he remained perpetually convinced that God would heal him.

Was it steadfastness in faith? Was it a stubborn and unshakeable desire that would settle for nothing less than full healing? Whichever it was, and his family and friends had varying opinions about it, John had utter confidence that one day the Lord would grant him the miracle he sought.

John's mother, Mary, felt that he was 'being unrealistic.' "John," she would say, "you can't be keeping going on like this or you're going to lose the run of yourself."

And his sister, Anne, kept trying to make him understand that the cross is an integral part of Christian life. Often she would say, "John, surely you must realise by now that this is a cross the Lord is asking you to carry. Suffering's part of life. You have to learn to accept it. You shouldn't be refusing it like that."

But John would argue vociferously, "I don't want this cross. I can be a far better person without this cross, helping God's people. Look at the good I could do, if only God would heal me. How is my being a cripple helping me to do good? If I had my health I could dig gardens for folks. I mean, there's so much I could do. He has to heal me. It's the only way."

Such extraordinary faith, such implacable determination, was, to John's friends and family, almost incomprehensible. They, too, from time to time sought help from God but like most sincere Christians, they tended to temper their petitions with some acknowledgement of God's will. John, however, would brook not the slightest doubt about God's will for him.

"The Lord wants me healed, there's no doubt about that. It's just that he's taking a terrible long time about it." And with renewed persistence and unassailable belief, he would return to his prayers.

"Lord," he would say, "I'm not stopping! I'm going to go on doing what I'm doing. Pain or no pain, I'm not stopping. If you want me to stop, you'll have to stop me yourself!"

Hope came again, suddenly, and with a force that left John shaking. Christina's mother worked at Musgrave Park Hospital in Belfast and one evening in 1984 she told John and Christina that she had met a famous surgeon that day called Mr. James. She looked at John, slightly hesitant lest she give him too much to hope for, and went on, "He's reputed to be one of the top bone specialists in Europe. I happened to mention your condition and he said he'd be happy to have a look at you." She pulled a slip of paper from her pocket. "This is his secretary's phone number. If you ring her, she'll set up an appointment for you."

John could hardly sleep that night, convinced that, finally, God was about to make his move. He phoned Mr. James' secretary the following day and was instructed to have further x-rays taken and bring them with him to the appointment. Speaking to Christina's mother in the interim, Mr. James told her that he wanted the fresh x-rays taken to see if he could determine why the surgeons at Merlin Park had been reluctant to attempt the operation.

"I know those men," he told her, his expression serious, "and they're very good. In fact," he went on, "one of them was once a student of mine. They must have had some reason for telling that such an operation would be contra-indicated." Then he said briskly, "But I'll know better when I make my own diagnosis."

A few days later, Christina's mother accompanied John to the appointment in Musgrave Hospital. John had the x-rays in a large envelope which he handed to the surgeon. Mr. James slipped the two plates into a lighted viewing box on the wall. He had been looking at them for barely a few seconds when he ran his hands over his face and sucked in a hissing breath. He turned to John, his expression offering little in the way of hope. His head was shaking from side to side when he said, "I can see right away why the surgeons in Merlin Park advised against this operation." He spread his hands. "I'm sorry, John. There's just nothing they could have done. You've got severe avascular necrosis … uh … bone decay, terrible wear and tear. Any attempt at a graft would only have locked the femoral head to the acetabulum … to the socket. You wouldn't have been able to move your leg at all. You'd have lost whatever mobility you have now."

John was devastated. What was the Lord playing at? "Are you telling me there's nothing you can do?" he asked, scarcely able to articulate the words.

"I'm afraid I am, John," Mr. James replied, clearly disappointed. "I'm sorry it has to be like this. I had hoped … But I have to tell you, the surgeons at Merlin Park clearly understood your condition." He stared seriously at John. "I have to agree with them. I have to say that I, too, would be very reluctant to operate on you under any circumstances. I'm sorry to be so blunt but you need to know the truth, there's not a surgeon in the world who could fix that joint, and, take my advice, never allow anyone to touch it, no matter what he says."

John's disappointment was palpable. His mother-in-law was almost in tears as she watched him. She said, "Did you not tell me something the other day about plastic hips?"

Mr. James glanced at her and nodded. But his answer changed nothing. "Yes, we've been experimenting with plastic hips for some time now but the friction going on with that joint of John's would have the new hip burned out in less than two years. What would he do then?"

John was having trouble involving himself any further in the conversation. He felt utterly deflated. The heartache was too much to bear. But he gathered himself as best he could to talk of practicalities. “Mr. James,” he said, wearily, going over old ground but still hoping for even the smallest light, “I have a family, a wife and two young children. What am I going to do now? How can I provide for them?”

The consultant was disconcerted. “Well,” he said uncertainly, “what is it that you do?”

“I’m a labourer, mostly on building sites.”

The consultant was visibly shocked. “A labourer … on building sites?” He scarcely knew how to respond. Then he said, “John, my goodness! You don’t appear to have much sense. Doing heavy physical labour on building sites with a hip and leg like that? What can you have been thinking?” He looked at Christina’s mother and shook his head, half bemused, half exasperated. “John, you have a serious disability. As far as work is concerned, that is, if you are contemplating doing any work in the future with that painful disability, all I can say is, and I’m sorry if this sounds blunt, just make sure you’re sitting on your backside. Otherwise your femoral bone and your hip socket will never last. They’ll just wear away.”

John limped from the clinic room, trudging down the corridor beside his mother-in-law. The outcome of the visit had been a terrible blow to his hopes and, in his bitter disappointment, he could not help but feel that somehow God had betrayed him. He walked in silence, his head bowed in dejection. His father had always told him that the Lord can do anything and John had always remained firmly in the belief, despite the years of torture and misery, that “… if God could make bones, He could fix bones.” Yet here he was, having been examined by the greatest bone specialist in Europe, being told that there was nothing he could do for him. Worse, he had been told there was nothing anybody could do for him.

Christina's mother walked alongside him, her head, too, bowed. She was deeply disappointed for John, disappointed for her daughter. She remained silent by John's side, acutely aware of the agonising heartbreak the young man was suffering.

John's mind was in turmoil. Hardly aware of the woman by his side, he prayed, almost desperately, "Dear God, where do I go now? I have prayed so hard and come so far with this suffering, and you let this happen? Where, Lord, where do I go next?" No answer came but, after a few moments, the turbulence in his mind eased. He seemed suddenly to be floating in a great darkness. And out of the darkness there came, half-formed and vague, a thought, a thought that he chased after and found heart in, a thought that made him believe that what had just happened was of no consequence. He tried to clarify it by responding to the Lord in prayer. "The idea that the surgeon would heal me was mine, Lord. Why am I accusing you? You never promised anything or hinted at anything. It was just me. I was the one who made the assumptions."

His brow furrowed as he struggled to apprehend the implications of what he was thinking. They were leaving the building now and at that point John lifted his head to the Lord. Over the fields he could see the dark shape of the Black Mountain and the huge orange ball of the evening sun beginning to settle behind it. And he said, "Lord, look at that! You have no bother keeping that sun up in that sky. You picked it up from the other side this morning and you're setting it down there behind the mountain this evening. You created those mountains, and that sky, and that sun. That's extraordinary. But it was no big deal for you. And yet, Lord, all I'm looking for is a wee hip to be healed. How hard can that be for you?"

And John knew suddenly, and with a fierce rising of hope again, that nothing had changed. He was still going to go on praying the way he had always done. He was still going to suffer. But he was still going to be healed. It was only a matter of time. He looked into the sky again and his mother-in-law was amazed to see him smiling. "Right, Lord," John was praying. "All I'm looking for, compared to what's up there, is a tiny wee thing and I'm coming back at you with a vengeance. This business at Musgrave Park Hospital was a mistake. We don't need surgeons; we don't need doctors. Whatever's in my body, whatever disease is in my hip, you'll cure with your own hands. It's time for violent faith now, Lord, and violent prayer, prayer that will knock down the very gates of heaven. And Christina will be there with me, praying at my side. This pain is not going to stop me. I'm going to go on crawling around, doing what I have been doing and, if you want me to stop, you're the one who's going to have to stop me."

Chapter Six

Succumbing

By 1985 it was clear to John that his younger siblings were able to manage the farm between them, so he felt he could now leave Donegal and move to Belfast to be near Christina's mother who lived alone. Unfortunately, their application for a house there was unsuccessful and they were put on a waiting list. In the meantime, however, they were able to rent a house in the Park Hall Estate in Antrim, an area where very few Catholics lived.

In those restless, often dangerous, times, minorities on both sides of the religious divide, in housing estates all over Northern Ireland, tended to suffer intimidation and aggressive forms of disruption to their lives. John and Christina lived quietly, however, drawing little attention to themselves. They became friendly with some nearby families, mixing with them easily and John, being John, helped them in various ways when occasion demanded. Thus they became recognised as safe and reliable neighbours and, because of that, were able to escape the excesses of "the troubles".

John had secured for himself a job on a building site on the Poleglass Estate in Belfast. Each morning he would make his way to the Antrim Roundabout, just outside the town, where he and a couple of others would be picked up by a van that took them directly to the Poleglass site.

Inevitably the damage to his hip was getting worse and pain was now as much a part of his life as breathing. Even as he lay in his bed at night, the pain would not ease. He experienced no comfort at any time, no release, no escape.

And, as always, there was no respite on the site. Heavy physical demands were made on him – digging foundations, lifting and heaving one hundredweight bags of cement to the mixer, wheeling barrow-loads of heavy bricks – all of which played terrible havoc with his dislocated hip. And even as he wondered how much more of this he could stand, he knew the hip was getting worse. The pain told him; the terrible clicking and grinding of the femoral head in the socket every time he moved told him; the increasing damage that his efforts to protect his hip were doing to his knee, indeed both knees, told him.

He was now dragging his leg after him, unable any longer to make a real pretence at walking. And he was praying continuously each day for the strength and the will just to get through the day. He prayed that he would be able to drag himself from his bed in the morning. He prayed for the stamina simply to make it to the van that would carry him to work. He prayed every time he had to lift something, or dig something, or shovel cement. He prayed every time he moved, when the femoral bone would jump out of its socket and crack back in again. He prayed for his knees which were almost as sore as his hip and he spent his days in a state of panic wondering how long they would be able to support him.

Towards the end of September 1986, the work at Poleglass ended. As John left the job for the last time, physically weak, racked with pain and exhaustion, he knew in his heart that he would never work on a building site again, at least, his indefatigable faith would argue, not until the Lord would heal him. He left in a state of utter depression, dejected beyond hope. A wife and two children to support, yet convinced that he would never be able to work again

John had never discussed such an eventuality with Christina although both of them had been uncomfortably aware that a day such as this had to come. Somehow he had always felt that if he gave voice to any thought of defeat, to any possibility of yielding to his infirmity, it would be tantamount to admitting that the Lord had let him down, that his belief, his prayers, his hopes, had all been in vain. Yet here he was, still a young man, with no job, no prospects, no way to take care of his family, and nothing he could do about it. That brought as much pain to his pride and to his heart as his hip was bringing to his body. He had reached the lowest ebb of his life and his misery was compounded by the fact that now he could scarcely move his leg at all. Walking the shortest distances demanded supreme effort and fierce determination and, of course, since he stubbornly refused to use a walking-stick, he suffered all the more as a result.

For how long did Job rail at the Lord, crying for succour? For how long was misfortune upon misfortune piled upon him? For how long did Yahweh remain silent and unresponsive?

"I cry to you, O God, but there's no answer,
I stand but you merely look on.
You have become cruel to me ... [Job, 30:20 -21]

Job roars his anger and indignation at his condition. His friends give him answers that reflect the wisdom of the world but bring him no peace. Yet Job knows that it is only in dialogue with God that he will truly understand his place in the world, even if his words are filled with complaint and demand. But how wrong is that? How very human is that? Do people who love not feel hurt at the other's silence, at the other's recalcitrance?

"So I will not restrain my words,
I will speak out in anguish,
And complain with embittered soul."[Job.7:11]

In the end,

"Yahweh restored his fortunes, giving him twice as much as he had before."[Job 42: 10]

Thoughts of Job may never have entered John's head but, like Job, he preserved his trust. He remained steadfast in his prayers, arguing perhaps, demanding certainly, but never wavering in his belief that, despite the world's understanding of evil, of suffering, of the cross, that one day his prayer would be answered.

Chapter Seven

Encountering

John's test, if test it was, was far from over. One evening, not long after the Christmas of 1986, John had been visiting some friends who lived quite near them. As he was returning home, walking very slowly, he was afflicted with a stab of pain so sudden and so crushing, that he had to stop. His leg, which for some time now had been causing him to limp very badly, became suddenly useless. Sweat covered his forehead and dripped into his eyes and he leaned against a nearby fence, wheezing, breathless, trying to find some way of placing his leg that would diminish the terrible stabbing in his hip. Despite the fact that he was barely a hundred yards from his own house, he wanted to lie on the ground and simply surrender to the agony. But he fought the impulse. "I will not give in," he gasped through clenched teeth. "I … will … not … give … in."

It was not raining but it was dark and the raw January wind was bitterly cold. For that reason there were few people about and somewhere on the periphery of the red miasma of pain that filled his being, John experienced a vague gratitude that he was spared the indignity of the pity, or possibly the contempt, of passing eyes, depending upon how they might have interpreted his incapacity.

He knew that he could not complete that short distance to his house without significant intervention from the Lord, and so he lifted his head to the sky and prayed in his hopelessness, much as Job had done in the depths of his misery, "Lord, I'm weak here. I'm exhausted, utterly spent. I'm in severe pain and I just can't move one more inch. How much longer are you going to allow this to go on? I have prayed to you faithfully and fervently all these years, asking you to heal me." He looked up into the sky, stared across its immense expanse, at the huge, heavy clouds barely visible in the winter darkness, and he said, just as he had said that evening he emerged from Musgrave Park Hospital, "Lord, I know you are there. I know with all my heart that you have the power to heal me. And, Lord, I want with all my heart to be healed." Then he made an earnest and agonised promise. "Lord, if you will heal me, I will go out and help your people whatever way I can. Whatever help they need, I will do all in my power to see that they get it." He continued to gaze into the vast sky. "And know this, Lord! Know that I know, and that I have always known, that you have the power to heal me! You love me … and you have the power. This so-called cross is no good either to you or to me. How can I help your people when I am like this?" And his head fell on his chest, his mind quiet, his spirit still intensely with the Lord.

While he was making his promise, John had visions of the many practical ways he could use his skills to help unfortunate people. He had nothing more significant than practical support in his mind. But somehow, at a level of consciousness far below his normal awareness, he had a sense that he had a vocation to 'help God's people' without actually knowing what that meant. It was this deep, instinctive apprehension that drove him to make his despairing promise to the Lord in exchange for healing.

John's prayer was not, perhaps, the form of prayer that priests and religious would instinctively recommend to supplicants seeking help on how to pray. It is unlikely that such an approach to prayer is to be found in manuals about praying. But John's prayer was intense; it was real; it was loaded with a single-minded, if unsophisticated, worship that poured from his heart and his immense faith. And what he did not know at that moment, although he was to be made aware of it a day or two later, was that his patience, his faith, his determination, had finally broken through the divine, utterly incomprehensible defenses of this silent but ever-loving God.

Somehow John found the will to drag himself from the fence and stagger the hundred yards, the long, pain-racked hundred yards, to his house, where he collapsed on to an armchair and prayed miserably for even the smallest ease, the slightest comfort.

Two days later, John had accompanied Christina and their two children into Antrim's town centre to buy a few groceries. John was finding unemployment difficult to endure and, despite the unceasing pain and his now seriously debilitating limp, he looked forward to the short family walks into town. It gave him something to do, something that helped break the interminable monotony of the day. The shopping done, the family was making its way home again along the main street of Antrim. They were passing the Public Library when John heard a voice in his head, clear, real, unmistakable. "John! Go into the library. There's a book there for you."

John was stunned. He stared at Christina, half convinced that it was she who had spoken. But the voice, a soft, gentle male voice had not been Christina's. He looked right and left as well as behind him but there was no-one nearby who might have spoken the words. He could scarcely deal with the complexity of thoughts and emotions that were assailing him, but one thought above all was forcing itself into expression: "God is finally going to do something."

Elated, frightened, hoping yet afraid to hope, he turned to Christina and said, his voice sounding odd to his ears, "Christina, I need to step into the library for a minute. There's a book I want to get."

Christina stared at him, half amused, half bemused. They had been praying fervently for some time now, both separately and together, for something significant to happen to end this distressing phase of their lives. Christina's faith was strong and John had little difficulty in saying to her, his face a mix of seriousness and wonder, "A voice in my head is after telling me that I have to go into the library."

Christina's grin faded as she stared at her husband. This was strange but Christina knew her husband, knew his faith, knew the depth of his spirituality. Like John, she was filled with a sudden hope but one which she fearfully tried to quash even as it burst into being "Oh, John," She could not take her eyes from him. "Do you think …? Is it possible that ...?"

John simply looked at her and said, "I'll go way in here and see what this is all about. I'll not be long."

"We'll come with you," Christina said. We'll wait in the foyer until you find the book."

With the children, Christina followed behind John as he turned and limped slowly into the library. They found a seat in the foyer while John continued on into the reading area. He stood there, somewhat self-consciously, and stared around him - at the reading area, at the corridors of bookshelves - and wondered where he was supposed to go. Something about one of the sections to his right seemed to call to him. He made his way down through the rows of shelves, looking at the serried rows of books, his head moving this way and that without the slightest idea of what he was looking for. Then again he heard the voice, as if someone was standing beside him, "Stop. Turn around."

He did so and found himself facing the section on Mind, Body and Spirit. The books were an eclectic mix of New Age philosophy, Pseudo-psychic mind-control manuals, books on reading Tarot cards, and a number of Christian books on theology and self- improvement. Somewhere at the back of his mind, John had expected to come across a book detailing some new surgical discoveries about bones and hips. But all he could see were books about various religions. Then he heard the voice again, telling him to look down at the bottom shelf. There were more religious books here, too, but in among them was a small green book, insignificant, almost impossible to see, surrounded as it was by much larger books. But even as he cast his eye upon it, the book seemed to grow, to expand in width, until John could easily read the title from where he was standing. "Your Healing is Within You", by Canon Jim Glennon (Hodder & Stoughton, 1978).

Excited now, filled with curiosity, John pulled the book from its place and quickly turned the pages. He skipped the early pages and went straight to Chapter One. The first three sentences burned themselves into his mind. "Is the healing power of God still at work in the world today? Can we be sure that God wants to heal us? Does the sick person need to have faith?" (p.19) His eyes flew over the pages. He rushed through an early story of the healing of a boy with several severely collapsed vertebrae and a pronounced hump and the final sentence almost sucked the breath from him: "And anyone seeing him today would never know that he had once been grossly deformed." (p.21) John closed the book and held it to his chest, his mind in turmoil. All the answers were here. He was sure of it. He clung to the book as he made his way back to the reception desk where he took out immediate membership of the library and left with the book.

Christina and the two children rose as he came back into the foyer. He dragged himself to her as quickly as his useless leg would allow and waved the book at her, saying breathlessly, "This book is what I need for my healing. The key is in here."

John began to devour the book as soon as he arrived home. He read intensely the amazing stories of healings that had taken place at the hands of Canon Glennon. He and Christina had been praying assiduously for John's healing but they were to realise, after spending time studying Canon Glennon's book, that their prayers had been possessed of a wild, undisciplined fervour. Now they were learning how to pray the prayer of faith, about the key ideas that surround the concept of healing. They began to realise that God wants to heal us all but that there are some stipulations that must be met, what John was later to term "Rules for Healing".

They discovered that there can be blocks to healing within the heart and mind of the supplicant. One of the greatest of these, for example, is a grudge or a bitterness that does not allow us to forgive. This directly reflects the request in the Lord's Prayer that asks, "Forgive us our trespasses as we forgive those who trespass against us."

We ask God to forgive us, to heal us, only in so far as we forgive, as we heal, others.

John learned, too, that the Prayer of Faith is a hugely important stage in healing. He had instinctively employed this prayer for years without knowing precisely that it involved not only a total belief in the Lord's power to heal, but a full and complete acceptance that we have been healed even though the healing may not yet have manifested itself. But he learned, too, that prayer must be supplemented by fasting, to show to God sincerity and determination of purpose. Fasting gives God more access to the supplicant and a greater opportunity to exercise His loving will over human will.

Christina was as thrilled and amazed as John was at the discovery of the book. They felt as if a huge window had opened for them, showing them what they must do for John to be healed and making it clear that John could be healed. It was for both of them, a time of a new and surging hope, not only because of what the book was teaching them but especially because of the miraculous manner through which the book had been brought to their attention.

Chapter Eight

Fasting

John and Christina began praying and fasting together. Sometimes they would fast from early morning until dinner time; sometimes dinner would only be a light snack. Gradually they progressed to fasting for whole days, from one morning until the next. They prayed as they fasted, filled with new hope, new belief. Their new hope was based on a different understanding of Mark (11:23): 'Ask and believe you have received." As John was frequently to say in later life, "Mark didn't say ask and keep on asking. He said, 'Ask and believe that you are healed!!' In the early days Christina and I just kept on asking and asking. It had never occurred to us at any time to believe that I had actually been healed."

Thus from that time onward, despite his obvious physical distress, John began to fast and to thank God for the healing that he "knew" had been given to him but that just had not yet manifested itself. Initially, however, all that happened was that John's pain increased. Despite his new philosophy of believing, fasting and thanksgiving, despite the wondrous introduction to the book that taught them this new way to pray, John's suffering increased. What a test of faith that must have been. What a test of acceptance and belief their lives had become. Both he and Christina were now unemployed. They had barely enough money to put food on the table. There was no money for taxis or any other form of transport, so, despite the terrible physical demands walking now made upon him, John had to walk anywhere he needed to go, to Church, to the shops, to the houses of friends.

Worse still, inexplicable to John but very real, were the doubts that began to assail them. They began to wonder if the healing would ever take place, to question the validity and usefulness of their new form of prayer. But they persevered in spite of these attacks. It was years later that John was to learn that it is precisely at times such as these, when prayer is at its strongest and most effective, that Satan does everything in his power to create doubt and capitulation in the mind of the person praying. In this future time, John was often to warn many of those he was helping, "When you're praying hard for something serious, the devil is not going to be far away."

Still hoping, still believing, still fasting, John and Christina continued to pray assiduously, morning and evening and odd times in between. There was a devout Catholic woman in her early forties who lived across the street from them. One evening, about two weeks after John had encountered the Lord in the library, their neighbour called in to tell them that there was a nine-day novena to Our Lady in St. Joseph's Chapel on the Greystone Road. It was not a great distance from where they lived but for John it would be a long and painful walk. John knew his neighbour to be a woman of great faith, however, and he listened with serious attention when she went on to say, "I don't know why, John, but I have an intense inner feeling that you and Christina are supposed to attend that novena."

The fact that the novena was to be held at St. Joseph's did not escape John. The name immediately brought to his mind his daily prayer to the saint, given to him a few years before by his bed-neighbour, Hugh, at Merlin Park Hospital in Galway. John told the woman about this prayer and his devotion to St. Joseph and, as the conversation progressed, little by little they revealed details of their new regimen of fasting and prayer and how they had come upon this knowledge through an extraordinary intervention of the Lord himself.

Their neighbour was reverent in her response to their tale yet, somehow, not awed. She simply said, “With all that you’ve told me about your prayers and your fasting and the mysterious circumstances by which you were brought to knowledge of that book … I just can’t see the Lord passing you any more, John. Something is going to happen soon. I’m sure of it. And I am even more sure that both of you have got to go to that novena.”

The novena was to be a significant event in the parish and the priests requested the parishioners to take nine days in advance of the novena to prepare themselves for it. People were expected to come to St. Joseph’s to pray, to ready themselves for the novena, to attend confession and have their sins forgiven, to focus their spiritual energies towards God and His Holy Mother.

Christina went to St. Joseph’s alone one evening for confession while John remained at home to look after the children. The chapel was quiet at that hour. As Christina knelt before the crucifix to say her penance after confession, she became suddenly overcome with emotion, an emotion she could neither explain nor identify. She began to cry and put her head down for a while to hide the tears from anyone who might pass by. A short time later she raised her head again and a wondrous event occurred. As she looked up at the cross, she saw a hand, followed by the rest of the arm, coming out of the cross. The hand seemed to be moving towards two objects hovering in the air. The hand clasped the two objects, what Christina could only objectify as "things", held them together in the closed fist for a moment, pulled them slowly back into the crucifix and disappeared.

Christina was filled with awe and wonder but prayed only briefly after that because she was anxious to rush home to John to tell him what had happened.

"What do you think it was all about?" John asked, mystified.

"I have absolutely no idea, John. I can't begin to understand it. But I did see it. I wasn't imagining it. I could see it as clear as anything, grasping these two things together, like a vice, and pulling them back into the cross."

"But what sort of things?" John asked. "What were they like?"

"I can't say. I could see them as clear, but I don't know what they were."

"They must have looked like something," John persisted. "What did they look like?"

"I'm really not sure. Maybe one of them was like a stick. The other was like a rough, shapeless piece of flat rock or something, sort of saucer-shaped."

"Humph! That doesn't make much sense to me," John said, musing. He stared at her for a moment, his mind puzzling over the news. Then he said positively, "Well, we might not understand it but it definitely must have something to do with what we've been praying for."

They continued to talk about the vision, John pressing his wife for a more specific description of the objects that the hand had grasped. Try as she might, however, Christina could offer no further clarification about what she had seen. Eventually John said, "Do you think you could maybe try to draw them so that I could have a look at them?"

Christina shrugged. “You know I’m no artist but I’ll give it a try.”

She got some paper and a pencil and John waited as patiently as he could while Christina made a number of attempts before finally handing him a sketch that she thought was the best effort she could make at reproducing what she had seen. John stared at the sketch, initially mystified but gradually sensing that here was something that he might have seen before. Something about it definitely seemed familiar.

“I think I’ve seen this before,” he told Christina.

Christina’s face expressed mystification. “Are you sure?” she said. “Do you know what it is?”

John continued to study the drawing and suddenly enlightenment dawned. He looked up at Christina, his head shaking from side to side at the wonder of it. “I know what this is,” he said. “It’s the x-ray of my bone and hip socket that I brought to Mr. James at Musgrave Park Hospital.”

“I never saw that x-ray,” Christina said.

“I know,” John replied. “But your mother did. Take it from me, that’s what this is.” Again he stared at the sketch, his head still moving in mystification from side to side.

Christina, too, was amazed. How could she have sketched a reproduction of an x-ray that she had never seen? John was filled with an enormous longing, a yearning he could not explain. But here was a certainty there too. He could scarcely squeeze the words out but when they came they were forceful and determined.

“Christina, we have to do that novena. It doesn’t matter what comes or what happens. God is telling us that if we do this novena, that … that this is my chance.” He feared to use the word “healed”. “We absolutely have to be there, or I’m going to miss the boat.”

Chapter Nine

Laughing

There were now two days left before the novena was to begin. John awoke that morning and, as he tried to get out of bed, discovered that his hip was completely locked. Try as he might he was unable to move that part of his body. He could move the lower part of his legs from the knees down, but he could not bend or turn his hips. He felt as if a huge clamp had been placed around his hips and, with the thought, came the memory of the vision Christina had had a couple of evenings earlier, a hand clasping his femoral bone and hip-socket. And he realised, too, with a sudden and heart-wrenching start, that for the first time in more than ten years, even though his back and hip were totally frozen, he was feeling absolutely no pain. And it was wonderful. He had great trouble getting out of bed; he could only make steps of five or six inches; he almost fell down the stairs, so great was the difficulty in moving down the steps; and for the first time in his life, he had to ask Christina, who was already up and making the breakfast, for help to put on his shoes. But there was no pain … no pain … no pain. The words sang like a refrain in John's brain. No pain. No pain. He held Christina in his arms for a long time before he was finally able to tell her what had happened.

John's movements were very restricted after that. Each step was barely inches long but they religiously attended every service of the novena - morning mass each day, afternoon prayers, evening devotions. John was to say, laughing, many years later, "There we were each day, walking to St. Joseph's, and pensioners with walking sticks and zimmerframes flying past us."

But he did not care. To be pain-free, no matter how much he had to hobble, was such a blessing, such a miracle. And he knew in his heart that this was only the beginning. The Lord would bring this healing to fruition when the femoral bone and the socket had properly fused together. He believed that; he believed it with all his heart.

Eleven days after that extraordinary morning when the Lord had clamped John's hips, the novena ended. Two days later, on the thirteenth morning, John awakened. His hips were still heavily clamped but as he struggled to get out of bed, the clamp began to release. "It was," he was to say later, "like snow melting." All the tension and stiffness had left his hips leaving him free to bend or to turn or to move in any way he wanted. He turned to Christina who was still in the room and said, with a huge smile, "My hip's after releasing."

Scarcely daring to breathe, Christina whispered, "Do you think you're healed?"

"Well," John replied, almost matter-of-factly. "It'll be very easy to test it."

He knew a number of body twists that would normally cause the bone to move. Only a few days before, if he pulled his knee up to the hip, the femoral bone would have scraped in the socket and had him almost screaming with pain. So he raised his knee, expression set tight against the possibility of a renewal of the pain, and jerked it upwards. There was no grinding. There was no scraping. There was only the simple, fluid, up-and-down movement of a healthy leg. Christina was watching him from the side of her eyes, almost afraid to look. John went out of the room and held on to the banisters. He twisted this way and that, up and down, back and forth, and still the bone remained in place. He experienced no pain whatever in his hip. He began bending, stretching, jerking, making small jumps, the grin on his face growing wider as he did so. Christina threw herself into his arms and they laughed and laughed with the sheer joy of it until they fell silent and stood together for several minutes, lost in the wonder of God's miraculous grace.

What St. Peter wrote in his first letter might well have been written for John.

"... even though you may for a time have to bear being plagued by all sorts of trials ... your faith will have been tested and proved like gold."

Chapter Ten

Accepting

On July 17th 1987, John and Christina finally made it to the top of the Belfast housing list and they were given a house not far from where Christina's mother lived. John went back to the foreman on the Poleglass building site to seek work. He had never told anyone of his disability, so he did not have to explain his cure. And since his previous stint on the site had ended with the completion of the building, there were no questions asked about why he left. He had always been a good and reliable worker so the foreman was happy to rehire him. He did have a limp when he last worked there, of course, but as things were to turn out, he still had a limp when he reported for work on the site again.

John was happy now, full of joy. He was working full-time again, earning money to feed and clothe his family and buy them the little luxuries that had for so long been missing from their lives. Life was great … almost.

What had happened was that over the years, in order to favour his hip, John had exerted extreme pressure on his knees. This had resulted in torn ligaments and muscles that were now stretched and weak. After a day's work, he found himself limping home again, in severe pain once more. The pain was in both knees, although the right knee was significantly worse than the left and had developed a substantial swelling. Because of that and because he had begun to experience a looseness in the knee, movements that were quite disturbing and extremely painful, John was forced to wear double-strength elastic strapping to support it.

One evening on his way home from work, he called into the chapel and prayed. "Lord, you healed my hip and it works wonderfully, and I truly thank for this miraculous healing. But what was the point of that if you're going to leave me with a knee that's nearly as bad as the hip was?"

He paused and stared at the altar, still filled with faith and love of God but trying to find the words he needed to explain that what had been miraculous was, in real terms, in physical terms, virtually pointless and deeply disappointing. While he knelt in front of the altar, staring at the tabernacle and his mind drifting from words to contemplation almost in spite of himself, he was conscious of a divine locution, something that, in later life, was to become a natural part of his normal living.

Somewhere in the depths of his soul he heard the words, "John, you only asked me to heal your hip. You did not say anything to me about your knee."

"Ah, come on, Lord!" John ejaculated, almost without thought, ready to defend his prayer. But he arrested the embryonic argument and reflected on the broader implications of what he had heard. Then he made a decision. "All right, Lord. I'll go back to the prayer of faith again … and the fasting, Lord. But this time, it's for my knee." He looked intently at the tabernacle and added, "Okay?" He made to rise and leave but turned back again, and said to the tabernacle with a half-grin on his lips, "Uh, that's both knees, Lord. Okay?"

He went home and later that evening, in his bedroom, speaking to the Lord all the while, he pulled the bandage from his knee. "Right, Lord," he said, determinedly, "I'm serious about this." He threw the bandage in the waste-paper basket in the corner of the room and continued, "There's no further support going on to this knee, Lord. You're the support. I am putting everything into my prayers now for my knees to be healed … and, Lord, I now know and believe firmly that my knees are already healed."

But yet again John was tested. The following morning he limped to work. The same evening he limped back home. And he limped to work the morning after that. Every morning and every evening over the next two months he was still limping to and from work. It was a trying time for him, and a testing time. The pain was unrelenting. There were times when doubt began to erode even his great faith. He began to wonder if finding the book and having his hip healed were, somehow, unrelated and ultimately meaningless events. But he fought Satan's insidious murmurings and stuck rigidly to his prayers, sometimes praying with more fervour than at others but always with faith, always determinedly thanking God for a healing that had not yet manifested itself but which he firmly believed had been granted.

After a couple of months, almost without any awareness of the healing process, John found that his knees had grown stronger, that the ligaments and the muscles were giving him virtually no pain. By the end of 1987, the inflammation and the burning pain had left his knees. His hip, occasionally perhaps not as strong as it might be, was fluid and painless in its movements. John was completely healed. From time to time over the next few years, God would allow his legs to fall victim to occasional weakness but John always accepted these moments as tests, reminders to persist in his prayer of faith and to pray with fervour through the moments of physical weakness. It would have been easy during such times to fall into doubt and believe that he had not been healed. But he prayed, he believed, he gave thanks, and always the weakness would leave him

Over the years of suffering, his limp had become ingrained and habitual but during those wonderful days in late 1987 he discovered that, if he chose to, he could walk perfectly well without a limp. When he experienced the first realisation of this, he closed his eyes and offered a silent prayer of thanksgiving. He had learned an important lesson, one that he would never fail to pass on to those he would help in the future. As he was to say some years later, “You’re not always healed for now. You’re healed for the future.” And then add with a laugh, “You call things that are not, as though they were, until they are. This is God’s way of praying.”

Chapter Eleven

Resisting

From 1987 until 1994, John lived six peaceful years in the sheer delight of feeling his body heal and grow in strength. He worked full days of hard, manual labour without pain or hindrance, loving every minute of it and enjoying his family life. Sinead was born in 1988, and now with three daughters, John could not have asked for anything that could have made him happier. He settled into this peaceful and comfortable life, delighted with what the Lord had done for him, completely at peace with himself, with the world, and with God.

It was around this time that Christina began attending Charismatic Renewal services and, from time to time, she would bring home books and pamphlets, books such as Sr. Briege McKenna's book, "Miracles Do Happen", and others which told stories of healers and healings in America. Browsing through these on one occasion, John came across a story about a man who had been healed of five medically incurable diseases. Filled with gratitude, the man made a promise to God to help His people and accepted God's call to a healing ministry. It was while he was reading this story that John remembered his own fervent promise to God to help His people in exchange for healing his hip.

John, however, had given no thought to any kind of spiritual ministry. Instead, he would now spend many of his evenings doing work for old people in and around his neighbourhood. For these tasks he never charged anyone a penny, simply happy that he was keeping his promise to God to help His people. As far as John was concerned, his life had run full circle and he arrived at his 'happy-ever-after' phase. He wanted nothing to change and he had no sense that anything was going to change.

From time to time, however, he would have to fight off niggling thoughts about the man who repaid the Lord by undertaking a healing ministry. He had a vague suspicion that God might be calling him to something similar but his immediate and instinctive response would be, "God, I don't want any of that! That isn't me! I'll do voluntary work, help people, do odd jobs. That's the way I'll help your people. Don't be talking to me about praying for the sick and stuff like that."

Nonetheless, he began to sense that God wanted him for something else. During his evening prayers especially, he felt that God was trying to say something to him about the life he was living, asking him to think about what he was doing. John was unhappy that anything might jeopardise the peace he had arrived at and did not want to hear what the Lord was saying to him. But in the ordinary intercourse of life, he would hear people complaining about being depressed or sick and he was always tempted to say to them, "Sure a prayer or two would soon sort that out."

Somehow John was conscious of an instinct to involve himself in the spiritual side of their lives in order try help them. At that time, however, he did not have the sophistication to make such an offer, so he remained silent. But he remained also internally disturbed by these inclinations he was experiencing. He would listen to the people voicing their distress and it seemed so obvious to him that they could easily be healed if only they would pray. “Look at me, for goodness’ sake,” he would mutter to himself. “Look at what God did for me and I was far worse than any of you.” But though he continued to remain silent, he would pray anonymously that their ailments would be healed.

After some time John began to realise that what seemed to him to be a simple matter of faith, was not quite so simple for others. At times during his prayers he would sense God telling him that these people did not have the same gift of faith he had and that was why people like him were chosen to help them. But John would answer, almost before he had fully grasped the sense of what the Lord was saying to him, “But I didn’t ask to be chosen!”

“Did you not ask to be healed? Did you not promise to help my people?”

The words were clear. John was now hearing rather than sensing them.

“Yes, I did, Lord. But this healing stuff is not what I had in mind. It might have been in your plans, but it was never in mine.”

But as the days and weeks went on, John became more and more aware of the suffering and sickness and hurt that were all around him and he could not curb the overflow of compassion that he felt. And he was increasingly tortured by the thought, by the real knowledge, that if medical intervention could not help these suffering people, there was great power in the healing of the Spirit. “All that’s needed here,” he would say to himself, almost exasperated by the seeming lack of awareness he saw in others, “is faith.” Indeed, he had more conviction in the power of faith than he had in any medical solution. But his exasperation would wane with the realisation that not everyone was granted the steadfast, determined faith that was needed to trigger God's healing.

God has His own way of making things happen. It was sometime in1994 that John attended a series of Life in the Spirit seminars, organised by the Holy Trinity Prayer Group. Such seminars are common in prayer groups throughout the Church. Part of the process involved the sharing of experiences and John told the group the story of his own healing. The organising Core Group asked John to speak to other groups about his healing and he was happy to do so. He continued to attend the seminars and, as was customary at these meetings, he joined with the others in praying for the nine gifts of the Holy Spirit.

These nine gifts are usually organised into three categories. There are the three 'gifts of power' – faith, healing and miracles; the 'gifts of the mind' – wisdom, knowledge and discernment; and the 'gifts of language' – the gift of tongues, the gift of interpretation of tongues, and the gift of prophecy.

One evening, after the seminar was finished, two of the women from the group approached John. One of them he knew to be a pious woman who would from time to time, receive some form of prophetic intuition from God. Now she had a message for John. "God is now ready to give you the nine gifts of the Holy Spirit. He will soon call you to a healing ministry and you will also receive an extra gift, attached to the gift of discernment. God is going to show you in particular during many of the healings you will work, demons who lurk in the background of people's lives, demons who cause physical sickness, mental illness, and other forms of oppression. God will give you the ability to see when these demons are part of the cause of some petitioner's illness and you will have the power to cast them out."

Despite his natural instinct to step back and reject what these women had said to him, John found that, as a result of his attendance at these seminars, much about his way of thinking and praying was changing. He began to read more than he had ever read before. And his reading was specifically focused on books about approaches to healing through the Spirit, books about spiritual warfare, books about demonic oppression and possession. He found this research fascinating. He also found himself ill-at-ease and unsettled. He was happier now on the building sites than he had ever been. He loved the work. He loved the way his body was growing stronger, and he revelled in the hard physical activity. To come home each evening, pleasantly weary but with no pain, was a source of never-ending joy for him. He felt that he wanted nothing more from life and was content to serve God as a builder's labourer who did his work to the best of his ability with an honest awareness of his responsibilities to his employer.

But somehow what he was reading was affecting him. He was beginning to intuit that he would have no peace if he was not doing the things he was reading about. He began to feel as if he was engaged in a spiritual struggle; to sense that, happy as he was on the building site, it was not the work God wanted him to do. More and more he came to know that what the two women had said to him at the seminar was nothing less than a message from the Lord himself, a message to leave the building site and begin labouring among God's sick and oppressed people.

But John's natural humility fought against the Lord's appeal. He was happy with the anonymity of his existing state, with the simple pleasures of his life. He did not want to be thrust into the public eye. He did not want to hear people asking, "Who is this guy? Where did he come from? Why pick him and not somebody else? He's only a labourer … what education does he have to be healing and telling others what to do?" The questions John feared echoed unconsciously the same treatment Jesus had received from His own people in Nazareth.

"*Where did this man get all this? This is a carpenter, surely?*" [Mark. 6:2]

Such arguments, of course, carry little weight with the Lord. He has heard them over and over down through the centuries. When the Lord selects a disciple with singular gifts to carry out His work, there is little that person can do to resist. Even in biblical times, thousands of years ago, Amos made the same complaint to Amaziah:

"*I was no prophet, nor am I the son of a prophet. I was a shepherd and looked after the sycamores; but it was the Lord who took me from herding the flock and it was the Lord who said, 'Go prophesy to my people Israel.'*" [Amos 7:13 – 15]

And John would pray, "All I have is a stubborn faith, Lord. I am only a labourer. How does this equip me for this sort of life?"

Chapter Twelve

Exorcising

The year 1994 was also significant for another, deeply disturbing, reason. It was the year John's fourth daughter, Fionnuala, was born, a lovely child, healthy, and physically perfect. She slept happily in a cot beside John's and Christina's bed during the first few months of her life, giving them no cause for concern whatever. After a year and some months had passed, however, she began to become restless and unsettled. She would occasionally cry loudly in the night but her parents knew that it was not the normal night crying of a child who had hunger pains or some form of colic. This was a high-pitched keening that seemed filled with fear.

Christina was particularly upset by what was happening, praying for their daughter, and comforting her as best she could, but both she and John knew that something was not right, that something strange was upsetting the child. John wondered, but without any serious conviction, if what was happening had anything to do with God calling him into ministry, something his mind was full of at the time. He began to wonder if perhaps this was some form of demonic attack, if Satan was somehow using the child, frightening the child badly, and creating in Christina and himself such a fear for their child that he might be persuaded to step back from a healing ministry even though it seemed to be what the Lord was calling him to.

They prayed. They sought help. The local priest thought it might be just "childhood nightmares" and suggested that they leave a low light on in the room and to watch out for foods that might be making Fionnuala hyper-active at night. They did as the priest said but their efforts had no effect. The terrible night terrors for the child continued unabated and the worried parents knew that something more was needed.

Something about the atmosphere of the room, however, disturbed Christina. She felt ill-at-ease there, and somehow the normal light in the room seemed to have dimmed. One evening Christina woke from sleep and saw a hooded figure, cloaked and faceless, standing at the bottom of their bed. She knew at once that this was what had been frightening their baby daughter. She immediately rebuked the figure in the name of Jesus, commanding it to leave. The shadow disappeared but it was then that they knew with certainty that their lovely little daughter was under demonic attack. But how could that be? The child was born into a good home, had sincere Christian parents, lived in a house where God definitely was present. It seemed far-fetched and unreal that such a child could be the victim of some form of demonic attack. John was to learn later, from frequent and painful experience, that God had a plan for him and that Satan would attack him wherever he could, that he would employ every evil trick he could to attempt to thwart God's plan.

And certainly, at this time in 1994, John did fall victim to a dreadful fear. He knew that Christina's brief abjuration of the demon would not be enough to end the oppression. He did not know what to do. He had no help. He turned to God again in violent prayer. He fasted for three days, a long and difficult fast. Coming home each evening from a long day of hard physical labour left him weak and exhausted. The hunger tested him but he persisted. And he continued to plead with the Lord, "Lord, I don't know what to do here. I don't have any help. I know there's an evil force coming against my child. Show me how to free my house from this and I will go and set other people free from the same thing. Just show me, dear God! I need you to show me what to do to get rid of this thing."

They went seeking help again, talking to anyone they thought might know what to do. They went back to the local priest and explained what they now knew was happening. He could not understand why the holy pictures and angels were not enough to prevent the manifestations but John persisted.

"What would prevent a demon attacking a child's mind?" he asked.

"Oh, well, now," the priest replied, hesitating, "that is a totally different area of difficulty."

"Well, it's the area that we're having trouble with," John replied, with some force, trying desperately to wring more information from him. The priest knew John and his reputation and assured him that he could deal with the deliverance himself. He advised him to use a prayer that he already had in his house, the prayer of exorcism and the rejection of Satan from the Rite of Baptism. It was sound advice. The Catholic Catechism (p.281) states:

"*Since baptism signifies liberation from sin and from its instigator the devil, one or more exorcisms are pronounced over the candidate.*

the celebrant then anoints him with the oil of Catechumens, or lays his hands on him, and explicitly renounces Satan."

On the third evening of John's fast, Christina had gone to pray in St. Agnes' Church. She had Fionnuala with her. During that week a lay-missionary and writer of spiritual books, Frances Hogan, had been conducting a retreat in the chapel. Frances had been teaching scripture for many years and had a great knowledge of how the evil one works. Christina had been hoping to meet her to ask her how Satan operates and whether he could work through children, especially a child as young as Fionnuala.

By some divine coincidence, Christina found Frances Hogan at the front of the chapel and sat down to talk with her. She told Frances the full story and said, "We're terribly concerned. We can't seem to find the help we need. We don't know what to do. Is there any help you can give me?"

Frances said seriously, "I believe that God has a plan for your child … and Satan knows in advance what it is. He's trying to upset the child, disturb her in some way. He'll do anything he can to disrupt God's plans."

Christina was desperately worried. "But what can we do?"

"When you move her from your bedroom to her own room, you should get blessed salt and give it to the child. That's very efficacious."

"Where can I get that?"

"Just take some salt to a priest. He can bless it for you. When it's blessed it becomes very powerful for both healing and deliverance. You should also put a miraculous medal on the child. But try to get the salt. That's the best help."

Christina told John about her meeting with Frances. Late that night, however, indeed it was one o'clock in the morning, John and Christina were still sitting downstairs, talking about the situation. They heard sudden cries from Fionnuala upstairs and dashed up to the child's cot, terrified at the volume of the screaming. Fionnuala, who was now twenty-two months old, was pointing towards one of the corners of the room, continuing to scream in terror, her eyes focused on that corner. Christina immediately seized Fionnuala from the cot. As the child fell against her, she clung to her mother with extraordinary strength and Christina could feel the tiny nails digging into her shoulders.

The child's terror was frightening, and the atmosphere of evil in the room was now palpable. Satan was no longer attempting to hide his presence. John rushed downstairs, found some salt and sprinkled it with holy water from a bottle they always kept in the kitchen, praying that the Lord would bless the salt and make it efficacious in the desperate circumstances for which it was now needed. He ran back to the room and grabbed the baptismal rite from beside his bed where he had been previously reading it. He lit a blessed candle that he had earlier acquired and rushed to Fionnuala's cot where he read the baptismal prayer of exorcism with all the strength and fervour he could muster. He placed a little of the blessed salt on Fionnuala's lips and sprinkled what was left around the dark corner and the rest of the room, shouting as he tried to hide the tremor in his voice, "I command anything here that is not of Jesus to leave now in Jesus' name, never to return."

The effect was almost instantaneous and unmistakable. Immediately the atmosphere in the room changed. The child quietened, became calm, and began drifting off to sleep. They placed her back in the baby cot, left the candle lit, and said a decade of the rosary. The dimness that had fallen over the room during the previous days lifted and there was now an aura of soft brightness which remained in the room for several days afterwards.

John was later to learn that God had permitted this event, not only to teach him how to discern the presence of demons and to deal with such demonic incursion, but also to make him aware of what was happening in other homes, to draw to his attention that such instances of demonic attack often go undiagnosed and overlooked. There are many people in similarly dire circumstances who need help but who do not know what to do or where to go. When ailments can be given a medical name or a medical diagnosis, then help is almost always possible; but when the problem is supernatural, when a diabolical force that is threatening people is not recognised for what it is, then, as the Lord pointed out, "… that, John, is where people like you are needed."

Chapter Thirteen

Surrendering

One Sunday evening in 1996, John dropped a friend off on his way home from a prayer-group meeting. When he was driving back to his own house, alone in the car and half listening to a spiritual music cassette playing on his tape-deck, he returned once more to the mental tug-of-war that had become so much a permanent feature of his life. He had been wrestling constantly with the conflict between his desire to remain in his settled life and the urges he was experiencing from the Spirit to take an entirely different path.

One of his key defences was that he did not see how he could take any radical steps away from his present life unless he was given some indication of what was required of him, what he termed "a real sign from God!" But he remained uncomfortably conscious of the fact that this argument was thin. How does one interpret signs? What is a 'real' sign? He had become painfully aware that people were hearing that John Gillespie was a man of prayer, a man of faith, who could help people simply by praying for them. For some time now, friends and acquaintances, even occasionally someone he did not know, would ask him for prayer, usually for some form of healing. John could never refuse these requests and gradually word began to filter back to him that many of the people he was praying for were experiencing unusual healings, and this without John even having touched them.

Signs? He could almost see Jesus with one eyebrow raised and a quiet smile, saying, “Are you going to go on pretending this isn’t happening, John?” John could not escape the feeling that Jesus was trying to bring him into some form of healing ministry, yet, despite increasing evidence that he had indeed been granted a gift of healing, John continued to argue with the Lord, constantly claiming that he had no history or background that would enable him to undertake such a role. But he did not want to deliberately thwart the Lord’s will. He loved his present life but if the Lord truly wanted something else from him, then he would have to consider it. So he prayed constantly, fasted regularly, seeking some form of unmistakable confirmation that a healing ministry was what the Lord wanted from him.

His mind was so fogged with the pros and cons of the arguments that he shook his head to clear it and tried simply to listen to the music that was playing in the car. At that moment, a female singer was singing a song entitled, “I’ll be with you wherever you go!” John listened to the words and felt in his heart, knew in his spirit, that the Lord was talking to him through the words of the song. To John, every word was significant and penetrated deep into his mind. “Feed my lambs…pray for my sick…come back to me over stormy waters.” John’s heart and spirit were charged with the nearness of Jesus as he listened to these words. And again he was torn. At times such as this, he wanted with every fibre of his being to do what the Lord wanted, but even with the thought he wondered how he could justify walking away from the perfect life the Lord had given him.

Sitting at home a short while later, his mind still filled with the words of the song, John felt a tingling in his fingers, almost like pins and needles. He opened and closed his fists a couple of times in an effort to restore his fingers to normal but the feeling continued. Then from nowhere he experienced a sudden surge of immense power, like a bolt of electricity, charging through his body. His hands in particular were shaking with the force of this … this potency that was coursing through him. And John knew instinctively, without thought of any kind, that if he were to touch anyone at that moment, no matter what or how serious their ailment might be, the force pouring from him would heal that person instantly.

John was exhilarated and disquieted in equal measures. He had never experienced anything like this in his life before. The spiritual energy that was flowing through him did not abate and he paced agitatedly around the room, his hands held awkwardly in front of him, trying to explain to Christina what was happening. Christina managed to get him to sit back in his chair and she fetched a couple of beers from the fridge to help him to settle. Eventually she persuaded him to go to bed where he spent a restless night, muttering and praying, tossing and turning.

The following morning at the kitchen table, he reached for his bible "to read a verse or two to start the day". But as he touched the book, the power surged through him again and he began to see vision after vision of himself laying hands on crowds of sick people who would then walk away cured. John was aghast.

"Oh, my God!" he prayed. "Oh, my dear God! How am I to cope with something like this? What are my friends on the building site going to think? Dear Lord, turn this power down, way, way, way down. I can't go to work with this stuff buzzing through me. Enough's enough, Lord." He raised his eyes to heaven. "Lord, please! Turn this down. I need to go to work. I can't have this stuff sizzling in me all day. You have to turn it off, Lord."

He rose, washed, breakfasted, mumbling almost incoherently the entire while and eventually left for work. As he travelled to the site, he sensed some diminishment of the power in his body but then he began to feel a pulse, a rhythm, in his right hand. It felt like a heartbeat in the centre of his palm and he knew that something of God's power was working its way into the hand. Then, a short time later, a similar pulse began to beat in the left hand, and now he had a strong beat, pulsing vigorously, in both hands. And even as he wondered what was happening, he received the clear impression that the Lord was anointing his hands … and still he fought against it. "Lord, this isn't me. I wouldn't be any good at this!"

The pulsing, the force in his body, lost some of its intensity as he worked but it did not leave him. All day his mind remained filled with visions of people calling to him, their arms outstretched, crying for healing, and a voice would repeat from time to time in his head, "I'm calling on you to go out and answer these poor people's needs. Someone has to help them, John, and I want it to be you. How can you ignore my people, John?"

John worked with an almost manic intensity that day, involving himself little with his fellow workers, continually debating within himself how he should react to this strange phenomenon. But he was so inflamed with the potency of the spiritual energy that was coursing through him that he wanted "… to climb up to the roof of the house and stretch out my arms to God. I was so filled with him, so alive, knowing that He was speaking to me personally, touching me, filling me. It was just amazing."

But despite the glory of that spiritual experience, despite his love for the wonder of God's closeness, John's natural intransigence reasserted itself and he continued to wrestle all day with the Lord. "Jesus, you're not doing this to me. You need to turn this thing down a bit till I go home and figure it out." Then he would opt for matter-of-factness. "Look, Lord! If there's something you need to talk to me about, we'll discuss it tonight. But I'm up to my eyes here, and with all this going on, I'm going to get nothing done."

Despite his stubborn and frenetic work pace, the day remained a strange day of inner conflict, of preternatural psychic and mystical experiences. When he arrived home that evening, he knew, with blinding and sudden certainty, that his life would never be the same again. He tried to explain to Christina what he thought was happening but she had already understood, and fully believed, even before he spoke, that God was calling John into a healing ministry.

Eventually John went to a quiet room in the house, still in turmoil, and prayed, "Lord, if what is going on is really from you, then there's one way you can prove it. I don't think you're fooling around Lord, but neither am I. Before I go to bed this evening, I want you to send three people to me. I have nobody in mind, any three people. You're the one who keeps sending them to me. So, you send me three people here this night, anybody at all, who are seeking prayer for healing, because I need to test this stuff that's buzzing around inside of me."

Three people did contact John that night, each at a different time, and none of them having any connection with the others. The first was a phone call from a lady

John had helped before with physical work. She had a deformed hand which she could not use. But on this occasion, she had fallen and hurt the wrist of her other hand, leaving her helpless. She phoned to ask John if he would come to set and light a fire for her. She explained that her wrist was very painful. John prayed over the woman while he was there, asking her to point out where the pain was. As he prayed, he gently rubbed the sore section with his thumb. The woman winced, experiencing a sudden burning pain in her arm. But equally suddenly, she discovered that she could move her fingers easily and she was no longer feeling any kind of pain. Later x-rays were to show that there had been a hair-line fracture in the wrist which had mysteriously healed. An early hospital examination had somehow missed it.

John had scarcely arrived home when the phone rang again. It was Christina's mother. Some years previously, while she was looking after her grand-children in a play-park, she had fallen on her knee and shattered the kneecap and some of the other bones around it. She had had surgery which had helped but the consultant had warned her at the time that the maximum effect of the surgery would be ten years. Recently she had been experiencing considerable pain in the knee and she deeply regretted that the pain was preventing her continuing her role as an extraordinary minister of the Eucharist. Climbing the altar steps was beyond her. That night she was sitting in her chair at home praying her rosary when she received an inexplicable urge to phone John to ask him if would come to the house and pray over her. John immediately went to see her, prayed over her, and the knee was suddenly healed. To this day, years later, she remains trouble free.

John was to learn an important lesson that night from the third supplicant. A co-worker of John's arrived at the door later that evening. His nephew, scarcely nine years old, was lying in hospital dying of leukaemia. He asked John to go with him and comfort the boy in his final hours. John went with him and sensed immediately that here was a child of immense faith and he gave him a present of a small Benedict crucifix that he had taken with him from the house. He prayed over the child but he was to die on Christmas Eve, two days later. God had wanted the boy to share his suffering with Him and then join Him in heaven. It was as simple as that. Shortly after the child's funeral, John's co-worker showed him the crucifix. The child had clasped it so tightly and with such faith during his last couple of days, that the tracks of his fingers were ground deep into the surface of the cross. John was sad that the child had died, but he learned, not only that the Lord wanted the boy with Him in heaven but that there would be times when it would not be God's will for earthly healing to take place. John's role on that occasion had simply been to bring the boy peace and acceptance as he faced his death.

That was the night when John surrendered to the Lord. That was when he experienced the great conversion in his life that enabled him to accept that from then on he would devote his life and his energies and his new gifts to the delivery of Jesus' healing and comfort to His people.

He continued to work on the building site for a couple of years. Initially the healings he was instrumental in bringing about were sporadic and occasional. But as word-of-mouth spread about what he was doing, the demands on his time for prayer and healing continued to grow and he was having difficulty responding to all the requests that were coming to him.

The time he needed, however, was to materialise in an unexpected way. The building project he was working with was closed down and within a couple of days John found himself out of a job. Perhaps the Lord felt that John needed to devote more time to this work and decided to make it easier for him! He did find another job as sacristan at the chapel but even after a year or two of that, he was able only to attend on a part-time basis.

He was to hear a prophecy a year or so later, in 1998, from a priest, Father Ronnie Mitchell, who often celebrated mass for the Holy Trinity Prayer Group. Father Mitchell, who was well-known to have the gift of prophecy, told John about a vision he had of a huge ship, very heavily laden with cargo, coming into a port where John and Christina were standing. Jesus was at the helm of the ship, which was called The Miracle Ship, and He was pleading with John to distribute its cargo, thousands upon thousands of miracles, to His people. That was when John finally knew that there would be no turning back, that working for the Lord would be his life from then on.

Pope Benedict XVI, when he was Cardinal Ratzinger, once had a sequestered academic life planned out for himself. He saw himself comfortably ensconced in a good university, teaching doctrine and theology, studying and writing. But at the behest of John Paul II, the cardinal was forced to accept, most reluctantly, an appointment as Archbishop of Freising and Munich. As he signed his acceptance in the presence of the Papal Nuncio, the cardinal said resignedly, “Sometimes we even have to accept something that does not seem at first to lie in our own line of life.” John Gillespie may not have had these words in his mind when God insisted that he accept a healing ministry, but by 1998, their general import had finally made its way into his heart.

PART TWO: HEAL THE SICK

Chapter Fourteen

"The one who believes in me will do the same works that I do..." [John,14:12]

NOTE:

The stories of healing that are related in Part Two and in Part Three are all true and verifiable. In order to protect the privacy of the individuals concerned, however, the names of some the people and locations have been changed. A few have chosen to let their real names be used.

Note also that, while many of the stories were related to the author by John, there are some of them which were sent directly to the author by grateful petitioners who had heard that this book was being written and wanted to contribute their own first-hand accounts.

"Faith is the assurance of what we hope for, being certain of what we cannot see."[Heb.11.]

The Prayer of Faith

During the few years that John has been engaged in his ministry of healing, an extraordinary number of miracles has followed his prayer involvement with the supplicants. In Father Mitchell's prophesy, Jesus asked John to carry miracles to His people. There was nothing figurative or metaphorical about that. Jesus's request was literal. John is simply the conduit through which Jesus is able to deliver His healing to the sick or possessed.

Sometimes when John prays over a supplicant, the healing takes place immediately. This is not unusual nor was it unusual for Jesus in His day. There were times, as well, when Jesus required something specific from the petitioner, some sign of faith, for example. Mark tells us that when Jesus went to preach in His home town of Nazareth, He was rejected, and "… Jesus could work no miracle there though He cured a few people by laying His hand on them, but He was amazed at their lack of faith." [Mark, 6:5 -6]. Sometimes the person seeking healing was asked to repent of their sins before Jesus would perform His healing miracle. But there were times, too, when, moved with compassion, Jesus healed the suffering person immediately without stipulation of any kind.

This is not the norm, however. John's experience is that, more often than not, there are healings which require the prayer of faith, the prayer that demands belief that healing has taken place even before there is evidence of a cure. In the miraculous story that follows, the significant supplicants are asked to thank God for a healing where there were as yet no obvious indications that a healing had taken place.

***

Dermott's Story: Spinal Cord Injury

Dermott Hadden was sixteen years of age. Like any boy of his years, he loved football, all sports in fact, and lived an active, energetic life. At least, he did until the car crash that crushed the eight vertebrae in his neck, that squeezed the crushed discs into his spinal cord and caused a loss of all motor functions and permanent paralysis. Although the paramedics who arrived shortly afterwards at the scene did not expect the boy to survive the injuries, they rushed him to a nearby hospital. A priest, who had been called to the scene, accompanied the boy in the ambulance, giving him the last rites.

Dermott was operated upon immediately on arrival and afterwards the surgeon spoke to the parents. His news was devastating for the boy's mother. She was told that the worst of the injuries were in the neck and shoulders and, although a broken back or a broken neck can be healed, pieces of the vertebrae had torn into the spinal cord tissue causing serious damage. The particular location of this injury was the greatest cause for concern. The higher in the spinal column a spinal injury occurs, the more dysfunction will be experienced by the body.

"I'm terribly sorry to have to tell you," the consultant said, "that the damage to your son's spinal cord is irreparable."

"What does that mean?" Mrs. Hadden asked tearfully.

The surgeon hesitated a moment before saying, "The spinal cord is the major bundle of nerves that carry nerve impulses to and from the brain to the rest of the body. It is about eighteen inches long and extends from the base of the brain down the middle of the back to about the waist. It is that part of your son's body that has been most badly injured."

"What are nerve impulses?" the stricken woman pressed.

"Well … they are signals from the brain through the spinal column to various other parts of the body …" He was shaking his head when he added, "In complete spinal cord injury, the cord can't relay messages below the level of the injury."

"Are you saying that our boy is paralyzed from the neck down?" the father asked, horrified.

The surgeon nodded, his face serious.

Mrs. Haden was distraught. "Are you saying that Dermott can't walk? That he'll never be able to walk? But he's only sixteen … he can't be wheelchair- bound for the rest of his life … he …" and she broke down while her husband tried vainly to comfort her.

"We'll do what we can to rehabilitate him," the surgeon said. "We might be able to restore some movement to his hands but … we cannot cure a ruptured spinal cord. There's a lot of research going on about this at the present time but, so far, the scientists have not found a cure." He paused and took a deep breath. "I'm afraid you are going to have to accept that your son will be paralyzed everywhere below the level of injury."

During the following two days, members of the family came to visit the boy in hospital. He remained unconscious, head and shoulders encased in a rigid metal frame to prevent any involuntary movement. One of the visitors was Dermott's uncle, Seamus, who was distressed to see his nephew in this state. Seamus however, had been friendly with a family who were full of stories about a miraculous cure brought to one of the children by a man from Belfast called John Gillespie. He contacted the family, got a number for John, and begged him to come and pray over his nephew.

John agreed to come immediately. When he arrived at the hospital, he found the boy tightly strapped, wedged securely into the metal frame around his head and shoulders, and heavily sedated because of the extensive levels of pain medication he had been prescribed. John began to pray over the boy, asking Jesus for a miracle. And as he prayed, asking the Lord to heal Dermott's injuries, asking Him to allow the boy to walk again, he was granted a vision, an extraordinary vision. As clearly as if he was viewing it on a television screen, John could see the Lord weaving a new spinal cord up through the young boy's vertebrae. He could see the damaged lower motor neurones to the spinal cord being reattached to the spinal column as if by an invisible needle.

The Lord was allowing John to understand what he was seeing. The lower motor neurones are the spinal nerves that branch out from the spinal cord to other parts of the body. Their purpose is to ensure that the body can receive sensations and activate movement. Through the Spirit's unspoken guidance, John understood that the bundle of nerves being repaired was the boy's central nervous system and that, when the repairs were complete, Dermott would be able to walk again.

John said nothing of this to the parents. Instead, accepting the guidance of the Spirit, he informed the parents, that medical intervention would not be sufficient to help Dermott, that a miracle was needed. He instructed them to begin thanking God in faith for their son's healing and to encourage their relatives to pray thanksgiving prayers as well. John left then but promised to return soon.

The following day Dermott emerged from his deep sedation. The doctor, with the boy's father and uncle, were at his bedside. The boy clearly needed a few minutes to understand where he was and then, in a weak voice, he stared at his father and said, "Daddy, there was somebody here last night …"

Mr. Hadden knew that his son had been unconscious all evening and could not have known that John had been there. "Who do you think was here?" he asked his son.

"I don't know," Dermott replied, "but somebody touched me." He began to get agitated. "Whoever that person was, Daddy, you have to get him back." He became more insistent. "He's got to come back, Daddy. Some sort of a power went through me. If you can get that man back, I can be healed. I know it."

Dermott's father looked at the other two men and saw his own amazement registered on their faces. As the doctor moved forward to calm his increasingly perturbed patient, the father said quickly, "It was John, Dermott. He came to bless you."

"He has to come back, Daddy," Dermott was almost crying. "You have to get him back."

Mr. Hadden patted his son's hand. "All right! All right, son! Don't get upset. We'll phone him right away. Uncle Seamus is a friend of his. He'll go and call him now."

Dermott relaxed and his eyes closed as the sedatives again sent him to sleep. The doctor stood looking down at him for a moment, shaking his head in puzzlement. He nodded to the two men as he left the room.

"How could he have known?" Mr. Hadden asked, mystified. "I mean, he was unconscious."

Seamus shrugged. "God must have touched him in some way." He stared at his brother. "I know the doctor said he'd never move his legs again but …"

Dermott's eyes opened again. He stared wordlessly at the two men, sensing their puzzlement.

Seamus raised the blanket from the bottom of the bed and said, "Dermott, can you even move your toes?"

The boy's head remained motionless in its metal frame but his eyes moved to his uncle at the bottom of the bed. "I don't know. I'll try."

They waited for some minutes but nothing happened. The father said, "Can you try, son?"

"I am trying," Dermott said.

The two men stared at the motionless feet. Suddenly the big toe on the right foot quivered briefly but the feet remained still. Filled with a surge of hope, mingled with anxiety, the father pressed his son to try again. After some endless moments, the toe jerked again. Neither man spoke but the father ran out of the ward to find the doctor. The doctor dismissed any suggestion that the movement of the toe was significant. "Don't fall victim to false hope, Mr. Hadden," he said. "What you saw was simply an involuntary muscle reflex. It doesn't mean anything."

John came again that evening in response to Seamus's phone-call. After what he had seen in the vision the evening before, he had not been surprised to hear about the movement in the boy's foot. Again he prayed, asking God to send power down through the boy's other leg. Again, as he left, he encouraged the parents and the other relatives there, to thank God for healing Dermott.

The following morning, Mrs. Hadden came in with her husband and begged Dermott to try again to move his toe. There was an almost immediate reaction on the right foot and, in response to his mother's breathless encouragement, Dermott was able to move the big toe on the left foot as well. It was then that the parents knew that there was a greater power operating here, despite the doctor's conviction that the movements were unconscious reflex, and that evening they were fervent in their thanks to God.

For the next few days, all that happened were the toe movements but they became more regular and more obviously controlled. In addition, Dermott began to gain sensation in his feet. He could feel his mother's hands massaging them. John visited again and told the parents that as long as the bones were knitting in the straps and there was that restrictive metal cage around the upper body, there was little likelihood of any other movement. He advised them to continue to pray in faith and wait for the bones to heal.

The doctor and his colleagues were amazed and puzzled by this new development. Given the obvious control Dermott now had over his toes, however, they began to assume that their original prognosis of permanent paralysis had been incorrect. They arranged to have him sent to a hospital that specialised in the rehabilitation of broken bodies after serious accidents. After a few months, during which time John visited several times to pray over the boy, Dermott left that hospital, perfectly healed.

***

The prayer of faith knows no age barriers. As Jesus once said, "Everything is possible for God." The story that follows recounts a remarkable healing of an elderly pensioner. In this account we learn that healing can be progressive; that is, that there can be small, incremental indications that healing is taking place. In cases such as this, John will usually see the petitioner on a number of occasions, always encouraging them to pray the prayer of faith with increasing fervour and constancy until healing has taken place.

***

Robert's Story: The Four Blocked Arteries

Robert, a seventy-five year old pensioner, lives in a quiet village situated in a beautifully scenic area on the east coast of Northern Ireland. From his garden he can see the mountains on one side and the broad, majestic sweep of the sea on the other. Four years before he met John, Robert was a fit and healthy man who loved to walk for miles in the countryside around his home and spend hours working in his beloved garden. That was his life, a life of contentment, until the day the pains grabbed his chest, until the day when he could no longer tend to his garden, until the day when talking became difficult and walking became impossible. His doctor examined him and expressed concern for his heart. A consultancy was arranged and Robert went to see a surgeon at a hospital in Belfast. The surgeon was disturbed by what he found. Four of Robert's arteries were blocked and he would require a quadruple by-pass as soon as possible. The surgeon recommended that Robert's name be placed on the waiting list immediately.

A year came and went and still no call had come from the hospital. Robert was a strong-willed man who would never willingly succumb to weakness but this was a battle he simply could not win. His life became a misery of laboured breathing, and severe chest pains.

It was around that time that John Gillespie had begun visiting another house in the village, a house where he went to pray over people, a house he still visits regularly. Word about what John was doing soon spread and eventually Robert was taken to the house meet him. He told John his story and explained that his chest pains had become so severe that he was finding it very difficult to cope with them. He was also concerned that his heart might collapse before he would ever reach the operating table.

John expressed sympathy for Robert's obviously parlous state and prayed over him immediately. He prayed that Jesus would send his precious blood flowing through Robert's blocked arteries and free them from all obstruction. He then told Robert about the prayer of faith and said, "Now you can pray away yourself, sunning in the garden, lying in bed, sitting in the house, anywhere. You don't need to be on your knees. Just pray anywhere, no matter what you're doing."

Robert was somewhat uncertain. "What should I say? How will I pray?"

"All you have to do," John said, "is to thank Jesus for filling your veins and arteries with his precious blood and thank Him for healing you. It doesn't matter if you feel any pain. It doesn't matter if you still feel weak. Continue to thank Him for His healing."

"That's all I need to do?" Robert said, shaking his head, mystified.

"That's all," John laughed. "Do that and you'll do fine. And I will continue to pray for you as well."

Robert went home and did as John said. He prayed constantly, thanking the Lord for his healing and never doubting that John's word was true. The pains continued and his energy levels were very low. He was due to make a second visit to John a couple of weeks later and, when John prayed over him a second time, Robert said, "I truly believe that I am beginning to feel better. The pain is not bothering me anything like it was."

John just nodded. "Keep saying the prayer of faith," he said. "You're healed, Robert. Just believe it."

Robert went home and prayed even more fervently. He knew now that the changes he had felt on his last visit to John were not imagination. He was spending less time in the armchair. He was breathing more easily. The pains were much less debilitating. And so he prayed, continuing to thank Jesus for His healing, continuing to declare unequivocally his faith in it. When he went back to John again, two weeks later, he was a changed man. He was now doing small, undemanding chores in his garden; he was going for short walks; and his breathing was no longer troubling him.

John was delighted at his progress, but not surprised. He prayed over him again and asked Robert to call and see him the following week, just to report his progress. Robert returned in excellent form. There was no sign whatever of the illness that had laid him low. He was now back full-time in his garden, tackling all of the accumulated tasks with gusto. He was back to walking his usual few miles a day. He no longer felt any pain, not even little twinges. As far as Robert could tell he was completely cured. John prayed with him again, this time in thankfulness to the Lord for the healing He had effected in Robert.

About six weeks later, some eighteen months after Robert had put his name on the waiting list, a letter arrived from the hospital informing him that a date had now been scheduled for the quadruple by-pass. He was instructed to go to the hospital on a day the following week to have his chest x-rayed and to have a preliminary examination at the consultant's weekly clinic.

Robert obeyed the summons. His daughter, Margaret, went to the hospital with him and waited while the x-rays were taken. When the consultant saw the pictures a short time later he was amazed and mystified. Robert tried to explain what had been happening and told him about John's visits and prayers. The consultant could only shake his head and say, "This is something way beyond my experience. All I can say is that the pictures show that you now have the heart of a strong young man … no blocked arteries anywhere to be seen." He pointed to the viewing-box on the wall where he had placed the pictures, and switched on the background light. "Here is an x-ray taken eighteen months ago. It shows a heart with four seriously blocked arteries. Only surgery will clear those. Here is another X-ray, taken today. It shows a strong young heart. All the arteries are clear and the heart is as sound as a bell." He scratched his head, baffled. "A year and a half ago you were in desperate need of a quadruple by-pass. Now you don't need anything. There's no point in my going ahead with the operation scheduled for next week. You heart's in better shape than mine." He shook his head, still mystified. "You may as well go on back home, Robert. There's nothing I can do for you that God has not already done. I'll arrange to see you in a few months just to make sure that everything is as it should be. But," he stared at the x-rays again, seemingly unable to take his eyes off them, “from the looks of this picture your next visit will only be a formality.”

That was several years ago. Robert remains hale and healthy and has had no need for any further medical intervention.

***

The New Testament teaches that Jesus healed, that He healed all of the people who came to Hm asking to be healed. He refused no one. Jesus loved to heal. The reader may recall the story of the leper in the gospel who said to Jesus, “Lord, if You want to, You can heal me.”

And Jesus immediately replied, filled with love and compassion, “Of course I want to.” And He healed him.

It was this story that kept alive, all through his adolescence and early adulthood, John’s determination to be healed. What John Gillespie believed then, and believes now, totally in his heart, is that Jesus has never stopped wanting to heal. John frequently makes the point that before His death, Jesus left instructions for His disciples to carry on His work, preaching the gospel, healing the sick, casting out demons - three separate, yet inter-related duties. The apostles and disciples, long after Jesus died, continued to carry out this ministry as they wandered the Holy Land, and much further afield. They preached the Word as revealed to them by the Spirit, they healed the sick as they had seen Jesus do, and they cast out demons, partly through compassion for suffering and partly to convince their listeners that the Good News they preached came from God.

For two thousand years Jesus has continued to heal in all sorts of ways, through gifted people chosen by Him down through the ages and through His holy saints, before and after their deaths. John now acknowledges that, although he has done nothing to deserve it and that, in truth, he never wanted it, he too has been gifted with the healing ministry. He has finally come to terms with the responsibility that has been thrust upon him and now devotes his life and his heart to this new ministry.

John is occasionally referred to as a 'faith-healer'. It is not a term that he likes, particularly since it is a term often applied to people who do not claim to heal through the power of Jesus. He is constantly at pains to affirm that when healing takes place as a result of his prayers, it is not he who heals but Jesus.

"I don't do anything," he'll say. "It is Jesus who does the healing. Jesus can do anything."

And it is that sure belief in Jesus, John tells us, that we must take with us into 'the prayer of faith'. The story of Robert (above) is a perfect example of such faith. Nonetheless, John would be the first to admit that praying in faith is perhaps sometimes not fully understood. When we ask for a favour, he says, and we find the favour granted, we pray a thanksgiving prayer, a prayer of joy, perhaps a prayer of praise. In doing this, we believe that we are praying in faith. And, of course, we are. Any prayer implies a degree of faith but the 'prayer of faith' demands more.

Ordinary prayers tend to be prayers of hope or of thanksgiving. There is the example of a man who has a claw-hand, a hand that he has never been able to open or to use in any functional way during his life. He meets someone like John who prays over him and suddenly he is opening the tops of bottles, squeezing tennis balls, handling tools and implements with ease. There is delight. He prays in thanksgiving. But John says that what he is actually doing is praying the ‘prayer of sight’. He has the evidence of his healing before him. His prayer has been answered. He has asked in faith and his hand has been healed. But he no longer needs faith; he can see that the healing that has taken place.

But asking in faith, and believing that we will be healed despite the fact that there is no evidence to support this belief, is something more complex. For some people asking in faith can be difficult because of the confusion that can arise from their understanding of the Gethsemane prayer: “Father, not my will but thine be done.” This prayer can cause us to wonder, when we pray for something that we want, whether what we want is God’s will for us. In many ways, it is not a bad way to pray, understanding that we could well be asking for things that might not fit in with God’s plan for us. There are so many ‘ifs’ and ‘ands’ and 'buts’ when trying to distinguish between genuine ‘needs’ and what might be more properly categorised as ‘wants’.

But, by the same token, John is at pains to emphasise that Jesus told us that if we pray for something with faith we already have it. “If we do not receive what we prayed for,” John assures us, (and St. Paul tells us the same thing), “then we have not prayed correctly or we have asked for something unsuitable for us.” St. John is equally specific: “… and, knowing that whatever we may ask, He hears us, we know that we have already been granted what we asked of Him.” [John, 5:16]

However, we do know something from the bible about God’s promises to us, and it is what those promises contain that allows us to pray with certainty as well as with hope. It is in these promises that John finds his certainty. "It would have been quite pointless," he argues, "for God to have the made the promises that He had made if He were to deny us the fulfilment of those promises in our prayer."

If we search the bible we learn that God has promised us forgiveness of our sins, support when we are troubled, healing when we are sick. Once we have sorted out in our minds what God's promises to us are, once we have understood what God meant when He told us that if we pray in faith our prayer will be granted, then we are in a position to pray with conviction. St. James states, "The prayer of faith will heal the sick man and the Lord will raise him up …" [5.15]. John believes that this is a very clear statement that the promise of healing through prayer is a promise of God.

And this is why the 'prayer of faith', while it is a prayer that makes great demands upon us, is so powerful. Jesus told us once, "According to your faith, let it be done to you ..." In other words, the likelihood that your prayer will be answered is equivalent to the extent of the faith with which you pray it. The kind of faith that can be required is very clearly demonstrated in the early part of this book when John prayed unceasingly for twelve years for his hip and leg to be healed, fully believing that God wanted to heal him, never doubting that one day God would, yet always without ever seeing evidence of any kind that such belief was justified.

Until he read Canon Jim Glennon's book, however, John had not quite understood that a requirement of the prayer of faith is to know and believe that one is already healed. However, there is sometimes a need to understand that the Lord's healing and what the suppliant wants may not be the same.

Clearly, given the level of belief that it requires, it could well be said that the prayer of faith is not an easy prayer. It often happens that someone comes to John in faith for a healing and he is instructed to believe that he is already healed, to claim his healing in prayer. And yet the days go by, and the weeks go by, and the pain remains. There is no apparent easing of the malady that disturbs this individual. He goes back to John and says, "I did what you told me last month. I prayed the prayer of faith every day. I believed that I would be healed. But I'm not healed; I still have the pain, the sickness."

John will reply immediately that the problem is to be found in that very comment, "I am not healed!" Here lies doubt, and doubt is anathema to the prayer of faith. It is here that John uses the analogy of the seed in the ground. "A farmer," he says, "plants potato seeds one day. He's not going to go around the next day pulling his hair out because the potatoes have not yet appeared. He knows that those seeds have to be tended; they have to be watered and nourished. And it's the same with the prayer of faith for healing. We haven't seen it yet but we must continue praising and thanking God that it's on its way."

St. James instructs us to "... ask in faith with no doubting." [James 1:6] He goes on to say that "... a person who has doubts is like the waves thrown up in the sea when the wind drives. That sort of person, in two minds, must not expect that the Lord will give him anything." [James 1: 7-8] There must be no doubt in the heart of the person seeking healing. And regardless of how long the manifestation of that healing takes, the heart, the spirit, must believe that whatever it has asked for has already been granted. For that is what the prayer of faith asks us to do. We are asked, in spite of all evidence to the contrary, to pray with absolute belief in our hearts that we have been healed. We must accept it as an accomplished fact. Jesus has told us that "... whatever you ask for in prayer, it will be granted." It is almost as if every twinge, every moment of pain, comes to us as a reminder to thank the Lord for his healing. John constantly exhorts suppliants in whom immediate healing is not manifested, never to stop "... claiming your healing. While your back is aching, or your heart continues to palpitate, or your cancer is as debilitating as ever, or your body is racked with pain, you must still say to the Lord with absolute conviction, 'Thank you, Lord, for my healing', and when you can do that, you are beginning to understand what it means to pray the prayer of faith."

Regardless of how we understand 'faith', however, it is not of itself a sufficient description of the nature of divine healing. John points out that the healing ministry in which he is engaged is not just a simple matter of the laying on of hands or the saying of prayers. There are many aspects of his ministry that he had to learn through intensive reading, through experience and, most wondrously, through direct teaching from the Spirit.

Among these elements, of course, is 'the prayer of faith', in which John believes very strongly. But he believes equally strongly in the importance of forgiveness as part of the process. He believes, too, that illnesses or physical misfortune are often, although not in every case, caused by some kind of ancestral link or by a problem in the bloodline of the person who is suffering. It is because of this that John says that he needs first of all not to pray that the person who is ill should be cured but rather to ask God to help him discern the root cause of the illness. Only when he knows this is John best able to identify the approach and the kind of prayer required.

John believes, too, that there are barriers to healing which must be overcome - spiritual blocks in the petitioner, some form of engagement in alternative therapies that are not of Jesus or, indeed, demonic influences that require some form of deliverance. These barriers will be discussed in detail in Part Three of the book but they are mentioned briefly here to indicate that John's ministry is fraught with complexity.

For the moment, however, the focus is on the 'prayer of faith'. Below is another account of a miraculous healing in which Grainne, encouraged by John, prayed the prayer of faith through pain to healing.

***

Grainne's Story: Crippled with Osteoporosis

From time to time, when John has been instrumental in bringing about a healing for a petitioner, he will be offered the use of that individual's house on a particular day each week as a meeting place to pray over other sick people. The petitioner's gratitude will frequently extend to organising a diary of appointments for John, a great boon, because over the course of a week John sees many, many sick people.

Thus John did not know Grainne when he first met her. Her appointment had been made for her by the lady who owned the house. Grainne, a retired Catholic woman, sixty-two years of age, had to be helped into John's presence by her husband because she was virtually crippled with osteoporosis. She told John that she was living with severe and constant pain in her bones and, although she had recently asked her doctor to prescribe stronger and more efficient pain medication, he had refused her request. She had had several increases in her dosages already and the doctor felt that any further increase in the strength and quantity of the drugs she was taking would be more harmful than productive.

Grainne, who lived in a coastal town not far from Belfast, regularly visited one of the large hospitals in Belfast every three months for observation and scans and she told John that the latest reports showed that her osteoporosis was accelerating. She was clearly suffering as she explained to him that she did not know how she could possibly cope with any more suffering. “I’m not asking for a cure,” she pleaded, “but can you do something to ease this awful pain?”

John sensed her pain and put his hands on her shoulders for a little while. He bowed his head in silent prayer and was immediately given to understand by the Lord that the woman’s condition was indeed very serious. Her only hope was to be given new bones, a solution, of course, that was medically impossible.

John stood back. He looked at Grainne and said seriously, “Quite simply, you need a miracle.”

Grainne’s face crumpled. It was clear that she thought John was telling her that there was nothing he could do to help her. His next words were no more comforting. “I can’t perform miracles,” he said. “Neither can you.”

Grainne’s heartbreak began to give way to confusion as she looked at John because he was starting to smile. “But luckily,” he continued, “God can.” He held her shoulders again and went on, “Now, what I have to say to you is very important. Running around talking about osteoporosis and saying you have it and telling people it’s getting you down, is not the way to healing. You have to say the prayer of faith ... I’ll tell you a bit more about that in a minute. But the important thing is, you have to pray it yourself. I will pray for you as well, of course, but there is a big onus on you, too. Now, the key point here is that you must constantly claim your healing. You must believe as you pray that you are already healed, that God is already starting to give you new bones. I don't know how long it will take Him, but believe that He has already started." He prayed over Grainne for a while, then, and pleaded with her once more to pray with faith, to remove all doubt about her healing from her mind.

Grainne was stunned into silence at that point but she agreed that she would try to do what John had told her. As she was leaving, John asked her to come back again in two weeks when he would pray over her once more.

Grainne came back two weeks later as agreed and, as John prayed over her again, she told him that she believed that the pain was now less. John cautioned her to keep on praying, anywhere and everywhere, whether she was just walking about or washing dishes. He told her to pray as constantly as she could, with full faith that the Lord was already working on her bones. He prayed over her again, thanking the Lord for His goodness to Grainne in healing her osteoporosis. Grainne bowed her head in silent gratitude as John prayed, determined to pray ever more fervently over the following weeks.

Grainne made an appointment to meet John three weeks later, partly for more prayer, but partly to tell him that she could not believe how healthy she felt. She had no pain in her bones, in her joints, or anywhere in her body. She told John that she was shortly due to return to the hospital for her three-monthly scan. She felt that something amazing would result from that visit and promised to let John know what transpired.

Grainne went to the clinic a few days later. She had her usual CAT scan and met the consultant in his office a short time later. He had a copy of her previous scan on the table sitting side-by-side with the new one. He was staring at them in mystification, clearly unable to explain what he was seeing. When Grainne told him her story, the surgeon could only shake his head in bafflement. "I don't know what to believe," he said. "All I know is that here …" he gestured to the left scan, "… I have a scan of a sixty-two year old woman with severely advanced osteoporosis, a condition for which there is no medical cure." He gestured to the other scan. "But here …" He spread his hands, still unbelieving, "… with the same name, the same date of birth, the same hospital number, dated three months later, I have a scan that shows the bones of a healthy, eighteen-year-old girl."

The Prayer of Faith

John often gives a copy of Canon Jim Glennon's Prayer of Faith to supplicants who do not appear to have been immediately healed. It incorporates precisely the tenets of the prayer of faith and is worth repeating here:

Loving Father, we praise Your name that You have drawn close to us in Jesus Christ and revealed what You have provided for us and want us to have from Your hand. Thank You for Your promise to us that the prayer of faith will enable the sick person to be restored to health.

We praise You that You have also revealed to us how we are to pray. Father, forgive us that so very often we have not prayed in the way that Jesus taught us. We would repent of that and, by Your grace, so pray that Your blessing may be given to us now and at all times.

Father God, I now accept Your healing for my need. I accept it humbly, gratefully and completely. I accept it so that it is what I accept and the way I think of myself. I thank You for it and rejoice that I am giving You glory by exercising faith. I thank You now and will continue to thank You until faith gives way to sight.

Show me what I can do to put my faith into action. As my faith is small, I know that You will not expect me to act upon my faith all at once, but I believe You are showing me the first step I am to take.

Through Christ Our Lord, Amen [Glennon, 1979, p.52]

John also frequently suggests that the petitioner add simply:

Loving God, I claim that my body is healthy and strong, free from all ailments, all sicknesses, all diseases. I claim this in Your name. Thank You, Father; thank You, Jesus; thank you, Holy Spirit. Amen.

Chapter Fifteen

'... if you are bringing your offering to the altar and there remember that your brother has something against you, leave your offering there before the altar, go and be reconciled with your brother first and then come back and present your offering. [Matthew. 5:23-24]

The Power of Forgiveness

John Gillespie, referring to the lines from Matthew above, tells us that "... these words incorporate everything that Jesus had to say about love, about the two great commandments, 'Love God and Love your Neighbour.' There must be no impediment in your prayer, no spiritual lack, no unforgiveness that will cause your spirit to wane, to go cold, to drift away from the Lord. We cannot pray if we have bitterness in our hearts. We can go to mass, we can say the rosary, but we cannot truly pray because we have blocked ourselves from a real connection with God."

Unforgiveness is a major block to healing. In the individual harbouring the hurt, it can lead to resentment and bitterness and, in both spiritual and psychological terms, this closing of ourselves through resentment will not allow us to open ourselves to God. Unforgiveness as a theme runs constantly through the stories that John relates. It often happens, however, that some stories are combinations of ancestral curses, lack of forgiveness both generational and contemporary, and a miraculous healing. The following story has elements of all of these, including the dire effects of a curse that dated back four generations, but the story's significance lies in the fact that bitterness and unforgiveness had to be expunged from an individual's heart before a most miraculous healing could be wrought. John was to say later, "That was a brilliant miracle Jesus worked. Yet at first He told me to walk away from it. If Nancy had not recanted her bitterness, Jesus would have made me leave and the miracle would never have happened. That would have been terrible."

Joseph's Story: The Man in the Brain-Dead Coma

In May, 2000, a neighbour of John's had occasion to spend a few days in the far north of Ireland. Her married sister, who lived there, had recently undergone surgery in the local hospital and the neighbour wanted to be near her sister and spend time with her. She visited her sister several times each day and during her regular visits to the hospital refectory she became aware of a woman who seemed to be spending as much time in the hospital as she was. She eventually fell into conversation with her and learned that her husband had been lying in a coma for over three months, presumed to be brain dead. His name was Joseph, she told her, and he was hooked up to machines that were keeping him alive.

"They're trying to get me to have the life-support machines switched off," the woman, Nancy, told her, clearly in a distressed state, "but I can't do it."

When the neighbour enquired further about Joseph's condition, she was told that three months earlier Joseph had gone into the hospital for a simple appendectomy. "I'm not clear about what happened," Nancy said, "but I'm told that some kind of inexplicable force entered the operating theatre and went into Joseph's brain … I know, it makes no sense," she said, in answer to the incredulous look her companion gave her, "but that's what I was told. My husband's brain was seriously damaged by whatever it was." She was staring vacantly at the table in front of her but obviously needed to talk. "He had a … a tomography, and they told me that the damage was so severe that Joseph was in what they called 'a persistent vegetative state' and that his chances of recovery were very low. They put him in a ward on life support but after a week or so there was some sort of swelling in his brain that caused a build-up of fluid inside his head and they had to put a screw-valve into his skull in order to drain this off."

"Good gracious!" was all the neighbour could say.

Nancy looked her. "Yeah, except that during the past few weeks he's had to get three more of these spigots put in. They're constantly draining off this milky white fluid. I can't help feeling that it's part of his brain because now they're telling me that he's brain-dead, that there's no electricity in his brain, that there's no clinical evidence of any brain activity. He's had examinations by independent doctors but they say the same thing. There's no hope and they want to switch the machines off."

John's neighbour was shocked to hear this story but she could only shake her head wordlessly. She did not know what words of comfort could be used in this circumstance. Nancy went on, "There's a nun comes in to pray and a priest has given him the last rites. Everybody's amazed that his body's still alive. The nun says that she believes Joseph is still with us for a reason."

When Nancy mentioned the nun's comment, her companion was prompted to thoughts of John and she told the grieving woman that she had a neighbour who had brought about miraculous healings through prayer. She gave Nancy John's number and begged her to contact him.

Shortly after that, John received a call from the woman. John had an immediate sense that he should travel to this hospital to help Joseph and told Nancy that he would be there the following afternoon and that she was to keep her husband on life-support until he got there.

While he was driving to the hospital, John prayed to the Lord for information about the case. He sensed that there was an ancestral curse involved, one that dated back four generations and had originated from a dispute over land and property, one family member cursing another. But he also received the strong impression that there was an additional problem of bitter unforgiveness that was contemporary. He could not quite fathom how contemporary unforgiveness could be related to a four-generations-old curse. He knew, however, that he would learn the connection in due course.

He met Nancy in the corridor outside the ward where Joseph was lying. When he prayed over Joseph, however, he received the immediate knowledge that the force that had rushed into the operating theater was a demon that had impelled itself up through Joseph's nostrils and into his brain. He learned that the demon was an ancestral demon of death, and he received the same impression of a generational curse that he had sensed earlier but he could not sense any indication of a contemporary bitterness.

He left the bedside and told Nancy, who had waited outside to give John privacy, that he needed to go home to fast and pray and seek the Lord's guidance about how he should proceed with Joseph's situation. He instructed Nancy to pray as well and to keep her husband on life-support until he returned.

John prayed for one week, fasting for several hours each day. He finally learned that when he had prayed at the hospital his focus had been on Joseph who, the Lord told him, was not the one who had asked for his help and whose family was not the one in need of forgiveness. There was indeed an ancestral curse, John finally learned, but it was in Nancy's bloodline and, further, a similar dispute about property and land had happened again in the recent past. Nancy and her brother were to inherit a farm with substantial acreage around it but, through disputed claims of entitlement Nancy's brother had inherited the bulk of the estate, leaving her with nothing. Nancy fully believed that her brother had acted wrongly in a way that deprived her of her true share and entitlement. She was filled with hurt and resentment and had not spoken to her brother for several years. John now knew that he had to look to Nancy for the real solution to Joseph's problem.

When John returned to the hospital a week later, Nancy made to lead him back to Joseph's bedside. But John said, "The Lord has told me that I need to talk to you first, Nancy, before I go back to pray over Joseph."

Nancy said, "What about?"

John told her about the curse in the family bloodline and advised her that the curse would have to be lifted though prayers and Masses for forgiveness. Nancy argued that she could not see the relevance of that since the problem was in her family and not in Joseph's.

"The Lord frequently uses situations like this," John explained, "to draw attention to souls seeking spiritual support in the next life. Your husband's situation is the sign the Lord is using in this case."

Nancy remained unconvinced but was taken aback when John went on to tell her that the bitterness in her own heart would also have to be forgotten and that, if Joseph was to be healed, Nancy would have to forgive and pray for her brother.

"But how could you possibly expect me to forgive him … for what he did?" Nancy argued. "I'm left here with nothing and he's got everything and you expect me to forgive him?"

"I don't expect anything," John responded quietly. "It is the Lord who asks this of you, just as He forgave the executioners who nailed Him to the cross."

"Well, I'm not Jesus," Nancy said. "And I don't see how I could be expected to forgive that fella for what he did."

"I'm sorry to hear that," John said, "but forgiveness is part of the Lord's price for Joseph's healing. The Lord won't even let me go into that ward to pray, if you can't forgive."

"Well, how is that fair?" Nancy began to cry. "There's nothing to stop you going in there. Why should he get blamed for what's going on in my family? I just can't do what you're asking."

John shrugged. "I'm sorry you feel like that, Nancy. You leave me no choice. I'm going to have to go home to Belfast without seeing your husband, and I won't be allowed to come back. I can't go against the Lord's wishes."

With that, he turned and walked back down the corridor towards the exit. There was no response from Nancy and John continued walking. He had actually exited the front entrance when he heard footsteps chasing down the steps after him. It was Nancy, desperation written on her face and her manner defeated.

"I'm sorry, John. I can't leave Joseph like this. What do you want me to do?"

John spent almost half an hour explaining the importance of forgiveness, explaining how Nancy had to make the act of will needed to forgive her brother and pray for his soul, how she needed to get a series of Masses said for the person or person in her bloodline who also needed forgiveness. Nancy, in tears, agreed that she would do everything John asked and John then agreed to go back to pray over Joseph.

As they walked back down the corridor, a nurse came running out of the ward and, seeing Nancy, cried, "It's your husband. It's your husband. He's awake. He wants to go home."

Joseph did not go home that day but he did a week or so later, leaving behind two mystified neurosurgeons whose hastily arranged tests showed that Joseph's brain was functioning normally and that his memories were fully intact.

***

When we kneel down to pray, in the chapel, or in our own room at home, and say something like, "Heavenly Father, I know you can see me, I know you can hear me, I know that you know better than I do every thought that is in my mind …", then what can we else but continue, "… and Father, I know you can see into the very depths of my being." If our prayer takes us that far, if it takes us to an understanding of the Lord's loving gaze, then we know that we are laid bare in the eyes of God.

At that point, if we sense that there is any bitterness in our hearts, any grudge or unforgiveness, there is little we can say other than, "Father, I now realise that as long as this bitterness is in me, I cannot truly talk to you, for you have asked us to pray as Jesus taught us and say, 'Father forgive us our trespasses as we forgive those who trespass against us.' Lord, I need to rid myself of this bitterness. I need your help."

Or we can fool ourselves that the Lord does not see what is in us, or that what we harbour has nothing to do with our prayer - a futile pretence, since it blocks any real relationship with the Lord and, ultimately, any true form of prayer.

Matthew makes this very clear:

"Yes, if you forgive others their failings, your heavenly Father will forgive you yours; if you do not forgive others, your father will not forgive you your failings either."

[Matt; 6:15]

In this context, John constantly refers to the Our Father. "When we pray that prayer," he says, "we tie ourselves to the stipulation of forgiveness. We ask, 'Forgive us as we forgive those who trespass against us …', but what we are really saying is, 'Only forgive us, Father, to the extent that we are prepared to forgive others.'" John often says, with a smile, "That's the problem when we pray to a God of love. Love always implies forgiveness and forgiveness is a substantial part of love. There's no escaping it!"

Forgiving, however, does not mean that we are expected to forget or to excuse the wrong done to us or to, in some way, minimise its impact upon us. That would be false. But what we are expected to do is to remember that we ourselves are sinners, that many times we have wronged God, and yet, not only has He forgiven us but we have sought and expected that forgiveness. In seeking this forgiveness, we subject ourselves to God's requirement (to what John frequently refers to as 'God's stipulation') that we find the same forgiveness in our own hearts for the wrongdoing of others.

Jim McManus [2002] explains the point very concisely when he says, "We cannot have God's forgiveness and remain un-repenting people; nor can we be a forgiven but unforgiving people. Forgiveness received from God means forgiveness extended to others." (pp.178/179)

John explains that unforgiveness brings with it significant danger to our spiritual lives. "Unforgiveness," he says, "is spiritual poison. And sometimes we drink it deliberately." But how do we, fallible and weak human beings, suddenly empty our hearts of bitterness and anger in order to forgive? John agrees that if we depend simply upon our own human resources, we will not succeed. "We can forgive," he says, "only through, and with the help of, the Holy Spirit."

The way of the spirit leads us to the growing knowledge that as long as we harbour resentment we not only wound our spirit, we cut ourselves off from God. Eventually this realisation can spur us to seek the Spirit's help. We can perhaps do little more than make an 'act of will' to forgive. John says firmly, "It's a decision. It's something you definitely put your mind to and then pray to make it happen."

But that act of will, that 'wish', represents only a first and very basic step. All we might be able to say at this point is, "Holy Spirit, I do not know how to deal with this. I want to let go of this hurt. Please help me!" With this simple plea, however, we start on the path to forgiveness. John warns us that it may take time to be comfortable with the decision but it is this decision that will allow the Spirit to make it happen.

When John talks about unforgiveness, he is forthright and uncompromising. He says, "Go back to the Lord's Prayer. The Lord has only given us this one prayer and everything that we need is in that one prayer. He has given us plenty of instructions and commandments but He has only given us the one prayer. And the key line in that prayer as regards healing or sickness or disease is, 'Forgive us our trespasses as we forgive those who trespass against us.' John says, "We can all say these words but a lot of the time we need to say them from our heart and not from our lips because here the Lord stipulates that forgiveness is an essential element of being set free from evil. 'Deliver us from evil' is part of the same sentiment. Evil does not come from God … and unforgiveness, which is not from God, becomes an evil.

***

Medical science is familiar with the phenomenon of psychosomatic illnesses, illnesses that can afflict the body as a direct result of mental stress or a severe emotional state. The following case-study recounts the details of a woman diagnosed with a dangerous cancer. The significant point to this story is that the woman who sought John's help was willing to do anything John asked of her except forgive her husband. Yet when John prayed with her and helped her to see the importance of forgiveness, it transpired that the very cancer that was killing her had stemmed directly from her unforgiveness.

***

Sandra's Story: The Cancer of Unforgiveness

Sandra, a middle-aged woman who lived alone in a small house in Belfast, began to feel unwell. She had severe pains in her back and experienced a deadening lethargy that left her weary and incapable of carrying out the ordinary routine activities of her life. She saw her doctor who arranged an appointment for her at the Royal Victoria Hospital for tests. Sandra was diagnosed with a malignant tumour on her spine. She was informed that her situation was serious. The growth, however, had been caught early and she was also told that with an operation, followed by treatment and some periods of chemotherapy, it might be possible to control, perhaps even prevent, any further spread of the cancer.

Sandra was a respected member of her parish, well-known for her devotion to Mass and the rosary. She was a member of a number of organisations in the parish and, at one these meetings, she told a friend about the bad news she had received. Fortuitously, or more probably through God's grace, the friend was able to tell Sandra about John Gillespie and gave her a phone number through which contact could be made with John.

John knew nothing about Sandra other than the few words that had passed between them over the telephone. So, before he made the visit to Sandra's house, he prayed to the Lord, asking him if there was anything he needed to know about the case, if there any issues he needed to be aware of. As he prayed, John sensed that the Lord was telling him that Sandra was victim of a great bitterness, that, despite her attendance at Masses and her recitals of many rosaries, she nursed a deep and abiding unforgiveness that was the root cause of her cancer. John learned no more than that from this prayer session. As he was driving to Sandra's home, however, he sensed that the impending visit would not be pleasant but that "the Lord would lead him through it." He discerned that the Lord was warning him that Sandra was a "controlling personality" and that there would be "a battle of minds" during which Sandra's case would be presented to John in a way that would disguise the real truth. John felt that the Lord was instructing him to be very aware of what lay in Sandra's heart, that he had to focus essentially on the issue of unforgiveness and to ignore anything else that was calculated to disguise this spiritual problem. The Lord warned John that he would be told about Masses, rosaries, sodality meetings and other practices that were indicative of a strong spirituality but that John was not to be distracted by these from the true purpose of his visit. John knew that the Lord wanted him to find the root cause of the problem and, although he was given no clear information in the car about what this might be, he had some sense that it was a family matter.

When John finally arrived at Sandra's house, he met a pleasant woman who gave him a full account of her illness, of the hospital's diagnosis, and details about the tumour. She went on to say that another appointment had been scheduled for the following week for further tests and scans that would be needed to help the surgeon decide how she best might approach the forthcoming operation. It was at this point that Sandra revealed her inner concerns and fears to John, asking him to pray over her for God's healing.

As she was saying this, she went to a cupboard and took out a blessed candle. "I thought it might be an idea to light a blessed candle while you say the prayers of healing," she said, preparing to light the candle.

John held up a hand and said matter-of-factly, "No, that's all right! I don't need a blessed candle." Then he said, quietly observing Sandra's attitude and demeanour, "But if you feel happier with one, go ahead. I don't need it myself and don't normally use it."

Sandra didn't reply immediately but simply replaced the candle in the cupboard. As she turned back, she said, "It's all right. If you don't want it, we won't use it." Then, sitting down again, she said "Perhaps we could take out our rosary beads and recite the rosary together?"

John was now aware that Sandra was attempting to make suggestions about how the healing prayer session should proceed. This was precisely the kind of controlling influence that the Lord had warned him about. In a completely neutral tone, he said, "No, I don't particularly need that but if you want to pray the rosary after I've gone, that'll be okay."

Two ploys attempted; two ploys, in some subtle way, rebuffed. A certain stiffness appeared in Sandra's manner, indicative of an inner irritation, perhaps even a burgeoning resentment. John was aware that it must have seemed to Sandra that he was unwilling to accept any of her suggestions for prayer.

Sandra's next words confirmed that. Trying without any great success to keep her voice calm, Sandra said, "You don't want a blessed candle; you don't want to say the rosary. I'm afraid I don't know what way you want to pray or to go about the healing."

"It's really nothing at all to do with what I want," John replied, still neutral and matter-of-fact. "It's what the Lord wants."

"Well, what does the Lord want, do you think?" Sandra replied, trying but failing to keep the frostiness out of her tone.

"When the Lord brought me into this ministry," John responded calmly, "he always gave me only one stipulation, no matter where I go."

"What stipulation?" Sandra asked, clearly not happy with the way the visit was going.

"Just forgiveness," John told her.

When John said this, Sandra's manner became defensive. "Forgiveness? What's that got to do with me? There's no worry about that with me. I go to Mass every day. I pray the rosary at least twice a day. I am in the Legion of Mary sodality …"

As Sandra continued to defend herself with details about the spiritual activities in her life, John had a sudden sense that something cold and unspiritual was being defended. He was prompted suddenly by the Lord to ask about Sandra's husband. "How about your husband? Are there any areas in your marriage where forgiveness might be necessary?"

"Why are you bringing that up?" Sandra said, fighting anger. "He's irrelevant here. My husband and I are separated."

"Oh!" John replied. "Sorry to hear that." Then he added, "How do you feel about him?"

"He has earned nothing but contempt from me," Sandra said, her face tight. "In fact, when I heard about this cancer, I told my daughters to make sure that if I die, under no circumstances is my husband to be buried, when he dies, in the same grave with me."

"Contempt?" John stared at her. "You're a Christian woman and you have nothing but contempt for your husband? And you don't think you have a problem with forgiveness there?"

Sandra was struggling to retain her control but anger was getting the better of her. "After how he behaved in our marriage? After what he put me through? Do you think for one minute that the Lord would expect me to forgive that … that …?" She closed her mouth and stared defiantly at John.

"Of course he does," John said. "He expects all of us to forgive. Why do you think that Lord has told us, in the only prayer he ever taught us, to ask the Father to forgive us as we forgive others?" He stared seriously at Sandra. "Think about it! If you are asking the Father to forgive you as you are forgiving your husband, do you not think you're in a bit of trouble?"

Sandra was shocked into silence. It was clear that she had not given this element of the Our Father any real thought. She seemed to collapse within herself on the chair as John went on, "Before I even came here, Sandra, the Lord made me aware that your cancer is a direct result of a serious unforgiveness that you're harbouring. You have to accept and understand that that is the truth. And you would need to make a decision very soon about what you're going to do about it because, if you are not prepared to forgive your husband for whatever it was that he did to you, there's no point in my praying over you. It would be a waste of time me going to the Lord while you nourish this resentment in you and you're not willing to forgive."

He stared at the stricken woman who now sat in the chair, head bowed, all energy drained from her. "And I need to tell you something else," John said earnestly. "Whatever about your cancer, and that's bad enough, it's nowhere nearly as bad as what will happen to your immortal soul if you die with that resentment festering in you. Because unforgiveness comes from Satan, and it's his poison we take when we harbour unforgiveness in our hearts. And it doesn't matter how many Masses you go to; it doesn't matter how many rosaries you say, it doesn't matter how many prayer groups or sodalities you go to, you will not get into Heaven because by harbouring unforgiveness, you've made the decision to keep the gates closed on yourself."

Sandra was thoroughly distressed now. All attempts to defend herself were gone. In a faltering voice, she said, "But this resentment in me, it's been there so long. How do I suddenly get rid of it? What do I do?"

"It's a decision," John said. "You simply make the decision to do it. It's about the will … not the emotions."

Humbled and contrite, Sandra said, "Can you help me, John?"

John saw the woman's sincerity and recognised that Sandra would now accept the Lord's stipulation to forgive. He prayed some forgiveness prayers, asking Sandra to repeat each line after him. As John was leaving, Sandra said that he would offer up her Masses and holy communions for her husband and for the grace to find spirituality in his life.

One week later Sandra went to the hospital, as arranged, for the pre-operation tests and scans. The baffled surgeon could find no trace of any cancer or tumours that needed treatment. Sandra was sent home, her hospital records adjusted to show that her x-rays were clear and that no tumour was visible on or around her spine.

Chapter Sixteen

"It is a holy and wholesome thought to pray for the dead that they may be loosed from their sins."
[Old Catholic School Catechism]

Ancestral Links

John's ministry of healing the sick has taught him that there are many forms of illness that seem susceptible to natural and straightforward diagnosis in a doctor's surgery. Some of these illnesses, however, stem from causes that defy rational examination. If the root cause of the illness has a spiritual component, medical diagnosis will always fail to discover it. In the story that follows, a young woman has been diagnosed with leukaemia. A tragic case but the diagnosis was unquestionably accurate … or was it? Michael's story, like those in the previous chapter, is about the need for forgiveness but on this occasion it was not the victim who needed forgiveness but members of her bloodline for whom forgiveness had to be sought.

Michael's Story: Young Man with Leukaemia

Michael had been diagnosed with leukaemia at the age of sixteen. He had various medical treatments for it, including chemotherapy, and the cancer finally went into remission. For some time after that Michael was able to live a full and normal life. But four or five years later, sometime in the early 2000s, the disease returned. This time it was very severe and so debilitating that Michael was not only confined to hospital but was on a list of patients to be transferred to a hospice.

It so happened that an acquaintance of Michael had been prayed for by John for an illness of his own. When the man found himself cured and freed from the trouble that had plagued him, he suggested to John that he go to a hospital in Belfast to visit a young man there who was dying of leukaemia. Like Jesus, John never refuses a plea for help. He agreed to go and see the young man.

Very often, when John is faced with people with severe illnesses, he is led to pray for knowledge about the root cause of the illness, for information about something connected with the illness that would have to be resolved before he could pray for a cure. When he stood at Michael's bedside during his first visit to hospital, John prayed initially for what he terms, "the Word of Knowledge". Through this gift of the Spirit, John can be made aware of any peripheral circumstances that might have significant relevance to the case he is dealing with. After only a short prayer to the Holy Spirit, John immediately learned that the young man was dying because of a particular sin that was in his family, something that had happened within recent times, although at that point John did not know what it was.

John reached into his pockets for a small pouch that he always carries with him. It contains the holy oils with which he blesses his petitioners as he prays for their recovery to health. He blessed Michael with the oil and prayed that God might show him what was needed to bring this young man to healing.

As he prayed, John's mind was assaulted by visions of men wearing balaclavas over their faces, using guns, dragging people down alleyways to shoot them. He saw one particular episode of killing as clearly as if he was watching it through an open window and, even as he watched the vision, John could hear the Lord's voice saying clearly to him, "Some distant relatives of Michael's have been involved with paramilitaries. They have shed blood; they have maimed people for life; they have killed people. They have used the very blood of life for death and many people have suffered at their hands. Now this young man is another innocent victim. He is of the same bloodline as these paramilitaries. The sickness that has felled him, the disease he suffers, comes from that background. These people need to repent and seek forgiveness. They must be made aware that what they have been doing was evil. They claim that what they were doing was right, that they were involved in a righteous war. But what they have done was not righteous in my eyes. Now the family expresses concern for this young relation. If they are serious about wanting him to be healed, if they are serious about their concern for him, then they will take my message equally seriously. Speak to them on my behalf, John."

John said further prayers, spoke a few words of comfort to the boy and told him that he would be back to see him soon, that he wanted to talk to his family. John left the room and met with some of the family members in a waiting area further down the corridor.

Michael's mother was tearful. "This is very hard to understand," she cried. "Why does Michael have to suffer all over again? Why has this cancer come back?"

"I know this is difficult for you," John sympathised. "But there are some things I need to know before I can help him."

Michael's aunt, who was with the group, was a nurse at the hospital. She told John that she was currently working alongside the medical team, helping them to carry out a whole range of scientific tests in the hope of finding some answers.

"Have you discovered anything?" John asked.

"It appears that the trouble is located in his genes," she said, "although at this point we can't be definitive. But we've done a lot of advanced tests and different treatments and that is what we keep coming up with."

John said forthrightly, "Well, I am not a specialist and I don't know anything about all these forms of testing that you are doing. But I can tell you positively that the problem most definitely is in the genes."

The nurse expressed some surprise and said, "Em ..." but floundered at that point.

"Were you able to discover how it got into the genes?" John asked.

"Well," she said, somewhat uncertainly, "it is relatively easy, medically, to detect that it is the genes, but I don't think we'll ever be able to say how the cancer got in there in the first place."

John stared at her, and at the other members of the family who were listening intently. "I know that you'll have a problem with what I now have to say. I left school at the age of fourteen. I've never done an exam in my life. I have no medical experience whatever … so why should you believe me? But I can say with absolute certainty how the disease got into Michael's genes, and I can also tell you how to take it out."

Michael's mother's hands went to her face. The aunt looked mystified. "What do you think is happening, then?" she asked.

"It's very simple," John explained. "This disease got into the young man's system through sin. That young man lying in there, your nephew, is suffering because of evil done by other members of the extended family. These things often come about either through the sins of the individual who is suffering or through the sins of someone connected with him."

The aunt's mystification gave way to scepticism. "Are you trying to say that old belief in the bible about the sins of the father being visited upon the children is real?"

"Of course it is," John replied positively. "I see examples of it all the time. The Lord often shows me links like that in the bloodline." The aunt simply shook her head and John said to the boy's mother, "I would like to talk to someone who knows something about the family history."

"I'll take you to my granny," she said, her heart so full of hope at that point that she would have agreed to anything John asked. "She knows everything about everybody."

The following day John sat with an old woman, a lady of clear mind and strong personality. He explained the situation to her in straightforward terms.

"I'm going to be very stark about what I have to say to you," he began. "You have a young relative lying dying in the hospital. I have to speak the truth about the information the Spirit gave me as I prayed at the side of the boy's bed. I need you to tell me now if you know of any members of your family who belong to, or have belonged to, groups that have used guns and who have killed people down alleyways?"

The old lady stared for a long moment at John, clearly engaged in some form of internal debate. Eventually she said, clearly ashamed, "Yes! There are members of this family who have been up to their eyes in paramilitary activity. A lot of people in the Belfast area have been caught up in this conflict and some of them are nephews and cousins of mine. It's a terrible thing, and worse now, if all that stuff is the cause of that innocent child's illness. What can I do to help? I'll do anything."

"It's simple," John told her. "You need to get some of these people going to Mass. They need to confess their sins and ask the Lord for forgiveness for what they have done." He paused and continued seriously. "That's the only way. And these people will also have to pray for forgiveness for some of their ancestors who have been involved in the same kinds of woundings and killings, because in my visions I was able to see some of the things that were done by some of the people in your extended family."

The old woman, despite her obvious amazement at what John was saying, straightened and said resolutely, "I might not get through to them all but I know I'll be able to persuade some of them."

"Good!" John said. "But you'll also have to get other members of the family to Mass as well, even ones who weren't involved in the troubles."

When the grandmother said goodbye to John, she was filled with determination to do what she could to carry out the instructions he had given her. She contacted as many of the family members as she could, and many of them took John's message to heart. They began to attend Mass and Holy Communion, getting Masses said for their uncles and their ancestors and praying for forgiveness for the family's sins. Not all of the men who had been in the paramilitaries accepted the message but enough members of the family prayed with sufficient earnestness to allow the Lord to act.

And so Michael, who was dying in hospital, a victim paying the price for his family's sins, was suddenly cured through the power of forgiveness of all trace of his cancer. He left the hospital shortly after John's intervention and he remains fit and healthy to this day.

***

When he talks about bloodlines or connections with ancestral influences, John often refers to Kenneth McAll's book "Healing the Family Tree" (1986). "The Lord teaches me all this stuff," John says, "but if anybody wants to read about it, McAll's book is a good place to start."

McAll was a missionary-surgeon who later became a practising consultant psychiatrist. He, like John, has a ministry of healing and he has a particular belief that many of his "incurable patients are victims of ancestral control." In his book, he identifies three kinds of what he terms "controlling bondages" (p.6). The first kind he talks about is the loss of one's own identity in thrall to the control of a living person, the easiest form to diagnose.

The second form of bondage is exerted by the dead upon the living, sometimes by dead who are unknown. In cases like this, McAll suggests, the most effective way to find out whichever ancestor is causing the problem is to draw up a family tree and study the various members of it, looking particularly for excessive behavioural problems. (p.11) The third form of bondage, which will be dealt with in Part Three, is the bondage of the living to occult control. This, McAll claims, is the most dangerous evil to unravel.

The focus of interest of this chapter, however, is the second of these three states, the very important question of sin in the bloodline, of some ancestral evil that can bring illness and pain to family members down through as many as four, five and six generations.

John often points out that ancestral bonds or curses are nothing new. "They have been with us since the early times of the Old Testament," he says. In the Book of Exodus, the Lord told Moses that He *"... lets nothing go unchecked, punishing the father's fault in the sons and in the grandsons to the third and fourth generation." [34:9]* In the Book of Samuel, the Lord commanded Samuel's family to mend their evil behaviours. They did not respond to the divine warning, however, and in doing so, they brought a curse upon their family line. [Sam.2: 31–33]

Scriptural quotes for this phenomenon, therefore, abound. So, too, do the occasions when John becomes aware that there is a generational element to a healing he is praying for. Usually, when John is given to understand that the root cause of an illness he is praying about is ancestral, he would not normally engage in the depth of psychological analysis recommended by Kenneth McAll. His approach, however, is not dissimilar. Whereas McAll uses family and connections to pursue a detailed examination of the family tree, John relies much more on guidance from the Spirit, sometimes in transmitted thoughts, but frequently in the form of clear and very intense visions.

Nonetheless, the Spirit's guidance often demands that John speak to elder members of a family about the family's history in order to clarify visions that might require additional explanation. This, in many ways, is designed to elicit the same information that McAll seeks in constructing a detailed family tree. Both men, in their approach to the problem, search the family history for similarities in behaviours, illnesses or hurts than might bear some resemblance, however vague, to the illness they are praying to heal.

John's experience of dealing with ancestral bonds convinces him that we must do all we can to clean the family bloodline. He is strongly influenced by the plea in Psalm 78: "*Do not remember against us the sins of our fathers*." He believes that we must break the pattern of sin through the generations, to break any curse, or cure any illness, that threatens generations of children. His constant plea to the members of the families concerned is that they pray for and confess the sins of their ancestors, forgiving them any evil they have done and asking God's forgiveness for them.

But there is good news in this. Jesus, John assures us, can break any curse or evil that inflicts the bloodline. When we find the patterns of sin, what John often refers to as the "root cause of the illness", then we know that we can pray with confidence to Jesus to have the generational fault healed and save souls locked out of heaven.

In order to cut an ancestral bond, Kenneth McAll holds "a service of the Eucharist" with members of the family. A priest is normally assigned to Kenneth by a bishop to say a Mass and conduct the service. Its desired purpose and impact is similar to John's approach which is to persuade members of the family to confess their sins, attend the Eucharistic service and pray for forgiveness for the ancestral connection. In the case of non-Catholics, Masses can be offered along with special services in their own denomination.

Kenneth McAll originally suffered doubts about praying for the dead since he was under the impression that judgement came immediately after death: *"Just as man is destined to die once and after that to face judgement..."* [Heb.9:27] But as he contemplated and studied, again and again the line immediately following this statement, he came to a different conclusion. *"... so Christ was sacrificed once to take away the sins of many people; and He will appear a second time ..."* [Heb.9:27],

Pondering over and over these words, "He will appear a second time!" McAll came to realise that the time when the judgement will actually occur is not specified. The lines can equally imply that judgement could very well take place at the time of the second coming of Jesus.

On that basis, and understanding as we do now, the immensity of God's love, McAll believes that "*... we can ask Christ to help the dead to receive His love and forgiveness as He offers it through the Eucharist."* (p.89) John shares this belief and never fails to offer help to those whose bloodline is in some way contaminated. But invariably, he makes it plain that in cases where ancestral forgiveness is required, no prayers are stronger than the prayers of the descendants, and often a healing John prays for occurs only when the prayers, devotions and masses stipulated by John are willingly and sincerely offered by family members.

Francis MacNutt offers a prayer for freedom from ancestral predispositions. It is a great help during Eucharistic services offered for the dead but it is useful, too, for individuals who might be aware of a strong and problematic predisposition in their lives that has caused them a great deal of spiritual anguish.

***

Prayer for Freedom from Ancestral Bonds

Lord Jesus, gently reveal to me through the Holy Spirit, those ways in which I may be living out certain patterns of inherited weakness or sin. (Here wait and see what you receive in prayer)

Now, Jesus, if there is any predisposition in me ______ (alcoholism, lust, etc) *that has come down to me through my ancestry, I ask you through your power to set me free. Send your Holy Spirit, and by the power of your Spirit and by the sword of the Spirit, cut me free from that disposition to* _______.

For any sins I have committed - or my ancestors have committed - in this regard, I ask your forgiveness, Lord. In the name of Jesus Christ and His precious blood, set me free, Heavenly Father.

And now, Lord Jesus, in the place of this weakness, fill me with the power of your Spirit; fill me with your Spirit of ______ (self-control, courage, sobriety or whatever gift counteracts the weakness you have). *And Lord, I ask you also to cut my children free from any harmful disposition they may have inherited from me or my ancestors. Amen.*

***

Medical science today is capable of extraordinary feats of diagnosis and analysis. Even the smallest germ, the minutest microbe, the most inexplicable virus, can eventually be examined, identified, and categorised. And yet, faced with an illness that stems from supernatural roots, faced with an anomaly that exists in the bloodline, even the brightest brains in the medical profession can be baffled. Nonetheless, they continue to seek only rational contemporary causes and rational contemporary solutions. That is the way of modern medicine. While faith is seen as an element of the healing process, its influence is invariably seen as psychosomatic. Consideration is never given to a supernatural component in the diagnosis. Madeleine's story, however, is a particularly impressive illustration of how sometimes the answer to an inexplicable malady can only be found in the spiritual dimension. It demonstrates also how easily unfathomable secrets are, after a brief prayer, immediately laid bare to John through the gift of Knowledge.

***

Madeleine's Story: A Baffling Illness

Madeleine, a young woman in her twenties, suffered from a strange and debilitating illness. She was constantly weak and without energy; she suffered acute abdominal pains which often travelled to other parts of her body. Numerous times her system would seem close to total collapse and on these occasions she would receive the final rites and anointing with holy oils. She was unable to work and was obliged to live at home with her parents because of her condition.

Visits to several specialists and consultants resulted in no clear diagnosis. There were those who suggested that her symptoms were indicative of some form of poisoning but that created more questions than answers. The doctors could not specify what kind of poison it might be nor, indeed, how this diagnosis might have any validity since there was no obvious evidence of any poison in her system. Others wondered if there might be some form of intestinal malfunction or, perhaps, a microbiological infection that had not been detected. But again, no evidence for either conclusion could be found. Madeleine was subjected to scan after scan, test after test, x-ray after x-ray, with no useful diagnostic outcome.

The young woman's parents were desperate to find help for their daughter and, losing confidence in the medical profession, resorted to seeking help from prayer-groups. From a member of one such group, Madeleine's mother was told about the work that John Gillespie was doing. She was given John's telephone number and one evening, in near desperation, she contacted him and told him about her daughter's illness.

As John listened to her story, his first thought was that if the best medical brains in the country were at such a loss, the chances were that the solution to the problem would be spiritual. As he repeats so often that it has become almost a mantra, "there's always a root cause somewhere and, when it is not immediately obvious, more often than not it is supernatural."

John listened sympathetically, assuring the girl's mother that he would begin to pray for Madeleine immediately and that, although where Madeleine lived was a considerable distance from Belfast, he would try to get to see her as soon as he could.

That night John prayed about Madeleine, asking the Spirit to help him find the cause of the young woman's illness so that a cure might be found. Almost immediately he began to receive visions which, while quite clear, did not make a great deal of sense to him. He saw what he describes as "… a war situation. A lot of smoke and noise, guns being used, people being shot."

He received little more that evening that he was able to understand and when he prayed again the following day, he still could not decipher the visions that were being shown to him. He saw the same kind of war scenes but he could not see any specific individual being shot or any repetition of a particular scene that might hold some information for him. Nonetheless, as he watched the visions, the gift of Knowledge was working in his subconscious. He began to sense that someone related to Madeleine had been shot during this battle and that poison from the lead in the bullets that had killed the man had something to do with Madeleine's illness. As he prayed further, John became convinced that Madeleine's illness was definitely linked to this shooting.

John contacted Madeleine's parents and told them what he believed. He asked them if they knew about any family member who might have been shot in a war, but they professed themselves baffled. They had never heard of anything like this in any discussions about the family. Certainly no contemporary relative of theirs had been shot during "the troubles" or in any other war that they knew about. They promised to talk to other members of the family about it, however, particularly older relatives, and told John they would let him know if they learned anything.

John prayed again in private, however, seeking further clarification from the Holy Spirit. On this occasion he was given the impression that the shootings he had been seeing had occurred four or five generations earlier. He was allowed the visions again and this time he could see the battlefield more clearly. Now he was seeing a young man, about twenty-two years of age, who had stumbled into or had been somewhere close to an explosion. The front of his abdomen had been torn open and his entrails were hanging out. As he lay dying on the field, he was crying out for his father and mother while two comrades who were with him did what they could to comfort him. There was little, of course, that they could do. They simply tried to hold the young man still as he writhed on the ground, shrieking in pain and cursing the people who did this to him.

While John was seeing this vision, he was also given an understanding that whatever poisons were in the explosions were transferred at that point into the young man's bloodline. He also learned that not only was the young man angry and bitter as he cursed those who had mortally wounded him but that neither his father nor his mother had ever forgiven the people who were instrumental in their son's death. In addition to this, John received a further message from the Lord that no forgiveness had ever been requested for the person or persons who had caused the explosion.

John was to meet the family a few days later in a neighbour's house where he was praying with some people who had asked his help. He spoke to the family about the new understanding he had gained about their situation, but still they could not give him any information about such an event in the family's history.

As they were speaking, John was studying the young woman. He had a sudden impression of something in her left side and he said to her, "I believe that all of your pains originate …" and he pressed a finger gently on a small section of her intestine, "… from this one spot."

The girl looked at him, stunned. "In all the years that I've been going to consultants and doctors, of all the scans and x-rays I have had over all that time, this is the first time that anyone has actually been able to pin-point where the pain comes from."

John nodded but said, "I'm not sure that your situation will be resolved by medical means. I still believe that the root cause of your illness stems from this war situation I was telling you about ... something has been transferred down through the bloodline …" And he prayed over her again asking for guidance about the best way to find a cure for the young woman.

Madeleine's parents, strongly influenced by what John had told them, decided to take their daughter to a specialist in Dublin who had a reputation for diagnosing the origins and causes of difficult illnesses. After a battery of tests, he reported to the parents that the results he found were extraordinary.

"I have to admit I am baffled by what the results show," he told them. "If my results are accurate, and I have no reason to believe that they aren't, your daughter's body is full of lead." He shook his head, mystified. "I've never seen anything like it before. But I have to say it's alarming. It's poisoning her whole system." He gathered up the papers he was studying. "I have prepared a set of these results for you to take back to the young woman's consultant. My field is diagnosing strange phenomena like this … but I can't offer any medical advice. You own consultant will need to do that."

When the family reported these results to John, he told them that he believed that the poisoning had come from the lead that was used in the explosion that had killed the young man several generations earlier.

"The problem stems from a lack of forgiveness," John said. "First, there was the young man, raging during his painful death. Then you had his parents, holding the bitterness of their son's death in their hearts, never forgiving, never finding peace. Then there was the person who caused the explosion. He needs divine forgiveness for the sin."

"But nobody in my family had that sort of illness," the father said, still struggling to understand.

"Nor mine," the mother added.

"These things can skip generations," John told them. "I don't know why, but I've come across that many times. But the Dublin diagnostician has confirmed what I saw in the visions … about the lead poisoning."

"But they've all been dead for years," the girl's mother interrupted. "What can we do now?"

"You'll have to pray," John said. "You'll need to get Masses said for the young man, and for his parents, and for the perpetrator of the explosion. And it'll have to be you. It has to be descendants of the blood line"

The parents, and the girl herself, agreed that they would do everything that John directed.

Some weeks later John got a grateful call from the young woman. The family had had several Masses said for their ancestor and had said many prayers themselves. Now she was ringing to report that her symptoms had all disappeared several days before and that she was now fully healed.

PART THREE: CAST OUT DEMONS

Chapter Seventeen

***I have given you authority to trample on snakes and scorpions and to overcome the power of the Enemy, so that nothing will harm you.* [Luke, 10:19]**

Our battle is not against human forces but against the rulers and authorities and their dark powers that govern this world. We are struggling against the spirits and the supernatural forces of evil. [Eph.6:12]

Spiritual Warfare

The twenty-first century is not a place where talk of the devil is easily tolerated. At best, he is mostly seen as a personification of evil; at worst, he is dismissed as a mediaeval fantasy. What is the truth about the devil? How many would argue that claims of his influence on our lives is delusional, a superstitious placing of blame on a mythological entity for events that are susceptible to natural explanation?

These questions require answers and it would be instructive at this point to examine John's personal experiences with the devil. John has had his wars with the devil. As he progressed in his ministry, healing the sick and delivering many from the clutches of Satan and his demons, he became more and more frequently a target for Satan's wrath. He has fought the devil's attacks in his own life and he has fought his attacks in the lives of others. There were, and continue to be, numerous occasions when John has been subjected to physical pain that was clearly supernatural in origin, occasions when his car has been damaged or wrecked in inexplicable circumstances, occasions when his family has been subjected to demonic attack. These are not stories that are intended for these pages, although, in Part One, we have already seen how John's daughter, Fionnuala, was subjected to demonic threat at the age of eighteen months in order to put pressure on John to give up his ministry.

***

Claire's Story: The Child who Died

There is one of such stories, however, that would bear telling, the story of the occasion when the devil actually killed John's six-week old daughter, Claire. John introduces that event with these comments:

"I was brought into ministry with the gifts of faith and healing but as I began to read more about what I was doing, I learned that apart from the gift of healing, there is also the gift of miracles. I was reading a book by Bob Dugrandis and he said, I can only tell you it in my own words, it was something like, 'If you are going into the ministry of miracles, ponder it very carefully before you do because if you're looking for the gift of miracles you are signing up with the Lord to go on the front line against Satan. Satan will detest you and everything connected with you. He will use every weapon in his arsenal to take you out.'

"But I'd been remembering what Father Ronnie had told me about the miracle ship and could not help feeling that somehow this was a vocation I should be following. So I prayed and fasted for months for the grace to make a decision about whether I should go for the miracles ministry. I couldn't go into it lightly because I knew the price that would have to be paid for it and the extent of what I was stepping into … it was no less than a spiritual battleground. My family was certain to be affected and I discussed it in detail with Christina many times. In the end we both agreed that the decision should be made in favour of accepting the Lord's ministry of miracles and help as many of God's people as possible.

"The day I made the decision was the day that Satan launched one of the worst attacks on my family that we've ever had to endure. That morning I had gone to mass as usual, and prayed to the Lord. 'Lord, if you choose me, if you think I'm worthy of it, I would like to serve you in a ministry of miracles. I have made the final decision and I am prepared for whatever consequences come to me or my family as a result of this decision.' Then, after I went up to receive the Eucharist, I said, 'Lord, I am taking this Eucharist and I want to help you deliver your miracles to your people.'

"And that was the night that Satan attacked my six-week old daughter. Satan knows no mercy. He's totally evil. He threw everything he had at our child, and it literally died."

Christina's Prologue

In a handwritten submission, Christina introduces the story of the attack on her infant daughter, Claire.

My fifth pregnancy was the only one out of the six during which I felt that I was under spiritual attack. From the very beginning of the pregnancy I was over-anxious about the development of the baby and I had a constant sense of ill-boding which I could not explain. I just felt it. By the time I was three months into the pregnancy, I knew for sure that I had a battle on my hands for I was being constantly told by a voice that the child would die.

By the time six months had passed, the midwife had become very worried about me and suggested that I talk to a "white coat doctor". But I refused and, instead, I went on retreat to Dromalis with Father Ronnie Mitchell. He prayed with me and for my baby. I did feel better after that but the voice never let up. That demon taunted me the whole nine months of my pregnancy and I knew that there was a battle for our child, a battle that Jesus, John and I simply had to win.

Claire, our fifth daughter, was born on the 11th August, 1997 on the Feast of St. Clare. I spent a week in hospital after her birth and one week at home. During the third week I took her out in her pram a couple of times. Two days later, I went out to do some messages and left Claire with John. When I returned he told me that she had been coughing badly and that a blue line had appeared above her upper lip.

She seemed all right by that time but the next day I heard the coughing and witnessed the blue line myself. I took Claire immediately to the Hospital for Sick Children. The physician there suctioned her lungs, telling me that her nose and throat were probably clogged up with mucus.

For the next few days she was fine but then she started coughing again, this time holding her breath for long periods during the coughing fits. I went back to the hospital with her and she was kept in overnight. As parents, John and I were shown how to carry out CPR. Claire slept peacefully again in the hospital, with no coughing at all. She was released the next day and we brought her home. At that time she was five weeks old.

Nothing happened during the next few days and we thought all was well ... until the beginning of her sixth week. It was Sunday evening and Claire started coughing again. At 9:50 pm she stopped breathing. We carried out the CPR we had been shown and other tactics that the hospital staff told us about such as flicking the child's face with cold water, turning her over, face down, and gently slapping her back, but nothing worked. She was unresponsive to all of this and by 10:00 she still wasn't breathing. John took her from me and I was in a panic...

***John takes up the story*:**

"We were sitting there in the living room when Claire took that coughing fit. Then she stopped breathing and went totally blue, and no matter what we tried, we couldn't get any response, no response at all. There was no pulse; there was nothing. We tried everything but to no avail. The wee thing was lying there lifeless, and totally became a whitish grey within minutes. There was just no life in her and we knew the child was dead. Christina was doing everything frantically to try to get the child back, everything in her power, she'll tell you that herself. But she knew, despite her efforts that the child was dead. The child was lifeless. I have seen dolls with more life in them.

"Ten minutes had elapsed by this time. The children were roaring and screaming because Christina was screaming, "She's dead! She's dead!" and she was holdin' her away from the children, down at the worktop, and the children were frantic, hysterical, and they were screaming as well, "Claire's dead. Claire's dead."

"At that point I felt the Lord saying to me, "Take the child from Christina immediately. Just do it and listen to my instructions." So I went over and grabbed the child but Christina wouldn't let her go, so I just pulled the child from her and ran out of the kitchen into the hall with the child in my arms and I rushed to the holy water font because I felt God saying to me "Remember Agnes Sanford's husband." She was a Presbyterian minister. One time there were eighteen children dying and her husband went out and blessed them all with holy water and rebuked the evil and all eighteen were saved. So I got the holy water and I put some on Claire's lips. The child was still lifeless but when I touched her lips with the holy water, they moved, just the slightest bit. But there was no breathing. Then I felt the Lord saying to me, something we weren't told in the hospital, that there was a blockage around the throat area and that I was to put my lips down to hers and to suck the blockage out. As I did that, I felt that the mucus in her throat was dislodged but there was still no movement. So I took the child in both hands and held her up towards the ceiling and prayed aloud, "Jesus, with you there is no death, there is only life, and I claim life for Claire now in your name." And I kept saying that, over and over. "I claim life. There is no death. There is no death. I rebuke death. I claim life for Claire's body in Jesus' name."

"I continued to hold the child up to God, claiming life for Claire, claiming it and claiming it. Suddenly Claire spluttered and coughed and she started to breathe. Christina was still roaring and crying in the kitchen and I shouted to her, "Claire's breathing again. She's back to life." Christina cried, "No, she's dead." and wouldn't come. And I had to run back to Christina and hand her the child. Claire was still struggling to breathe and spluttering, and I said, "Right, we have to get her to the hospital."

So we jumped in the car and we prayed and we prayed the whole way down. Our child had been dead for ten minutes, without any oxygen to the brain for all that time, and three minutes is the limit. So I prayed to God, "Thank you, Lord, for bringing our child back to life but, please, dear God, do not allow her brain to be affected. Jesus, I know your power is flowing through her brain now and I know that there will be no brain damage. Let her brain be normal, Lord. I claim your promised healing, in Jesus' name."

"We rushed into the hospital with Claire and told them that she had been dead for ten minutes. The nurses were shocked, one shaking her head at the other one. But they were very efficient and they quickly got Claire on to a monitor and they were amazed when they saw her responses. Christina would be better at telling you about that. But, anyway, a doctor was called and asked me what I had done. I told him about dislodging the mucus by sucking at it and he was astonished. He had never heard of that before. He said that it was something new and that I couldn't have known about it. And he said that he believed that I had indeed been instructed to do it by the Lord.

"To be on the safe side, they kept her in intensive care for eight days. We have a friend who was a nurse in the hospital and she told us that the word of what had happened went round the whole hospital and different consultants and doctors and others went down to the Intensive Care ward to see that child that was dead for ten minutes but whose brain had been unaffected."

Christina's Account (continued)

Claire started to breathe after a full ten minutes and we rushed her to the Children's Hospital where she was admitted to the infectious diseases ward. We were later told that she had whooping cough. They said that, as she was still so young and had not had any immunisation jabs, she had probably picked up the infection in that third week when I took her out in the pram. That would be the explanation that they would best understand, though John and I know different.

Claire spent eight days in the Infectious Diseases ward and then a further week in an open ward. I stayed with her all the time and, since the children were not allowed to visit, I had not seen any of them for a fortnight. When Claire was eventually given the all clear, it was a joy to me to be finally leaving the hospital, taking my baby home and being with my family again.

Thankfully that was the outcome. We did lose Claire for ten minutes that Sunday night but the Lord got the better of our enemy and Claire survived. She is now a happy twelve-year-old. I went on to have another baby after that, in June 1999, without incident, thank God. We called her Siobhan and she, also, is a happy ten-year-old today. The Lord has now blessed John and I with six beautiful daughters and it fascinates them to hear true stories about their births and other incidents that happened when they were young, and the things that John and I have experienced both with the Lord and His blessings, and with He who is against the Lord. We tell them stories about how the enemy operates but it is not scary for them. It makes them knowledgeable and, as John often says, 'Ignorance is more scary than truth.'

John's Final Comments

"I believe that Satan, or a dark spiritual force, caused that death in my house to deter me from going ahead with my decision to spread the Lord's miracles. Although it seemed like a physical situation, and the doctors saw it like that, it was definitely a spiritual attack and I was able to turn it around and thwart Satan by using the miraculous power of the Lord. Just as Jesus raised Lazarus from the dead, so He also raised Claire. It was a terrible attack but the thing is, the higher the level of spirit that you are operating from, the more dangerous the force the demons will use against you. You don't go into spiritual warfare imagining that you can do what you do for the Lord and expect to get away with it without reprisals from the dark side."

***

It is often said that one of Satan's greatest deceits is his success in convincing the world that he doesn't exist. In some cases, however, that was not particularly difficult to achieve. People who do not believe in God, for example, find the idea of belief in a personal devil equally preposterous. There are many scientists who believe that the only realities are those which are tangible, empirical and observable. Supernatural entities are, for them, the stuff of myth and imagination.

So what are we to believe? Is evil personal or impersonal? Is evil an active or a passive force? Is the devil real or symbolic? Is evil simply an element of our dysfunctional nature or something real and malignant outside of us?

John Gillespie is under no illusion that any belief that disregards the notion of Satan or diabolical influences upon our lives is one that simply serves Satan, that helps him to do his evil work unhindered. "I always say that if there's no devil, then why do we need a God?" He finds it particularly painful to observe that there are many who have been entrusted with the responsibility of combating Satan on the behalf of their flock, who have been given the power as Christ's disciples to do so, but yet who chose to ignore this aspect of their vocation. "If they're going to pretend that the devil has nothing to do with them," John argues, with some heat, "how can they truly preach the Word of Christ? Was not the very first miracle recorded in the gospel, in St. Mark, a casting out of an unclean spirit? The first thing that impressed the people of the time about Jesus' ministry was that He cast out evil spirits." Derek Prince, at a lecture, made the same point, stating that, while Jesus never made a distinction between deliverance and healing, today's Church seems to have done so.

In light of these conflicting opinions and attitudes the issue might seem complex. But it does not need to be. Nowhere is the truth laid out more simply or with more force than in the address of Pope Paul VI to a general audience some years ago. *(Confronting The Devil's Power, November 15, 1972)*

The Pope began his address with a simple question: "What are the Church's greatest needs at this present time?" Few would have anticipated what the Pope was to say next. "Don't be surprised at our answer and don't write it off as simplistic or even superstitious: One of the Church's greatest needs is to be defended against the evil we call the devil." Pope Paul VI went on to examine the evil in the world and to discuss something of the nature of evil which led him to make a point about the devil, a point clear, unambiguous and unequivocal. He said,

"Evil is not merely an absence of something but an active force, a living spiritual being that is perverted and that perverts others. It is a terrible reality, mysterious and frightening … He is a malign, clever seducer who knows how to make his way into us through the senses, the imagination and the libido, through Utopian logic, or through disordered social contacts in the give and take of our activities, so that he can bring about in us deviations that are all the more harmful because they seem to conform to our physical and mental make-up or to our profound and instinctive aspirations."

Thus the message is clear. There is a huge supernatural universe of demons around us with all sorts of capacities and powers. They labour feverishly to challenge and destroy God's world and God's people while the vast majority of us pass our daily lives in ignorance of this spiritual warfare that is being waged around us. Nonetheless, despite this ignorance, and despite the tendency of many modern theologians, the Vatican has spelt out very clearly that the traditional belief in the devil remains compulsory for today's Roman Catholics, that such belief is, in fact, a tenet of faith.

John also makes it clear, however, that while it is important for Catholics to be very aware of the supernatural battle that we are engaged in, to be aware of the reality of the devil and his works, we should not fear him or become overly preoccupied with the topic of the devil. Fear of the devil, he assures us, is completely unnecessary for those who seek the Lord's protection in prayer and in a Christian life. (See prayers at the end of this chapter).

Nonetheless, although not every sin is due to diabolical interference, there are times when we open ourselves to demonic influence by spiritual hard-heartedness or living in constant sinfulness. Sometimes our sinfulness becomes so habitual that our conscience becomes atrophied and we are no longer aware of our sinfulness. This is a dangerous state to be in. John is all too familiar with the results of such a state and he constantly advises us to be vigilant, to restore ourselves to innocence and grace through the sacraments and the constant reiteration of that powerful line from the Lord's Prayer, "Father, deliver us from evil. Amen"

John says, "When you're at prayer, you're shooting arrows at Satan. Do you think you can shoot arrows at Satan two or three hours every day, especially when you're praying for other people, and he's not going to shoot back? And when he shoots back at you and you have not laid down some form of protection for yourself, well, you're in some sort of trouble, especially when we go into this heavy spiritual warfare stuff.

"I have to protect myself first of all when I am engaged in these kinds of struggles, but the victim has to learn to pray for self-protection as well. We're right at the front line taking on Satan and if we don't have the proper defensive armour, we're not going to last. You can believe me when I tell you that where there is some serious prayer or God's work going on, the devil is never far away. He hates to see anything like that and will do all he can to stop it.

"Protection is particularly important for healers, of course, but everyone needs to pray and to claim protection. I have found, over and over again, that there are people who pray ten times more than I pray, who pray for hours every day, but they do not pray for protection. They believe they are automatically protected just because they pray … but they are not automatically protected. There's a certain level of protection, of course, that comes from prayer but when Satan ups the ante, especially when you're praying for something big and he doesn't want you doing that, it's like being out in the elements, in the snow and in the wind and you in your summer clothes. It's like being on Mount Everest without a coat … you won't last. You need proper protection. You might be a good-living Christian, but if Satan takes a notion to have a go at you, he won't give up easily. So it is important to proclaim that power of God and His angels to protect you … people should be claiming the power of God to protect their bodies, their minds, their spirits, their thoughts and emotions, from any incursion by the evil one or his minions.

"Take the prayer of St. Michael, that's a good one for physical and spiritual protection and many people use it. But people don't realise that there is a deeper spiritual battle going on, the battle of the mind. That is where a high percentage of the spiritual war is waged. That is where there is great subtlety. Satan can implant tiny thoughts in the mind that can cause us especially to lose hope, to convince us that when we pray, we won't get what we're asking for, that the help we might need to overcome some spiritual lack is not forthcoming. Then there'll be times when we are convinced that when we go to confession that we have not confessed properly and we're not absolved of our sins. There are all these subtle wee demons working on us and very few people seek protection from them."

There are many prayers that can be used to protect ourselves from the guile and the duplicity of Satan. For physical and spiritual protection, John mentioned the prayer to Holy Michael, the Archangel. This prayer has a curious history. Pope Leo XVIII once fainted in conclave with his cardinals in 1884. When he regained consciousness he told the cardinals that he had had "a terrible vision" of the devil overrunning the world but that he would be eventually defeated by St. Michael. As a result of this experience, Leo XVIII wrote a long prayer to the Archangel. This powerful petition, with its pleas and responses, was seen as a highly effective defense against the devil and it was said at the end of all low Masses until the 1970s when it fell into disuse.

The longer version is seldom prayed nowadays but the shorter version is still well-known:

Invocation to the Archan

The Miracle Ship

St. Michael, Archangel, defend us in battle. Be our protection against the wickedness and snares of the devil, may God rebuke him, we humbly pray. And do thou, O Prince of the Heavenly Host, by the divine power, thrust into hell Satan and all other evil spirits who wander through the world seeking the ruin of souls. Amen

John also makes the point that physical and spiritual protection is not enough, that we must seek also protection of the mind. For this, we should always appeal to the Holy Spirit:

"O Holy Spirit, please give us the discernment to know when our hope in your guidance of us is being challenged by the evil one, when our faith in your mercy and forgiveness is being threatened by his insidious voice, when our desire to make new beginnings in our spiritual lives is impeded by false discouragement. Help us in this we pray, O Holy Spirit. Protect our bodies, minds and spirits, our thoughts, our emotions. Give us the strength to know and resist the snares of the deceiver and to remember that we live always in your glorious grace. Amen.

Chapter Eighteen

You must not have in your midst ... anyone who practises divination, who is a sorcerer, or one who practises enchantments [Deut. 18:11]

The New Age Illusion

John Gillespie has little tolerance of what are termed 'New Age Therapies.' "They are too close," he says, "to seeking and using powers that are not of God." There are those who openly resent his stance on what they see as perfectly innocent alternative and homoeopathic ways of healing. But John has seen people driven to the point of suicide by the depression and blackness in their lives occasioned by their involvement in New Age therapies. Many suppliants who have come to John seeking help for debilitating and undiagnosed illnesses are horrified to learn that their involvement in New Age therapies are the source of their problems. They did not have the slightest idea that their involvement in what seemed like 'harmless healing therapies' could lead to any danger. Most were shocked by what John was to tell them. The story that follows contains its own warnings about the practice of therapies that seek energy from sources other than God.

***

Colleen's Story: The Social Worker who Supplemented her Income

Colleen knew almost all there was to know about suffering, at least that was what she believed. She had endured hurt and brokenness throughout her life. As a child she suffered rejection from her family, particularly from her mother who never showed her any love or affection. Colleen, through no fault of her own and for reasons she was never to understand, was always treated differently from the other children in the family. Her mother simply did not warm to her and Colleen spent her childhood in silent heartache and secret tears.

The psychological effects of this upbringing clung to her and as she grew to womanhood she experienced difficulty in forming a real connection with the men who entered her life. She finally found herself in a troubled, unsatisfying relationship with a work-colleague which continued to stutter along, however, with some semblance of love.

Living alone, she was obliged to fend for herself and, even though she was a qualified social worker with a good salary, she felt the need to supplement her income in order to maintain her mortgage repayments. She was given advice by a friend to train in reflexology and other New Age therapies. It seemed that many professional young women were making a comfortable second living in this way.

She began to train with a well-known proprietor of a herb-shop, learning the use of crystals as well as reflexology. (Crystals are glass stones used in New Age healing. They reputedly have a form of universal energy coming from them.) Colleen was an intelligent young woman and had no trouble picking up the fundamentals of the therapies. Soon she was out visiting clients at the weekends, supplementing her income by bringing relaxation and healing to tired and pain-racked bodies. She became very successful and soon had a full calendar. But as time passed, her life, which had been relatively calm and peaceful at that time, suddenly began to disintegrate into chaos again. It seemed that while she was successfully bringing healing to her clients, her own personal life had become full of hurt and disaster. Her relationship with her boyfriend broke up in acrimony. She began to experience levels of stress far beyond anything she had known before. Her social work became demanding, difficult and demoralising. She found that she no longer had any peace in her life. Her health began to deteriorate and she became victim to moods of deep depression. Her life seemed to be crashing down around her, and her head, as she was later to say to John, "… was churning and churning. If I thought my life was bad before, I didn't know the half of it."

During this troubled period, Colleen sought help from a variety of sources, from priests, from counsellors at the offices to which she was attached, from other work colleagues, but from her perspective it seemed that nobody cared what was happening to her. Nobody seemed interested enough to try to help her.

Eventually, she felt that she could take no more. She packed a small bag and went back to the little town in the north-west of Ireland where the family home was. She had made the decision to commit suicide that evening and wanted to be near her family when she ended her life. Before she carried out the act, however, she went to the local church to pray for forgiveness.

"Lord," she prayed, "this is not what I want to do but I can't put up with this situation any longer. Please send me someone who can talk to me, Lord, or who can help me. Otherwise, I truly will have to end it all."

When she came out of the chapel, she sensed that there were two people that she should go to see, a married couple whom she knew and who often prayed with, and tried to help, people in trouble. She had the distinct impression that she should go to their house which was only a short distance from where she lived.

The couple, Ciaran and his wife, Mary, invited her in and expressed concern and understanding when she told them her story. Mary said immediately, "Somehow or other you have opened yourself up to something that's of Satan and now you are under severe attack from him." She had discerned that Colleen had been involved in something un-Christian and asked her if she had been involved in any New Age practices.

Coleen was shocked at what Mary had said but she told them her story as frankly and as honestly as she could. Her older listeners were very sympathetic and told her gently that she needed some kind of deliverance. They said that from time to time deliverance was something that they did themselves but that in this case they felt that they would not be able to do all that was needed.

"We can pray over you, if you like," Mary said, "but I honestly feel that you will still need further and more penetrating deliverance. There's a man from Belfast we know about who has had great success with this sort of thing. I can get you an appointment with him, if you like."

Mary was speaking about John Gillespie, and a day or two later, Colleen found herself meeting with John at her new friends' house. John, as always, was his uncompromising self but somehow nothing he says offends. Colleen listened to all he had to say about the dangers of New Age therapies. “These oils you use,” he asked her, “do you know where they originated or whether they have been interfered with?”

“What do you mean … interfered with?” Colleen asked.

“A lot of these oils come from Eastern Europe,” John told her, “and it is the custom in many of those places to prepare the oils using pagan rituals to invoke powers of healing into them.”

“But, sure if they heal …?” Colleen started.

“There’s nothing of God in pagan rituals,” John said firmly. “And if there’s power in them, where’s it coming from?”

John went on to explain how easy it was to open oneself to the occult and to dark, malevolent powers. “It’s easily done,” he told the young woman. “Once you start drawing power from sources that are not of God, you are immediately connected to the demonic.”

Colleen was disturbed and upset by what John had to tell her and very soon, realising what a terrible mistake she had been making, she was happy to allow him to accompany her to her house to examine the materials she had gathered up during her practitioner phase. She was persuaded by what John had said to renounce immediately her involvement with New Age and the attitudes and practices she had adopted. She also willingly renounced any allegiance she might have unwittingly made with a demon and promised to go to confession and receive Holy Communion as soon as possible.

John went around the house with her, pointing out hundreds of pounds’ worth of materials that were demonic or dangerous to her spirit – books, ointments, symbols, crystals, herbs and other paraphernalia that she had accumulated. They cleared all of these items from the house and threw them on to a small bonfire in the back garden. John then prayed over Colleen, once more asking her to repudiate and repent what she had been doing.

Over the following few weeks, John had to revisit Colleen for further prayers of deliverance because, as he explains, "When you take a demon out, a person is very vulnerable. Taking a demon out is one thing; keeping it out is something else entirely. You can take five or six demons out of a person in a few minutes, perhaps even less, but keeping them out requires prayer, repentance, a raised spirit and new hope in the victim. The victim has to have the courage and the faith and the hope to resist the demon. That's why I have to go back a few times. In the aftermath of deliverance, there is a point of weakness and vulnerability where the suppliant greatly needs my help. I have to encourage them, to help them to build up their spiritual hope and strength, to try to ensure that they stay optimistic. Without a renewed and buoyant spirit, they are vulnerable to the demon's return. It takes prayer to block this. As it says in the bible, 'He waits until the house is made clean, then he brings in seven more.' So I have to teach people not only to pray, to learn how to connect with Jesus, but also to protect themselves."

Colleen now feels as if a huge weight had been lifted from her shoulders. Her life, and her attitude to it, changed dramatically almost immediately after her first meeting with John. She is experiencing happiness that she has never felt before, has found a new relationship, and is thriving in the profession she was trained for and in her new life.

***

It is relatively simple to recount a story such as Colleen's and use it as a warning against the practice of New Age therapies. But there are those whose minds and intellects will be less than satisfied with a generalised warning from a single example. As was the issue of Satan, this subject, too, is one that needs examination.

Some fifteen years ago, young people in America and, indeed, in the rest of the world, developed a strong interest in the environment and in ecology. "Save the Planet" was their watchword. Many Christian idealists shared in this noble aspiration but as time passed, subtly and imperceptibly, the push for harmony between man and nature, the growing awareness of the need to improve the world, the disillusionment with the extreme materialism of modern life, the determination to mobilise the forces of good for a new world order, led to a movement in which 'the best' ideas from many religions were combined, leading to the anti-Christian belief that all religions are one.

While this movement is not an organisation or an institution, there are many people who adhere to the same loose set of principles and ideas that tend to fall under the title, 'New Age', a term of hope, a hope that humanity would now evolve into something new and better. For New Agers, a new era emerges every two thousand and one years. In the year of 2000, many believed that the world was leaving the era of Pisces (with its sign of 'the fish' and its connections with Jesus Christ) and entering into the "dawning of the Age of Aquarius". Initially positive, the movement incorporated many elements of Christianity but by mingling these with elements from eastern mysticism and other oriental religions, the truth of Christianity was altered and its true meaning was lost. Fr. Benedict Heron (1997) states:

"There are a number of important differences in the NAM [New Age Movement] which are diametrically opposed to orthodox Christianity and it is most important that Christians should be aware of these differences. There is a real danger of a woolly fuzziness which ends by sacrificing important elements of the Christian gospel." [p.39]

The NAM is thus a great challenge for Christianity. The 'fuzziness' of thought Fr. Heron referred to, has led to grand but utterly unchristian concepts such as 'cosmic energy', 'everything is God, 'we ourselves are God'. NAM has arrived at a stage where new divinities have begun to appear, for example, Gaia - the Mother Earth, the divinity that purportedly pervades the whole of creation. God is no longer a separate, external source of divine authority. He is sidelined into simply being a part of His own creation. Dr. John B. Shea explains it:

"The New Age does not believe in a God who transcends His creation, does not believe in good or evil, has no room for judgement or blame, and holds that belief in evil is negative and causes only fear. It also fails to distinguish between God who created the universe and the universe He created."

Thus New Age leads us away from God and His Church and away from authentic forms of healing, from an authentic understanding of our environmental issues, and from authentic solutions to their problems.

It comes as no surprise, therefore, that the Vatican (2003) felt obliged to publish a warning to retreat places, seminaries and religious formation houses about the dangers of dabbling in New Age spirituality. In a lengthy document, some 90 pages, the Pontifical Council for Inter-religious Dialogue makes some effort to understand the phenomenon of New Age and the confusion surrounding it for Christians but, ultimately, the document leaves no doubt that New Age is incompatible with, and hostile to, the core beliefs of Christianity.

The Vatican document (2003) explains that New Age spirituality appeals to people imbued with the values of modern culture but that while "… it [NAM] claims to satisfy people's spiritual appetites … it does not demand any more faith or belief than going to the cinema … [and] … its attempts to respond to the legitimate spiritual longing of human nature run counter to Christian revelation." The obvious conclusion we must draw from the Vatican statement, therefore, must be that since NAM ideologies are incompatible with Catholic doctrine, they cannot be viewed as positive or even innocuous.

Indeed, there are many dangers for Christianity in the New Age Movement, not least in the new drive for 'syncretism', a move which is as insidious as it is destructive to the spirituality of the unwary. On the surface syncretism seeks to promote a kind of ecumenical mix of ideas and practices from various spiritual traditions and religions but it makes no attempt to define or understand the truth or values of any. The consequent impact of this approach is particularly harmful to the truth and values of Christianity.

There are influential people in the New Age Movement who are trying to supersede existing religions in order to allow the development of a single universal religion that could unite humanity, a lofty goal which utterly denies revealed truth. This is a worrying trend which, unfortunately, is creeping into many Christian organisations. In 1994 the 'National Catholic Reporter' ran a story about a Catholic Feminist group who, in a desire to be accommodating and 'inclusive' to all women, held a conference at which different spiritual traditions would be viewed as equal to the Catholic faith. The Reporter informed its readers that at the Conference, "… in addition to rituals by witches *[there would be]* rituals led by Buddhists, American Indians, Quakers and Jewish leaders, as well as Catholic nuns."

Disturbing though this report is, there is little new in this kind of drifting. In biblical times, the Israelites angered God by much the same behaviour. The Book of Judges tells us: "*They prostituted themselves to other gods and bowed down before these.*" [Judges 2:16] Today, John Gillespie says, "New Agers are going into drawing powers from Hindu, Shinto, Taoism and other Eastern religions and are trying to adapt them into Christian practice. They're breaking the first commandment which is 'Thou shalt have no strange gods before me.' And the thing is, when people from the Hindu, Shinto, Buddhism or Taoism or any of those Eastern religions convert to Christianity, they renounce all their own practices. They stop them completely … but modern Christians are promoting it. That's dangerous."

In the *Alive.* newspaper, October 2009, Patricia McNally, a Catholic who now works in Pastoral Ministry, tells how she had once developed an interest in angels and healing. She attended courses in … "'*energy healing', Yoga classes, various types of meditation classes and doing angel readings* (what Father Owen Gorman refers to in a separate article the following month as "tarot cards dressed up in angels' wings.") *I went all holistic in 'mind, body and spirit' fairs and basically before I knew it I was right in the middle of a New Age web of occult practices ... I began to take on board a new set of beliefs, contrary to my Catholic faith. Over time these beliefs slowly phased God out of my life ... Eventually I was overcome with a terrible state of anxiety and fear. I felt stunned and numb. I didn't know what was wrong and believed it was something physical ..."*

Much of what Patricia says here is reflected in the cases that John has had to deal with, time and time again. Patricia tells us that eventually she *"... met a person who enlightened me about idolatry. It was what I was involved in even though I was not aware of it."*

It is for reasons such as this that the Vatican document argues that it is not possible to isolate some elements of New Age religiosity as acceptable to Christians while rejecting all of the others. The NAM has to be rejected as a whole.

The irony of New Age is that its proponents search back through aeons of legends and magic for a 'new' spirituality. The more ancient the better, it seems. They seek answers from mediaeval alchemy; they embrace a form of neo-pagan pantheism, creating for themselves, in a twisted version of the truth of creation, new gods and goddesses similar to those of the ancient Greeks and Romans. Such myth-filled philosophy inevitably had to arrive at a belief that its adopted deities have powers, that they have 'energies' that can be used for healing and good fortune. Thus New Agers seek information from 'spirit guides' who are supposedly tens of thousands of years old. They seek healing from 'earth spirits' in the use of many herbal or 'natural' remedies. They seek well-being from practices imported from ancient religions, practices such as reiki, reflexology, yoga, channelling, divination, and many others . [See Appendix 3] These approaches to healing all share the common belief that each individual has within himself a spiritual energy that can be controlled and unified with the universe ... but precisely what is meant by the 'universe' is not easy to discover. Nor does it seem to be clearly understood by NAM adherents. For many of them, this vague connection with the all-embracing universe seems understanding enough.

It is probably fair to say that New Age ideals and philosophies are not intrinsically evil. In its adherents' desire to seek health and help from the new deities, however, there lies enormous risk because the 'new deities' *do* exist, and they *do* respond (in their own insidious way) to requests for action. But the question that New Agers do not appear to have asked themselves is, "Where do these 'middle-ground' types of spirit come from?" What they fail to understand is that 'spirits of the air' or 'earth spirits' cannot exist, at least, not in the identity the New Agers attribute to them. These 'helpful' deities are simply Satan and his minions. Satan is subtle and he will make use of anything that leads away from revealed truth. He is always present in disguise, being what people want him to be, appearing beneficial, deluding the unwary with what John calls 'the subtlety of the suggestive voice,' but always bringing with him a lurking malice that is designed to defeat goodness and ruin lives. In the NAM he has found rich ground for deceiving untutored minds and for harvesting unsuspecting souls.

In their innocence, New Age adherents frequently claim to use "white" magic, magic that is used for a good purpose. Fortea (2006) makes it clear that this is not simply wishful thinking, it is a dangerous opening of oneself to the influence of evil forces:

"Strictly speaking, any paranormal effect achieved through magic is accomplished through the intervention of demons, not as a result of a particular person's "magical" powers. Even if those who practice magic … deny it (or are even unaware of it), the devil is behind all their works." (p.113)

John constantly preaches this same message. He has had to bring healing to many people whose lives had been brought to the brink of despair by involvement in New Age therapies. John is unequivocal in his judgement of New Age. He makes the point that if so-called Christian versions of some New Age therapies seem to work they are working for one of two reasons. They work because of power that comes from specific demons related to that practice or they come from Jesus. "Power can only come from two sources on this earth," John affirms. "There is no in-between stuff like white magic, earth spirits, the energy of the universe, or anything like that. Power can only come from two sources. It comes from either Jesus or the devil. So you can be sure that if it is not coming from God, it has to be coming from Satan."

Thus John argues that if a healing sought using some New Age process is successful and has not been claimed through Christian prayer, then it is the result of demonic influence. Such practice is to be avoided at all costs. If the healing is successful because it comes through Jesus in response to Christian prayers, as Fr. Heron seems to imply, then why is it necessary to use the New Age techniques? "They are not necessary," John declares firmly. "They are dangerous and should always be avoided. Praying to Jesus is more than enough."

Staunch support for John's stance is found in Derek Prince's book (1998). Prince tells a story about a Chinese doctor from Malaysia who had been using acupuncture, apparently very successfully, for five years. What the doctor did not realise, however, was that his wife's chronic migraine and his own unexplained darkness and depression were a direct result of this practice. He learned eventually to make the connection and immediately renounced his practice and gathered "… all my machines,

needles, books, diploma and charts and
bonfire of them publicly. The total cost of t
about $15,000.00" [p.148] But this led to w
"priceless blessings." Shortly afterwards, ...ne's migraine was miraculously healed and his own depression completely vanished. The sad ending to the story, however, was that the Christian Brother who taught him acupuncture "... suffered severe depression and committed suicide under mysterious circumstances." [p.149]

Brian Incigneri talks about a "new age supermarket" in which "... there are many products available." As well as fortune telling, acupuncture, and reflexology, one of the most popular of New Age practices is 'reiki'. The name derives from two words: 'Rei' which means 'god-consciousness' and 'Ki' which means 'life energy'. In the practice of reiki, the god-consciousness guides the life-energy. This technique was invented in Japan in the late 1800s by Makao Usui. His guidelines explain that the reiki master seeks to facilitate the flow of the 'chi' (a universal life energy) from the practitioner to the patient.

Reiki came to America in the late 1970s and there are now over a million people practising the therapy. Literature on reiki frequently describes the practice as "a spiritual kind of healing' and a growing number of Catholic convents and religious institutions are incorporating the practice of reiki into their programmes. But the literature, more and more, includes also key-phrases like 'becoming attuned to the universal life energy', reference to 'goddesses', and 'spiritually guided life-force energy'. In this language can be detected a strong drift from Christian beliefs.

A German reiki channeller makes the following comment on a website blog: "You will find it easier to ɜt off old, outlived structures and you will notice that you are being led and guided more and more …" It is clear that the writer is impressed by this discovery but to the discerning Christian the implications of the statement are horrifying.

Concern occasioned by the growth of reiki, especially among religious, has prompted the Catholic Bishops of the United States to issue a document stating that "Reiki therapy is not compatible with either Christian teaching or scientific evidence." (2009) The bishops warn that reiki operates in the realm of superstition which "… corrupts one's worship of God by turning one's religious feeling and practice in a false direction," and thus, "… it would be inappropriate for Catholic institutions such as health care facilities and retreat centres, or persons representing the Church such as Catholic chaplains, to promote or provide support for reiki therapy."

John has a close friendship with a Poor Clare nun, Sister Briege, who shares with him his gift of discernment of demons. Sr. Briege has had to 'deliver' from demonic oppression many people who opened themselves to the evil one through the practice of reiki and other New Age therapies. Sr. Briege has this to say:

"Reiki is very fashionable at the moment but, and I'm afraid that many will be offended by this, from what I have been able to discern, it is diabolical in origin. There are those that are involved in reiki as an exercise or a way of relaxing who will tell you that it is just a gentle healing process. The healer does not even touch people ... he simply holds a hand so many inches from the patient's body and the patient is supposed to open herself to God and let God heal her. But it's reiki; it's not a Christian healing ministry even though it may be identical in appearance. People would say it is a harmless, if ancient,

art of healing. But in actual fact it originates from an ancient demonic cult. What most people don't know, including those who train to be reiki masters, is that when they reach 'level three' in the training, they have to do homage to their reiki 'guru'. It's a picture of some person who is not of the Christian faith. The trainee reiki masters have to learn some secret words, in a language they don't understand, but what they also don't understand is that these words are the names of pagan gods. They are then instructed to use these words over the sick person but what they are actually doing is opening the sick person and themselves to the demon god who is attached to the picture. So to administer reiki or to participate in a session opens one to demonic oppression.

"Now, this is frightening because there are doctors and nurses, priests and nuns, who do reiki, all convinced of its healing powers. There are hundreds of people doing reiki here in Ireland in all innocence, unaware of the terrible danger they are placing themselves in."

Asked if there could be a distinction made between good reiki and demonic reiki, Sr. Briege responded firmly, *"No! All reiki is demonic. The consequences are all too evident. I have come across so many people involved in reiki, practitioners and suppliants alike, who have ended up almost suicidal, deeply depressed, their lives dark and without joy. There are so many stories but I'll tell you just one.*

"A friend of mine brought to me a young woman in her twenties, telling me that the young woman was in serious need of help. I spent time alone with her and she told me she kept waking up in the middle of the night, panicking because she could feel a cold hand on her throat choking her. She couldn't breathe, and would have to throw herself out of bed gasping for air. And this

happened in other places as well, even when she was driving the car. When it happens in the car, she has to pull over to the side of the road to recover. 'Do you ever see anything?' I asked her. 'Mostly no," she told me, 'but I do sometimes in the night see a black figure ...'

"She was a good Christian woman, a practising Catholic, but I know by now the kinds of questions to ask in situations like these. I soon discovered that she was involved in fortune-telling and reiki and that she had trained to be a reiki master and had paid homage to a reiki guru. I told her that she opened herself to demonic oppression. 'You are not actually possessed by an evil spirit,' I told her, 'but there is an alien presence beside you which you have allowed to accompany you because you have given it entry to some aspect of your life. That's what's causing all your problems. I'll pray with you, of course, but you will also have to go to confession and communion and renounce all involvement with reiki and any other New Age stuff you're involved in.'

"She nearly fainted when I told her this but said she didn't believe me, and just left. But later on I met the lady who had brought the young woman to me. She had some knowledge of this kind of thing and had kept on and on at the young woman, who was still suffering the terrible choking sensations, to go to confession and renounce the reiki. Eventually the young woman relented and did what I had suggested to her. She is now completely free of her troubles and is a changed and happy woman."

What John has to say about reiki differs not one iota from what Sr. Briege had to say. "The thing about reiki healing," John declares, "is that a whole lot of people who are practising it do not know what they're doing or what's behind it. This sort of healing is promoted with extraordinary vigour and reaches many people. Many church and parish halls run programmes on reiki, and on aromatherapy, too, and reflexology and yoga and goodness knows what else, in order to gather funds for new building programmes or other parish needs. They don't know what they're messing with. The whole story about it is never told.

"You watch anyone who's at it. Everything changes around them, their mood, their health. Everything changes. They start praying to angels. They learn to do all these focusing diagrams and they … they draw on powers and crazy stuff like that. But none of it is from Jesus. There is nothing here about the forgiveness of sin. When we pray for healing, the Lord is always bringing up stuff about asking forgiveness about this and that. But there's none of that in reiki. There are no rules. Everything's okay! They call it God's power. But it's not God's power because God's healing always has stipulations, about confession, about the Eucharist, about forgiveness, something the person has to do. But these reiki people pray to what they call the 'Angel of Light' and they believe that Angel of Light is bringing healing. But what they forget is that Lucifer - the name means 'bearer of light' - is the 'angel of light' and he was kicked out of heaven and into hell. It's his force they're drawing on. There are no universal forces. It's either God or Satan. That's why all these New Age practices are so dangerous. They take you away from God and there's only Satan left."

***

John has lost count of the number of suppliants that have come to him with New Age related illnesses. "I get them all the time," he says, "and the most of them don't have a clue what they're into." The two stories that follow, each with its own specific involvement in New Age, are typical of the type of help John is frequently called upon to give.

***

Deborah's Story: The Priest Said It Was OK!

Deborah, a young woman working in Belfast, decided on advice from a friend to train to be a reflexologist. She had been studying and practising the technique for two years and was preparing for her final examinations. The more expert she became, the more she practised. She expanded her expertise into Indian head-massage, healing by crystals, homoeopathy, and was soon earning a good living. Over the next couple of years she invested hundreds of pounds in reflexology equipment and materials – crystals, candles, herbs, oils, books and other paraphernalia – and even secured a loan from the bank to convert a spare room in her house into a reflexology workshop where she intended to work full-time. By this time she had built up a substantial client list, all of whom told her that they were very happy with what she was doing for them.

Deborah was naturally pleased with her success but her own health seemed to be adversely affected by something which she couldn't explain. She felt weak and tired, losing much of her usual energy. She found, too, that her mental faculties were suffering as well. She had great trouble now in studying what before gave her no problems, and in other walks of life her mind seemed considerably less sharp than normal. To counteract this malady she began taking tablets, vitamins, herbs … but nothing seemed to help.

Over a period of two years her health continued to deteriorate. An acquaintance suggested that there might be some connection between her reflexology and the illness. Deborah worried about this and spoke about it to two or three priests whom she knew well. Each of them said that there were "… courses and programmes in reflexology in local Further Education colleges all over the place" and that it would be perfectly all right for her to go on working at it. One did say that he might have been concerned if she had been involved in reiki but he could see no problem with reflexology. "As far as I know," he said, "it is in line with Church teaching."

But Deborah continued to feel worse and finally decided to go on pilgrimage to Medjugorje. The experience was spiritual for her but had little impact upon her condition. One benefit, however, did emerge from the visit. She met a lady there who told her that a Belfast man, John Gillespie was great at finding out the causes of mysterious illnesses.

She found John when she returned to Ireland and told him her story. John immediately discerned that Deborah was heavily involved in reflexology and explained that her illness stemmed from that. She began to argue with him, saying that there could be nothing demonic about reflexology. "If it was demonic," she said, "how can I go to Mass and pray? I'm only just back from Medjugorje and I was able to do all those spiritual exercises. How can you tell me that what I am doing is not of God? And anyway," she finished defensively, "the priest told me it was OK."

John shook his head slowly. He had heard this same argument so often before. "Look, Deborah," he explained, "you need to know something about God's laws. There's a kind of line between what is of God and what isn't. If you stray one degree off that line, you might as well go ninety degrees off. There's the black and the white, the grey and the white. Step into the grey from the white and you are already into the demonic. God's side is always white. The grey areas, as well as the black, always belong to Satan. He might not have you in the black but if you're in the grey, you're vulnerable to him."

Deborah listened, shaken, as John continued to explain the true Christian view on reflexology, how it allows demons to tap into the hearts and minds of those who practise it. He explained that the New Age concept of universal forces was theologically untenable, that there were only two real forces in the universe, God and Satan.

"I've been around three or four priests during the past few years," Deborah said, drained and deflated, "and none of them told me that. You're the first person to point this out to me."

"I'm sorry," John told her. "You're not the first by a long way to fall into this trap. The sad thing is, you have several demons all around you now and I am going to have to deliver you from them." Deidre was shocked anew but submitted herself to John's prayers.

John was able to identify the demons that were affecting her health, those that were affecting her mind, those that were affecting her emotions, and others that were already starting to attack the organs in her body.

"My organs?" Deborah was aghast.

"That's the way they work," John told her, "They start attacking the bodily organs a bit at a time. They start to shut them down here and there and when you go to the doctor seeking medical advice, he won't be able to find a cause. He'll hum and he'll haw and he might send you for a scan. No good. Hospital scanners are not going to show up demons."

Deborah left John's study and, as she was to tell him later, "… turned my life around. I had been to reflexologists myself over the last two years of my illness, but you achieved more with me in ten minutes of God's healing than I got from two years of New Age therapy. I've cancelled the bank loan and thrown out all that New Age stuff, hundreds of pounds' worth. But I don't care. I'm back at my old job now, and that's it for me. I'm not earning as much but I'd rather earn very little than earn piles doing something that's anti-Christian and ruining my physical and my spiritual health."

***

Deuteronomy forbids any practices that take one away from the Lord and into avenues that involve sorcery, soothsaying or divination. Dervla's story is an object lesson on what can happen when we seek, from dubious sources, information the Lord does not intend us to have.

***

Dervla's Story: A Persistent Headache

Dervla's husband, Eamon, was plagued with back pains. She heard that John Gillespie held healing sessions every Friday in a house in a mid-Ulster town near where she lived. She insisted that Pat go to see John and, to ensure that he "… wouldn't back out of it," she would come with him and bring the baby, Eamon, as well.

They made the appointment and met John. John was to say later, "The man's back pain was perfectly normal. His spine was out of line and very easily cleared up … only the work of a couple of minutes. But there was something about the woman. I kept looking at her. I knew God was trying to tell me something."

John said to Dervla. "Are you all right yourself? I'm thinking you have pain, too?"

"Ah, it's just this headache," she said. "It's on the top of my head here, always on the same spot. It just won't go away. I've had it for years. I've been to doctors, I've had x-rays and scans, but nobody can find anything. I take tablets but they don't seem to do any good. It's just always there."

John immediately recognised that something about this headache was not normal. He prayed over Dervla and asked the Lord for the Word of Knowledge, for an explanation of the root cause of Dervla's headache.

"I'll have to find the root cause," he told her, "because there's no point in praying for relief of pain until you know where it's coming from."

The word John received from God, almost immediately, was that Dervla had been repeatedly visiting a fortune-teller, week after week. He soon discerned that she was being oppressed by two demons that were working on her subconscious. They were filling her with fear, fear that she would contract some dreadful illness which would cause her to die young, fear that she would never see her child grow up, her husband grow old.

"Have you been going to a fortune-teller?" John asked her.

Dervla, looking somewhat guilty, nodded. Eamon's face tightened and he looked stern. This was obviously a point of contention in the family. But Dervla then said, “Sure, what’s wrong with that?”

John said quietly, “It’s not of God.”

“Not of God? Sure it’s only a bit of fun. I know lots of women who do it. There are no thoughts in our heads about offending God.”

John said firmly, “What’s fun to you can still be sin to God. It’s totally forbidden. And heed this! If you go to a fortune-teller alone, it’s very unlikely that you’ll come home alone.”

Dervla looked puzzled. “You mean …?

“I mean that you open yourself to demons. It’s as bad as that.”

At this point Eamon interrupted. “Thank God somebody’s talking sense to her about this. Nobody’ll listen to me.”

Then he went on to explain that Dervla had brought a fortune-teller to the house one evening. The woman began to work with Tarot cards and Eamon felt distinctly uneasy about that. He made the excuse that he had to get up early for work the next morning and that he didn’t want this woman in the house keeping them up late. But Dervla sent him off to bed. During the time the woman was reading the tarot cards, Eamon was thrown out of his bed by an unseen force. “It frightened the life out of me,” he said. “I told Dervla about it and said that that stuff is bringing the devil into the house. But she wouldn’t listen. She said that I was imagining things, that I had fallen out of the bed in my sleep.” He looked grimly at his wife. “Thank God you’re hearing the truth now.”

“OK, Eamon,” John said, raising his hands to calm the man. “Let me deal with this.” He turned to the woman. “You’re going to have to listen to me, Dervla.

Fortune-telling? Tarot cards? You've opened yourself up to Satan, and any information you got from this fortune-teller, you got from Satan."

The husband and wife looked stunned. Eamon was taking no joy from the fact that he was being proved right.

"There's a bit in the bible about this," John went on. "It's in the Book of Deuteronomy, Chapter 18, verse 10, something like, "Thou shalt not consult with one who practises divination, or anyone who consults the stars, who is a sorcerer, or one who practises enchantments or who consults the spirits, or one who asks questions of the dead." This biblical injunction is authorised by God, Dervla and you cannot break God's commandment. It's having strange gods before the only God."

By now Dervla was looking thoroughly crestfallen. John placed his hand on her shoulder. "Look, you've unwittingly opened yourself up to Satan and I can tell you now that pain you have been experiencing in your head all this time is coming from him. Have you been getting these headaches before you started going to the fortune-teller?"

Dervla thought for a while and then admitted that John was right, that the pains had started only after she had first visited the psychic. John placed his hand on her head again. "You have a constant fear in you that you're going to get sick, that you're going to die young ..."

"I don't think that," Dervla interrupted him defensively.

John said, "Dervla, God's not telling me lies. You have to admit the truth of what I'm saying. I can't help you otherwise."

Dervla emitted an embarrassed laugh and said, "All right. I know it's crazy, but I do think like that sometimes. But I didn't want to tell anyone about it."

"They're crazy thoughts, all right," John said, "but they're not coming from you. There's two demons in your head, battering away at you, filling your head with this stuff."

Dervla paled. "What am I going to do?"

"You'll be fine, "John said. "You'll have to renounce all connection with that fortune-teller, pray for forgiveness for your trespass, confess and repent all your other sins to the Lord, and the pain in your head will leave you."

As they were leaving, he gave them some leaflets containing information about New Age practices, warning them what to watch out for and what to avoid. John was not to see Dervla again but, as he explains with a laugh, "That's usually because they no longer have problems. If there are still problems, you always get them back."

Prayer of Repentance for New Age Involvement

Heavenly Father, by the power of Your Holy Spirit reveal to me aspects of my life that are not pleasing to You, ways that have given or could give Satan a foothold in my life. Father, I give to You my sins; and I give to You all ways that Satan has a hold of my life. Thank you, Father, for these revelations. Thank You, for Your forgiveness and Your love.

In the Holy Name of Jesus, I break and dissolve any and all links and the effects of links with astrologers, channellers, clairvoyants, crystal healers, crystals, fortune tellers, mediums, the New Age Movement, occult seers, tea-leaf, palm or tarot card readers, psychics, satanic cults, spirit guides, witches, witch-doctors and Voodoo. In Jesus' Name, I dissolve all effects of participation in seances, divination, New Age practices and any form of worship that does not offer true honour to Jesus Christ.

Chapter Nineteen

But if you do not obey the voice of Yahweh, your God, and do not take care to practise all His commandments ... all these curses shall come upon you. [Deut. 28:15]

The Lifting of Curses

For John Gillespie, the real beginning of a healing is the diagnosis of the root cause of the illness. Often, before healing can take place, John needs to identify the source of the illness. If the source is natural, a simple prayer for healing will suffice. If it is supernatural, then other factors come into play. Often the illness is not a simple, natural physical malady; it can be a caused by sin in the bloodline, by involvement in practices that open the victim to demonic infiltration, or, as in the case of this next story, it can be caused by a curse.

***

Mona's Story: The Five Lost Babies

Before John Gillespie came into their lives, Mona and Kevin would have deemed themselves an average, modern Catholic couple. In the ten or so years that they had been married, Kevin's career proved successful and they were now comfortably middle class with plenty of friends and a good social life. They considered themselves honest in their dealings with others, believed that there was a merciful God and, while they did not go to Mass on Sundays, they still saw themselves as established members of the Church who lived good Christian lives without the necessity of the pomp and circumstance of the liturgy.

Their life together, however, was not without its share of sorrow. They both wanted children to complete their family but on each of the four occasions that Mona was able to conceive, she lost the baby. She learnt that although she was able to conceive, something abnormal kept happening to the embryo. Her doctors explained that there was a mysterious blockage somewhere between the fallopian tubes and the womb. Each time she became pregnant the embryo could not reach the womb and began, instead, to develop in the fallopian tubes. The foetus, they told her, could never survive the full term in this situation and miscarriage was inevitable. When her doctors finally admitted, after these four failed pregnancies, that they did not know how to help her, Mona was devastated and began to sink into a clinical depression.

John had helped someone near where Mona lived and when she heard about this miraculous healing, she made a point of contacting him. An appointment was made and when she arrived, accompanied by her mother, she was, as John was later to say, "… in a dreadful state emotionally." Haltingly, and with many tears, she told John her story.

John's immediate reaction was to say, "I have to say that this doesn't make sense to me. Why would an embryo get lost in the fallopian tubes and not make its way to the womb?"

"That's what the doctors said is happening," Mona replied, still tearful.

"All right," John said. "I'll pray over you now and see what the Lord tells me."

As he prayed, asking Jesus for an explanation of this unusual circumstance, John became aware that there had been an ancestral curse placed upon this family, that the women in Mona's father's bloodline were destined to be barren. Thus, although the blockage had appeared as a physical disability, it was, in fact, supernatural in origin. In the visions that were also given to John during this time of prayer, he saw five generations of barren women, all victim to the curse in the bloodline. Mona, because her womb was cursed, was unable to bring a child to term despite being normally fecund.

As he continued to pray, John also learned that other members in the family would need to return to prayer themselves. The Lord told him that they were not going to Sunday Mass, that prayer was not in their lives, and that, therefore, John himself could not take responsibility for the prayers needed to lift the curse.

Mona had been sitting quietly, hope on her face, as John prayed. She was not prepared for what he was next to say to her.

"The Lord has given me to understand," John said solemnly, "that your problem is linked to an ancestral curse."

"A curse?" Mona's voice was filled with disbelief.

John ignored it. He went on simply, "The Lord has told me to ask you if you go to Mass."

Mona did not answer immediately, a mixture of embarrassment and shame evident on her face as she looked down at the hands folded on her lap. Eventually she said, "No, we haven't been to Mass for a while."

"Why not?" John asked, with a small questioning shrug.

"I don't get much out of Mass. I … find it boring."

John nodded. "And what about your husband? Does he go?"

"No, he doesn't go either," Mona replied in a small voice.

"Well, God has already told me that," John told her, "but he asked me to make you admit it. The thing is, God is saying that if you want to have children, the both of you, you and your husband, will have to start going to Mass regularly, every Sunday in fact." He looked at her seriously. "But first you will both have to make a good confession and become reconciled to God. You'll have to go to Mass and take the Eucharist worthily, and you'll have to pray for forgiveness for your ancestors, especially for forgiveness for the person who uttered the curse."

Mona's mother said, "I don't understand. You said the curse was uttered five generations ago. Surely the person who cursed the family is dead?"

"Dead in mortal terms," John said, "but not dead in eternity. Your ancestors need serious help. These kinds of things coming down the bloodline like this are always a sign that somebody needs spiritual help. It's a sign, too, that with prayers they can be saved." He turned to Mona. "It's a supernatural blockage that causing your pregnancies to fail, not a medical one. That's why the doctors can't figure out a way to fix it." He paused to look at Mona who was staring at him, her expression crestfallen.

John raised his eyebrows. "What's wrong?"

"I don't really want to go to confession," she said hesitantly, "or to go back to Mass either. I don't really see the point of it."

John stared at her for a moment, shaking his head slowly from side to side. Then he said firmly, "The thing you and husband most want in the world is a child, and you know you need a miracle, and you're coming here to me looking for it. But you're actually saying to God that although you want that miracle, it's not worth an hour a week to go to Mass, to be in His presence, to join with Him in the Eucharist."

After a pause during which no one spoke, he turned back to Mona again. "I have to say to you that if you, and your husband as well, because he's part of this, could make up your mind to turn to the Lord, you might have a chance. But," again he spread his hands, "do you seriously think that you can ask the Lord for a miracle and you don't think it's worth going to Mass and saying a prayer or two yourself?"

Mona's eyes were filled with tears and her mother looked shocked. John's voice softened. "I'm sorry if I sound a bit hard, but wait till I tell you, even in His own hometown, Jesus was only able to work very few miracles because of the lack of faith He found there. It's still the same today. Faith," he went on, nodding, "makes you do things, Mona, and faith makes things happen. Go home now, and if you feel that you want to commit yourself to this, to really turn to God in faith for help, I will definitely be with you, don't doubt that for a second. You can come back and see me as often as you like."

Mona, crestfallen now, said "I will go to Mass, John, and I will go to confession. But I don't know … about Kevin."

"Well," John said. "You go anyway, and go with sincerity. And tell your husband that if he is really serious about your having a child, he'll not leave you to this by yourself. He'll go. If he doesn't, well then, you may tell him there's no use him expecting a child. But don't force him. Just let him know and leave it up to himself. It has to be his own decision."

Mona and her mother left. Mona went to confession as she had promised. The following Sunday, she and her mother went to Mass together, received Holy Communion, and prayed for forgiveness for the person who had uttered the curse. They also went to the Parish Office and procured several masses for this ancestor. Kevin did not accompany them that first week but almost immediately he began to feel guilty, worried that his lack of faith and prayer might inhibit Mona's chance of having a child. He went to confession the next Saturday and started going regularly to Mass.

A few weeks later the impossible happened. Mona conceived again and this time, despite all of the misgivings of the medical profession, the embryo was situated in the womb. Mona was thrilled. She continued to meet occasionally with John, praying continuously for a cleansing of the family bloodline, and praying for the ancestral curse to be lifted.

She carried the child for a number of weeks but again she miscarried. She telephoned, John immediately, devastated that yet again she had miscarried. Five children that she might have had, all dead. She had been filled with such hope and to have that hope dashed, especially after John's assurances, was almost more than she could bear.

John made a point of visiting her the following day.

“We don’t know what we’re going to do,” Mona cried when she saw him. “Why would God allow this to happen?”

John offered her his sympathies for her loss. He prayed over her again and sensed that, while the curse had been broken, there were still ancestral sins that had not yet been lifted. It was this supernatural incompleteness that had caused the fifth miscarriage. These sins, whatever they were, had to be released before Mona could bring a child to full term.

After a few moments’ prayer, he said to Mona, “I know you have lost another child, but the Lord told me to remind you that He has made the impossible happen once against all the odds and He can do it again. You still had a miracle happen, didn’t you? Didn’t you conceive a child in the womb, and didn’t the doctors say that that could never happen?”

Mona was staring at him wide-eyed, hoping yet afraid to hope.

“It was because you went to Mass and said all those prayers that this has happened. You’ll have to keep praying for the ancestral sin, God tells me, and you never know what might happen in the next few months. Keep praying with faith, always faith, and keep asking God to bless your womb. And above all, keep going to Mass.”

He left Mona feeling happier and more hopeful than she might have expected. She trusted John now and came back to him on a number of occasions during the ensuing weeks, asking him to pray over her, asking for help to pray for her ancestors. Again, amazingly, the impossible happened. In a very short time she became pregnant again, with the embryo safely cushioned in her womb. This time she carried the baby to full term and gave birth to a healthy baby boy.

***

What do we know about curses? Was John's claim that there was a curse in the bloodline any different from his diagnosis in Madeleine's case (Chapter 16) that there was sin in the bloodline?

In books about the psychology of education, there is frequent reference to Herbert Kohl's principle of "The Self-fulfilling Prophecy." Essentially what this means is that if a teacher harbours negative expectations of a class or of an individual student, the class or the student will perform badly. Conversely, if the teacher has high expectations of a class or of an individual student, the class or the student will perform well. The effect is due, for the most part, to the teacher's innate authority.

A similar effect is found in the relationship between a parent and child. If the parent, whose voice is the voice of authority, continually berates the child, saying, "You're stupid! You'll never amount to anything!" it is virtually certain that the child will fail in life.

MacNutt (1995) says that "... some judgements that others make about us have the same effect in our lives as curses." (p.121) This is often true and there are those who would claim that the reaction people have to negative judgements about them is what explains belief in curses. They claim that the concept of pronouncing curses is a myth that derives from the practice of Voodoo, from the superstition of the Middle Ages, from the realm of witches and dark magic. They choose to use psychology to explain the effect of curses, or to debunk them.

But in the intangible milieu inhabited by the mind and the spirit, there are areas where psychology and the supernatural meet, divide, and go their separate ways. One such area marks the realm of real curses, curses that invoke the demonic for their effect. In this realm, psychology has little to offer.

"Curses are real," John says. "They go back to the very beginning of time." Adam and Eve brought the first curse, the curse of original sin, upon humanity. In this particular case, the curse could be said to have been inflicted by the Divine although, in reality, they brought the curse upon themselves. God sets boundaries on our behaviours, through His commandments, through His revealed word and, when we transgress against those boundaries, we put ourselves outside God's blessing. In this we are cursed. We become what St. Peter terms *"... an accursed brood."* [2 Peter 2:14]

There are close to three hundred references to curses in the Old Testament. They begin even as early as Genesis. Yahweh cursed Cain for his brother's murder. *"Now be cursed and driven from the ground that has opened its mouth to receive your brother's blood ..."* [Genesis 4:11] And much later, Yahweh promised Abram that *"... whoever curses you, I will curse."* [Genesis 12:3]

The God of the Old Testament is, of course, the same loving, generous God that Jesus taught us to know in the New Testament. Although there is a strongly held theological belief among many Christian commentators that Yahweh 'cursed' His people for their sins, it would have to be argued that His 'curses' would not have come from arbitrary anger. They would have come from love. Yahweh would have allowed affliction to fall upon His people only as a consequence of their own behaviours, only because they had strayed so far from His true purpose that they needed a significant reminder, even significant punishment, to turn them away from paths leading to their spiritual destruction. It might well be argued, given the moral laxity of twenty-first century liberalism, that similar reminders might well be needed in today's world.

Further examples of curses in the Old Testament abound. When David heard that Joab had murdered Abner, he uttered a curse that was bloodthirsty and specific: *"May there be forever among them (Joab's family) some member who has discharge, or is sick with leprosy, or who is only fit to hold a spindle or who falls by the sword or who hungers."* [2 Samuel 3:29] MacNutt (1995) tells us that "… countless other Scripture passages reveal the truth that words can convey spiritual power for either good or evil, beyond mere human utterance." (p.101)

Today curses are recognised as evil, as the opposite of blessings. They are pronouncements of a desire for affliction to befall someone. They can range from a relatively unconscious wishing of harm to serious and malevolent intention to destroy the victim's life. John Gillespie says that "… anyone can bring down a curse. It demands venomous ill-will but if that is there, the curse comes."

It must also be noted that simply because a curse does not actually invoke the devil, it cannot be assumed that the devil is not involved. Amorth (1994) warns us that "Curses invoke evil and the origin of evil is demonic."

Words, therefore, are powerful, in psychological terms, and in supernatural terms. It is always necessary to exercise care in their use. Heightened emotion, together with clichéd intemperate language, has the potential to become a curse. During an angry exchange of words, someone might instinctively say, "Damn you to hell!" It is a common phrase but, if the anger and the animosity are strong, demons can seize the opportunity to gain access to the recipient's life. That is why almost all modern definitions of cursing include reference to the demonic. Fortea (2006), for example, offers the following definition: "A curse is an action that is done to harm another with the help of demons." (p.110) Amorth, too, uses this kind of language. He defines a curse as "… harming others through demonic intervention." (p.129) Thus curses work because they give demons permission to harass someone's life.

Anyone can utter a curse against another person but it is generally believed that a curse can be more powerful and more effective if it is uttered by someone who has some form of authority over the accursed. In addition, the more malicious the intent, the more damaging the curse. The misfortune intended by curses can range from harm, to illness, and even to death. Sometimes ordinary skills and abilities can be affected. The victim can experience bad luck like the loss of a job or a severe downturn in the quality of life. Victims in business can suffer serious losses. And many of these negative events occur in lives without the victims ever realising that they result directly from some form of curse.

John Gillespie tells us that cursing is very rife in Ireland today and that there are many people suffering the effects of a curse without any knowledge of the cause of their misfortunes. MacNutt (1994) agrees that such a state is regrettably common and not easily recognised for what it is: "Spiritual realities are discerned only spiritually. Experts may study the human dimensions of the problem from a purely rational point of view but never identify the supernatural component." (p.110) For this reason, people like John, Sr. Briege and others, are needed to 'discern' the source of the problems and help with their solution.

Sr. Briege says that there are often standard patterns to be observed that can lead to the discernment of a curse. "Families can have a pattern of terrible accidents," she explains. "Others seem to have to endure constant financial failures and disruptions, or continual runs of bad luck that seem to go from generation to generation. Until the curse is broken, these terrible things will continue to happen."

These patterns could, of course, be the result of natural causes. Only those with the gift of discernment of the demonic can truly affirm whether a curse exists or not.

"People who live in God's grace," John says, "who live good lives, normally need never fear a curse. The more one prays, the closer in relationship one is to Jesus, the more one is protected from curses and from evil. There's plenty of evidence for that in scripture." John has become very familiar with scripture. He reads the bible constantly. He refers to Romans 8:31 where we are told that 'If God is with us, who shall be against us?' He remembers a line from the Book of Proverbs as well, which also assures us that a curse will not fall on the blameless. '*The sparrow escapes, the swallow flies off, so the motiveless curse will have no effect.*' [26:2]

Derek Prince (1998) tells us that Christ broke every curse on Calvary. "There [on the cross] Jesus took on to Himself every curse to which our sinfulness has exposed us, that in return we might be entitled to every blessing due to His spotless righteousness." (p.258) The evidence for this is found in Galatians 3.13: *Now Christ rescued us from the curse of the Law by becoming cursed Himself for our sake.*

A life that is devoid of spirituality and prayer, however, a life in which sin exists, severely hampers God's protection. In bondage to sin, we are truly vulnerable to curses. It is often asked why God allows curses to fall on His people, especially the weak and vulnerable. There are three explanations.

Firstly, life normally has its share of suffering and misfortune and God can allow curses to take effect in order to bring about a significant element of His plan for the victim's life.

Secondly, where people are living sinful lives, the effects of a curse are permitted in order to draw attention to their parlous spiritual state, to encourage them to seek reunion with the Lord and reconcile themselves with him. This can be seen from the Old Testament in particular. There are several occasions in this history of the Chosen People when God visited affliction upon them in order to draw them away from sin.

Thirdly, when John encounters a curse that has dogged a family for generations, he sees in it a cry for help by ancestors who have not been freed to live in the bliss of heaven. They have been existing for all those years separated from God, and the family curse can draw attention to their need for prayers and salvation.

It is generally agreed that cursing can be effective, that is, effective in achieving its maleficent intentions. But what those who utter curses do not seem to know, but ultimately learn in wretchedness, is that the effect on the person who cast the curse is even worse than the impact on the victim. Fortea (2006) says that, "Without doubt, they will suffer some type of demonic influence, possession or sickness. The evil they wish on another will come back to them." (p.110)

There are two kinds of curses: i. those curses directed at an individual and ii. "generational curses'. Generational curses, briefly referred to above, are those curses that continue to affect the same family for generation after generation. Don Rogers tells us that "Generational or ancestral curses are similar to the curse of original sin only they have a temporal effect rather than eternal."

It might seem unfair that apparently innocent victims are doomed to suffer for the sins of their forefathers. But it is argued that the justice for it can be seen from God's perspective. Fathers have specific lifestyles which influence their children. If the lifestyle is sinful, it is passed down through generations as each child imitates and becomes the father. The punishment, the curse, applies equally to each generation until the sinful pattern is broken, until redemption and reconciliation are sought.

John makes it clear that a curse can only be lifted through forgiveness but he does not see this as a difficulty. For John, curses can be lifted easily from a person's life or from a bloodline, by the simple expedient of repentance for sin and seeking reconciliation. If an individual seeks freedom from a curse's bondage, John says, "… he must turn to prayer and the sacraments. He must confess, repent his sins, and take the Eucharist. There's no other way. And there's no use just going to confession and just saying the words. Your contrition has to be from the heart."

If the curse is generational, John enjoins that there still remains an obligation on members of the present generation "… to clean up their own spiritual lives" and, in addition, to ensure that prayers are said and Masses offered, seeking forgiveness for the ancestor who uttered the curse, or who earned the curse through bondage to sin. "As long as the curse lasts," John says, in his Christian way, "you know that the ancestor still needs help and that salvation is still possible."

***

The following two stories, both of which concern members of the same family of travelling people, recount the events leading up to a remarkable miracle but they also reveal how devastating and pervasive generational curses can be.

***

Maggie's Story: Two Generational Curses

Maggie was a revered and highly respected doyenne of the travelling community to which she belonged. She was renowned for her venerable age, her wisdom, and her great knowledge of the family and its ancestral connections. For some time, she had been concerned by a number of serious misfortunes that had been attacking her family and she had begun to reach the conclusion that what had been happening was not natural, that it was somehow demonic in its patterns and in its impact.

For a number of years, Maggie had witnessed an unusually high number of deaths among her family connections. Young men, boys, girls, even young children and babies, had been dying in fatal accidents. What had aroused Maggie's concern, and her suspicions, was that, regardless of the nature or manner of the accidents, the deaths of the family members were always attributed to one of two common causes - death due to head injuries or death due to burning, usually on the face, chest and shoulder areas. Maggie had, herself, lost more than one brother over a relatively short period of time, all killed through a variety of often violent and unexpected accidental causes. Even some of her own offspring had been affected. In all cases the common denominators seemed to be head injuries due to road traffic accidents or severe accidents that involved electrocution or burning.

Maggie tried to pray for an end to these terrible accidents but the more she prayed, the more aware she became that she needed special help. She had become convinced that, given the pattern of the deaths in her extended family, there was a curse on the bloodline, not an unusual occurrence among the travelling communities. But this curse seemed to be very widespread, affecting three generations, not only of her own immediate family but also those of cousins, second cousins and other relations.

Some years before, one of the community children had been taken to the Intensive Care ward in a hospital in Northern Ireland even though the attending consultant had diagnosed that there was no hope for the child. A man, John Gillespie, had been called to the hospital that day to pray over the child. He had arrived as the child was being wheeled to Intensive Care on a hospital trolley and simply prayed over the child as it passed him. By the time the child had reached the Intensive Care ward, however, it was suddenly and very definitely out of danger. Maggie had never forgotten that day, nor the quiet, unassuming man who had left the hospital before anyone could even thank him. She was convinced that he was the one person who could help resolve the tragic circumstances that seemed to have befallen her family.

Contact was made and when Maggie told John about what had been happening, he prayed to the Lord for information about the origins of this curse. He discovered that there was not one, but two, curses in the bloodline.

The first was an evil curse that had been uttered against Maggie's travelling community some six generations earlier by a rival travelling community. John saw in a vision that the effects of the curse had first been seen some time in the late 1800s when a member of Maggie's ancestral family had fallen from a horse and suffered a fatal head injury. For years after that, several members of the community were killed in accidents involving some form of travelling, usually caravans, horse-carts or horses. As time passed, the new forms of travel that emerged after the advent of the automobile – lorries, vans, cars, motor-bikes, trains, buses – became the principal cause of the deaths attributable to the curse. When John talked to Maggie about this, he was amazed by her memory and the accounts she was able to give him of numbers of people in previous generations who had died from head injuries caused in similar types of accidents.

But John went on to tell Maggie that that was not the only curse working in the family. The Lord had told him of a second curse, a curse in the bloodline of the same family, that had appeared a generation or two later but that now was running parallel with the first one. The second curse, however, John told the old woman, was attributable to bitterness and a lack of forgiveness locked into the family bloodline rather than a specifically uttered curse. After John had prayed earnestly about the burnings and had referred several times to the bible, the Lord had given him a vision of a young man in an army uniform and in a war situation. John saw an explosion and the head and shoulders of the young soldier in the trench suddenly being covered with flames.

"No one has ever forgiven the person who had killed the young soldier," John told Maggie, "and the effect of this unforgiveness is still running through the bloodline."

"But … how can we be blamed for that?" Maggie asked. "It hardly seems fair when we know nothing about it."

"The present generation may well know nothing about it," John explained, "but God knows about it and God is telling me the source and the root cause of the misfortune that has befallen your family so that you can do something about it."

Maggie was a great family historian and had access to significant amounts of information about the family tree, yet even with all of her knowledge and memories of stories from her childhood, she was unable to identify any of her ancestors who might have been killed in a war. John advised her to pray about it and promised that he would, too.

A week or so later, John called to see Maggie again. She told him that after she had prayed, she had remembered hearing, as a child, a story from her great-grandfather about a relative who had joined the army to fight in a war but who had never been heard of again. That was a story that had caused a lot of anger in the family, both at the government that had ignored the disappearance of their young family member and at the person or persons who had probably killed him.

John said, "That's obviously the young man that I saw in my vision, then, and that anger is more than likely the cause of the bitterness that has infected the bloodline."

With Maggie's help, he drew up a family tree, identifying all of the family and ancestral members who had suffered from the two curses. A significant number of

Masses was arranged, to pray for the souls of the travelling person who had uttered the first evil curse and for the soul of the person or persons who had killed the young man at war. There were Masses arranged also for the forgiveness of the ancestral family members who had held grudges in connection with both curses. John, himself, spent a significant time in prayer for the breaking of the two curses, beseeching the Lord to lift the curses and set the bloodline free.

Maggie admitted to John at that time that there was a strong tendency among some members of the travelling community to utter curses and she invited him to address a large group of travelling people at a hall in Dublin. When John got there, the hall was full, not only with members from Maggie's community but also with members from several other communities as well. John spoke at some length about the dangers of cursing, pointing out that although the accursed people would assuredly suffer, the curses would come back on the people who uttered them, not only in terms of significant misfortune in this life, but also in terrible danger to their immortal souls in the next.

He was to meet Maggie some years later and learned that since that time no member of the community had died from a head injury or any kind of burn. The two curses had been safely broken.

Davey's Story: Victim of a Family Curse

In the main street of a large regional town in Ireland, a young mother was pushing her child in a small buggy. The little boy, Davey, who was about two and a half years of age, seemed suddenly to leap, with extraordinary energy, right out of the pram. Somehow the child turned in mid-air and landed on his head, hitting the pavement with violent force. The mother screamed for help and a number of bystanders rushed to her support while one man called the emergency services on his mobile phone

Fortunately, the town had its own general hospital and within ten minutes an ambulance had arrived and transferred the child to the Accident and Emergency department for immediate treatment. However, when Davey's responses were tested, there was no reaction of any kind. A hastily arranged CAT scan revealed that the child was suffering from severe brain damage due to two acute subdural haematomas. The volume of blood released by the blow to his head had entered into the brain at a very high pressure, destroying all tissue in its path. The blood inevitably began to clot in two places but, while clotting is normally a part of the body's natural defence-system, in this case the clots were formed between the brain and the skull, putting severe pressure on the brain tissue and seriously damaging the brain's functioning.

The little boy was immediately brought to the Intensive-Care ward where he was placed on life-support machines. He was attached also to various monitors while the doctors tried to restore some of the brain's functions.

Throughout the first day there was no response of any kind from Davey, no response to pin-pricks or any other test. The next morning, the child's great-grandmother arrived. As soon as she saw the situation, she remembered stories that she had heard from friends about John Gillespie. Not even taking time to discuss her intention with her grand-daughter and filled with a desperate hope that this man might be able to do something, she contacted one of her friends, got John's number and phoned him, explaining what had happened and telling him that doctors were now saying that there was no hope of recovery. John was sympathetic but he had already committed himself to a number of visits in Belfast which he felt could not be ignored. He did promise, however, that he would finish all his calls and phone her again that evening.

All during the first day and for most of that night, doctors worked tirelessly to resuscitate the child but with no success. By the afternoon of the second day, they finally diagnosed the little boy as brain-dead and recommended that the life-support machines should be switched off. “There is no hope,” they told the family. “Prolonging Davey’s life in this state is pointless.”

Davey’s mother was devastated, as were the other members of the family. The great-grandmother pleaded with the doctors to leave the life-support machines on for a while longer and tried to phone John again, her mind still racing with stories that she had heard about him. She was unable to contact him, however, as his mobile was turned off but she left several messages, pleading with him to come as soon as he could since he was the family’s last hope.

John checked his messages late in the afternoon. He experienced a surge of empathy with the great-grandmother’s panic and phoned her to say that, however late he got his visits finished that evening, he would undertake the lengthy journey to see her great-grandson.

When he went home later for a quick bite to eat, however, it was already sometime after five-thirty and he wondered if he should attempt a long drive at the end of an already tiring day. The thought weighed heavily upon him and he experienced a nagging reluctance to pursue the matter. He discussed the visit with Christina who felt that he should go, saying that he would never know what the Lord’s will was for the child unless he went to see him and that the family would feel very let down if the child died and John had made no effort to help him. John was persuaded by Christina's arguments and, tired as he was, he phoned the great-grandmother and told her that he was just leaving Belfast and would get to the hospital as soon as he could.

As the miles passed, fatigue began to affect him. He was feeling increasingly exhausted and became convinced that he should turn the car around, go home and get some sleep, But somewhere deep inside, he felt that the child needed him and he would be turning his back on the Lord if he were to abandon the visit, so he forced himself to keep driving.

All during the drive, however, there was a constant battle waging in his mind. What seemed like a voice in his head kept trying to convince him that the whole business was a waste of time and, worse, that if he continued the journey and did not turn the car around and go back, a lorry would crash into his car, that he would be smashed off the road, and that he would never see his wife and children again.

As the voice continued to torment him, however, John became aware that thoughts such as these were utterly alien to him. With that consciousness came the realisation that the torment was demonic, that Satan or one of his demons was trying to prevent him from doing the Lord's work. John prayed immediately against Satan, saying, "You will not touch this car. I call on the protection of Jesus Christ and His angels. Nothing will touch this car and, in Jesus' name, I forbid you to come near it."

John then turned his prayers to the child, praying to the Lord for a miraculous healing, but even as he prayed, during the entire journey, the dark voice kept trying to assault his mind. He knew now that several minor demons were assailing him and that, as one was banished, another would take its place.

Eventually he reached the hospital and he went in to meet the family. They were gathered in a waiting room, some yards down the corridor from the Intensive Care ward. The young mother was crying and the father was pale and shaken. The old lady who had phoned him told John that the doctors were strongly advising them to turn off the life-support systems and take Davey home for burial. They had agreed, however, in response to the mother's tearful pleadings, to keep Davey physically alive until John arrived. Then the great-grandmother asked, unable to keep the fear from her voice, "Will you be able to do something?"

"Trust in God," John replied. "I'll pray a while and see what I can find out."

John told the group that, given the lateness of the hour and the long drive home that still faced him, he would not be able to stay long. He instructed everyone in the room, asking them to repeat his instructions to other family members waiting in a larger lounge (there were about thirty relatives visiting there that day), that they should immediately begin praying in faith for a miracle. "The child is brain-dead," he told them. "We need a miracle. Everyone must start praying for a miracle from God. If we don't pray in fervent faith for one, it won't happen. I certainly cannot deliver one. Only God can, so you must ask Him."

Everyone was exhausted with grief and tension but rosary beads began to appear in some hands while others left the room to wander the corridors in private prayer. John went into the ward where the child was lying. He went to the bed and saw a tiny, pale, fragile little boy, wires of different colours protruding from various parts of his body, attached to various machines around the bed. Some of the monitors which showed erratic, flickering lines, bleeped faintly from time to time.

There was a matron standing beside the bed, studying a chart. She looked up. “Are you John Gillespie?” she asked.

John nodded.

“I heard that you brought a brain-dead man back to life in this hospital a while back,” she whispered. Her tone made the statement a question.

“I didn’t do anything,” John said. “It was Jesus who did it.”

The matron stared at him. “My God! It’s true then?”

John moved to the bed. “I’ll bless the child now and say a few prayers over him.”

As he prayed, John was given the knowledge that Davey had been the victim of some kind of curse and he knew that the effect of the curse would have to be broken before any healing could take place. He had already prayed in the car, as part of a series of prayers that he often prayed while travelling to a supplicant, for the breaking of any curses that might be involved. Now, however he had a greater consciousness of what was involved. He sensed that there was indeed a curse involved but that it was contemporary, that it had been recently uttered against the whole community by someone who resented them or bore them a grudge. The ill thus wished upon the family had fallen upon the little boy.

He prayed prayers to break the curse, and prayed also for forgiveness for the person who had invoked the curse. Then he continued in a low voice, “Lord Jesus, I pray for healing for Davey. I call upon your miraculous power, Lord Jesus, and claim life over death for this innocent child in your name. I ask you to let your precious blood flow through every vein and artery and organ in Davey's body. Through your healing power, Lord Jesus, I ask you to command the two blood clots in his skull to disperse and that your healing blood flowing through the child's body will bring the miracle that restores his life. I thank you in faith, Lord Jesus, for the healing which you have promised to those who ask in faith."

As he prayed, he heard the Lord give him specific instructions and he carried them out just as the Lord commanded. He blessed the child and anointed his head with holy oils. He blessed and anointed the child's two hands. There was no response from the little boy. He prayed in Jesus' name that the Lord would bless the two little hands and bring movement to them. He prayed the same prayers over the feet, blessing and anointing them and claiming the power of God to go through the head, to the hands and down to the very feet.

John stepped away from the bed, putting the holy oils back in the little pouch which he then returned to his pocket. As he was doing this, the child lifted his right foot, which was attached to one of the monitors, and kicked with such force that the machine was dislodged from its stand and thrown with a crash to the floor. That was the child's only reaction at that point. His eyes did not open; his breathing did not change. The matron was first shocked, then baffled. John went back to the child's head, praying over it again. Davey began to breathe more strongly and the monitors began to go crazy. What before had been feeble sporadic blips and beeps, became a crescendo of shrieks and whistles. The matron rushed to them to turn down the ear-piercing shrillness just as another nurse, followed by the child's parents, came rushing into the room. The nurse looked at the monitors and then at the child for a moment, trying to understand what was happening. Her hands then joined before her face and she cried, “It’s a miracle! It’s a miracle.”

Davey’s father began jumping around, unable to contain himself. “Davey’s back,” he kept shouting. “Davey’s back!” Then he rushed to hug his wife who appeared to be in shock. “He’s not dead. He’s alive!”

As yet other members of the family came pouring into the ward, the matron said to John, “What did you do?”

“I didn’t do anything,” John said. “I just prayed for the child.”

“But there was no hope for that child. You must have done something,” she insisted.

“All I did was pray,” John repeated.” Any other questions you have, you’ll have to take them up with the Lord. He did it.”

He went back to the bedside. The child was breathing normally but his eyes were still closed. John blessed his eyes again, praying again to Jesus … and the child’s eyes opened.

“Oh, my God! Oh, my God!” the matron said.

The other nurse, who was now studying the remaining monitors, said, “His heart-beat is very faint.”

John held his hand over the child’s heart and prayed that the Lord Jesus would allow his precious blood to flow into the heart and bring His healing. The machine measuring the child’s heart-rate boomed into life and the heart began thudding strongly. There was immense excitement in the ward and the matron had to ask people to return to the corridor so that they could administer to the child. They left slowly, some crying, some laughing, others shouting, “It’s a miracle.” John left too, and, after a brief conversation with the old lady who phoned him, went to his car and drove back to Belfast.

After John had left, the matron phoned the consultant and told him what had happened. He came to the hospital immediately to see for himself and, although the evidence was there before his eyes, he could neither understand nor believe what he was seeing. He arranged for an immediate scan of the child's skull and the results revealed that the subdural haematomas, that had taken the child's life, were still there. Yet, miraculously, the child was alive, and apparently well. He contacted a specialist friend of his who worked in a Dublin hospital, explaining what had happened but emphasising the fact that the haematomas were still there. They agreed that the child should be sent to Dublin immediately by ambulance where a full team would be waiting to carry out a craniotomy that would safely remove the clots.

Davey left the Dublin hospital three weeks later, restored to full health.

Ordinary Christians need not concern themselves too much with curses. In God's good will, experience of this evil is unlikely for those in His grace. Nonetheless, it is useful, from time to time, to pray for protection from the evil one and the direful effects of human malice. John offers the following prayer which, he says, is particularly useful for warding off the effects of curses.

Prayer for Freedom from Curses

In the name of Jesus Chris, crucified, died and risen, I bind the influence of any lost or fallen souls who may be present, all emissaries of Satan, witches, warlocks, or Satan worshippers who may be present in some supernatural way. I also forbid every adversary mentioned to communicate with or help one another in any way, or to communicate with me, or to do anything at all except what I command in Jesus' name.

In the name Of Jesus Christ I forbid any lost spirits, covens, satanic groups or emissaries or any of their associates, subjects or superiors, to harm or take revenge on me, my family and my associates, or cause harm or damage to anything we have.

In the name of Jesus Christ and by the merits of His Precious Blood, I break and dissolve every curse, hex, seal, spell, sorcery, bond, snare, trap, device, lie, stumbling block, obstacle, deception, diversion or distraction, spiritual chain or spiritual influence; also every disease of body, soul, mind or spirit placed on us, or on any of the persons, places or things mentioned, by any agent, or brought upon us by our own mistakes or sins. [Repeat three times]

I now place the cross of Jesus Christ between myself and all generations in my family tree. I say in the name of Jesus Christ that there will be no direct communication between the generations. All communications will be filtered through the Precious Blood of the Lord Jesus Christ.

Mary Immaculate, clothe me in the light, power and energy of your faith. Father, please assign the angels and saints to assist me. Thank you, Lord Jesus, for being my Wisdom, my Justice, my Sanctification, my Redemption. I surrender to the ministry of Your Holy Spirit and receive your truth concerning intergenerational healing.

Glory be to the Father and to the Son and to the Holy Spirit. As it was in the beginning, is now, and ever shall be. Amen.

Chapter Twenty

Signs like these will accompany those who have believed; in my name they will cast out demons [Mark16:17]

Deliverance from Demons

Exorcism, more commonly referred to nowadays as 'deliverance', is one of those words that inevitably induce strong reaction in believer and sceptic alike. John sounds perfectly calm and matter-of-fact when he talks about deliverance. It is just another element of his healing ministry.

"All an exorcist has to do is to command with authority in the name of Jesus. I can usually take authority over demons very quickly. Once I identify, with the Spirit's help, the demon that's there, I can command it to leave very quickly. And if there are a number of them, I start to take them out one by one. Once I can persuade the victim to repent of whatever he or she was doing that allowed the demons to enter them in the first place, I can tell the demons that they have no right to be there any more. The repentance breaks the demonic links that handcuff the person and allows the straightforward working of deliverance prayers."

In terms of convincing the victim to repent, something that is not normally seen in movie exorcisms,

John finds himself in agreement with well-known experts. Benedict Heron (1997) tells us that "… there is nothing to be gained by trying to cast evil spirits out of someone who is not willing to renounce and repent the sins or practices which allowed the evil spirits to enter. We first need to pray that they will be given the grace to repent and renounce." (p.114)

But for many, such claims might just be a step too far. Several experts in psychology claim that exorcism is a form of hypnosis that allows the subject to play out the 'hypnotist's fantasies'. Others believe that the person who 'thinks' he is possessed has actually created in his own mind a devil that reflects some form of his own personality. Dr. Vincenzo Mastronardi, a psychologist who delivered the keynote address in 2006 at the annual congress of the Italian Society of Psychopathology, claimed that exorcisms are riddled with auto-suggestion, manipulation and misdiagnosis.

Tracey Wilkinson (2007) who interviewed several exorcists in Rome, and who was present at an actual exorcism, also remains unconvinced. "The capacity of some people to believe the patently unbelievable is limitless. And the capacity of the human mind to fool itself is also limitless … Most, but not all, psychiatrists, psychologists and other scientists dismiss demonic possession as a case of suggestible people acting on subconscious impulses or following the cues of a priest." (p.150) Michael Cuneo (2001) sees exorcisms as demonstrations in self-delusion, partly fuelled by movies like The Exorcist. "My central point is that exorcism-related beliefs took hold within certain sectors of (mainly white) America only when Hollywood began spreading the message … It is the power of the media [that] induces belief in diabolical possession."

Self-delusion? Hypnosis? Auto-suggestion? Misdiagnosis? John's healing ministry, the miracles that his prayers have wrought, are too numerous and too genuine to permit easy ridicule. But is it possible that in the area of 'deliverance' he might have fallen victim to the power of suggestion?

There is much need for a detailed examination of the concept of possession, of the nature of exorcism, of the question of who is capable of performing exorcisms, but it might be instructive first to read an authentic and verifiable account of one of the many episodes in John's ministry when he was called upon to cast out demons.

***

Raymond's Story: The Possessed Young Man

(Note: All names, dates and places have been changed to protect the identity of the individuals involved)

Raymond (not his real name) was born into a respectable Catholic family in a small town in rural Ireland. He was brought up in the faith and lived his childhood in innocence. During his teens, however, as John phrases it, "he fell in with bad company and soon got caught up in drugs and promiscuity and everything else."

Eventually Raymond met and fell in love with Tess, (not her real name) a fellow addict he met in a rehabilitation programme and, because he wanted to get married and settle down, he somehow managed to change his life style. He freed himself from his addictions, as did Tess. As a qualified bricklayer, Raymond had no problem finding a job in Ireland's burgeoning construction industry and, for a few years Raymond and Tess lived happily together, producing two children and living conventional and normal lives.

There came a time, however, when Tess began to behave erratically, accusing Raymond of behaviours of which he was totally blameless. She fell back into taking drugs again and was never at home to look after her family. It was generally known that she spent much of her time in bars and hotels with other men. Raymond was deeply hurt by these betrayals and, although he tried for a couple of years to keep the marriage alive, break-up was inevitable and they separated.

The effect of the break-up on Raymond was traumatic. Normally a happy, placid man, he began to exhibit extremes of aggression and anger. He would become morose and uncommunicative and his children eventually had to go to live with their grandmother.

Raymond's change of personality was attributed to the break-up of his marriage and to the hurt he was feeling at the loss of the wife he loved. By this time a local priest was called in by Raymond's mother, asking for prayers and counselling for her son. Father Thomas was a good priest, a holy man, but despite his best efforts he seemed incapable of helping Raymond. He began to suspect, however, a sinister malaise that had little to do with simple behavioural problems and he contacted two people in his parish, Miles and Sheila, members of a local prayer group, who had some experience in the past with deliverance. Father Thomas hoped that they would be able to help

Miles and Sheila met with Raymond and prayed for him. They soon discerned that Father Thomas's suspicion of demonic oppression was correct and they visited Raymond a few times in the hope of delivering him from the demon's bondage. They had had some success in the past with deliverance, and in the early stages of their time with Raymond they did deliver him from two evil spirits that they discerned were troubling him.

The deliverance, however, did not seem to help Raymond. There were times when he went to the chapel to pray, genuinely trying to find peace. But when he knelt before the Blessed Sacrament, he would suddenly start snarling and uttering imprecations of such a foul nature that Father Thomas had to drag him out of the chapel and send him home. At other times, he would be at work, behaving in perfectly normal fashion when he would suddenly lose his temper and begin fighting with his workmates and threatening them with unspeakable violence. He had been a popular worker on the building site but his employer would no longer tolerate these behaviours and Raymond lost his job.

From time to time, Raymond was capable of rational behaviour and friendly.interaction. He spent a lot of time with Miles and Sheila, desperate for some release from the malaise that was troubling him. He wondered if psychiatric help was what he needed, if he was now suffering some long-delayed after-effects of the drugs he had taken as a teenager. Miles told him that he was free to try that approach but assured him that he had a great deal of experience in these situations and that he was certain that Raymond's problems were not natural.

Despite their best efforts, however, and despite the success they had had with such cases in the past, Miles and Sheila could do nothing for him. They were puzzled. They knew that they had delivered Raymond from a number of demons yet nothing had changed. Raymond continued prone to behavioural extremes. He would flit from violent aggression to uncommunicative sulkiness, from a vocal and raging bitterness to sullen melancholy. Miles began to believe that, despite the deliverance that had been done, there were still demons oppressing Raymond, demons of such power that it was beyond their capacity to expel them. He discussed the issue with Sheila and eventually they agreed that their only recourse was to call on John Gillespie from Belfast in Northern Ireland for help.

Miles phoned John and told him about the case. He explained that the young man had been brutally honest in confessing all the sins of his past – the drug-taking, the drunkenness, the promiscuity – but that somehow, he was still seriously oppressed.

After some reflection, John said, "There must be something hidden somewhere that you don't see. Demons can hide in all sorts of nooks and crannies and it can be hard to discern them." Miles remembered, as John was speaking, that a holy woman had once told John that he would be given a gift of the Holy Spirit to discern demons that lurk in the background of people's lives. John continued speaking. "The young man was helpful in responding to all your probing about his past life and he seems to have renounced all the drugs and the relationships with other women." He paused again, thinking. "It doesn't make sense that his trouble could still be coming from all of that. I think the demons you have already expelled might have come from that. But the demon or demons that are troubling him now are not operating from there. I've no idea yet where they coming from or who they are but I'm certain there's something else, something serious that's got nothing to do with those sins."

"So you'll come and see him?" Miles urged.

"Of course, but I want a few days to pray about this to see what the Spirit will tell me."

During the next several days, John prayed fervently for the information he would need to help the young man. He was eventually granted some amazing visions. John describes what he saw: "The Spirit showed me a ship sailing on the water, like a cruise ship today but one going back four or five generations. He showed me a woman who was working as a prostitute on the ship. She became pregnant and there was a doctor on the ship who carried out an abortion for her. The child was suffocated and died as it was being taken from its mother's womb. The woman got pregnant a second time and another abortion was procured. As before, the child was suffocated and died in the womb.

"Then the Lord showed me that two demons, two very powerful demons, a demon of suffocation and a demon of death, were allowed into the family bloodline because of these abortions. The Lord showed me that the children were a boy and a girl, that they had never been baptised, that there had been no forgiveness asked for the two murders and that the effects of these terrible sins were now coming down on the young man."

John went to see Raymond a few days later. They met at Miles's house as had earlier been agreed. John was somewhat surprised to find Raymond completely normal, full of fun and stories and laughing a lot, the person he had been before this trouble had come upon him. But John knew that if what Miles had said was true, this couldn't last. There would have to be a radical change very shortly.

They put Raymond in a chair and John instructed Miles to stand to one side, in a corner of the room where he would not catch Raymond's eye while John was talking to him. Nonetheless, he wanted Miles there in case his strength was needed. Miles, who played rugby in his youth, was a large, heavy-set man, well over six-feet. He would be a useful support if Raymond got physically aggressive.

John stood above the young man, staring down at him. He was not sure how to proceed until he received a sense from the Spirit that he should "… simply confront the two demons head-on!" He first blessed the young man with holy oils, claimed the power and the protection of the Lord Jesus Christ over everyone in the room, and then spoke to the demons directly.

"You two are there from four generations ago," he said. "You came into this young man through his bloodline through suffocation and death. So I know you. I know you both. You cannot hide from me. I know you are there."

As soon as John started speaking, there was an instant reaction. Raymond seemed to go crazy, writhing and squirming in the chair, roaring in a loud raucous voice, shaking uncontrollably. "His spine was shaking." John was to report later. "You could see the demons pulling at his spine and Raymond screaming 'My spine! My spine! They're in my spine.'"

Miles, behind the young man, could visibly see the spine moving and contorting as if invisible hands were pulling on it.

John began to pray in earnest, directing all his energies towards the first demon, the demon of suffocation. He could feel forces around him clutching at his face but he knew that he had the protection of Jesus and ignored them. He looked directly into the young man's eyes and kept issuing strong commands to the demon, with all the authority of Christ, instructing it to leave the body of Raymond in the name of Jesus. “I command you, demon of suffocation, in the name of Jesus Christ, to depart, without doing harm to Raymond or anyone else in this house, or in his family, and without making any noise or disturbance, and I command you to go straight to Jesus Christ to dispose of you as He will. Furthermore, I command you never to return.”

As he prayed and commanded, John could feel forces gathering around him, seeking to squeeze him into submission. He experienced, as well, a terrible coldness that made it almost impossible for him to cling on to the Benedict cross that he always used in deliverances. Benedict is the patron saint of exorcists and there is always a special additional protection attached to that cross. He was holding the cross in his right hand which was now freezing and growing increasingly nerveless. Nevertheless he clung to the crucifix, repeating over and over the prayer of exorcism, his voice growing stronger with each repetition, feeling the demon’s resistance but knowing that it couldn’t last.

Suddenly, and without warning, at a final repetition of the name of Jesus, he felt an instantaneous release and an unseen and malicious presence flew past his right ear and disappeared from the room.

Without pause, John immediately turned his attention to the second demon. He began to challenge him, repudiating his right to oppress the young man and commanded him in the name of Jesus Christ to depart. John knew from his visions that this demon was larger and more powerful that the other one. The demon made Raymond roar and screech in a voice that was not his own. Horrific blasphemies and awful grunting noises were emitting from the young man’s mouth as John continued to intone, with all the force and authority of Jesus, the prayer of exorcism.

Sheila, who had been upstairs at the time, heard the clamour and came running down to the room. She saw the young man screaming and contorting in the chair, and detected the anguish of human pain among the other bestial noises. John looked at her quickly and took time only to utter sharply, the one word, “Now!” before returning immediately to the deliverance prayer.

Sheila quickly left the room, knowing what she had to do. Prior to the deliverance ceremony, John had been forewarned in his visions that the second demon was extremely powerful and would be massively resistant. The Lord had advised him to arrange to have a baptism of the two aborted children carried out while he was struggling with this second, more dangerous demon. John had earlier given Sheila the names of the two children and had instructed her to carry out the baptism when he gave her the word. The Lord had told him that the demon would sense the baptism and be weakened and enraged by it.

John, still feeling intense pain in his freezing right hand, struggled with all his strength to hold on to the crucifix as he continued to command the second demon to depart. Across the room, Miles stood stock-still, ill-at-ease despite his experience in these matters, as he felt the malignant force of the demon, felt the awful chill in the room, heard the nightmarish noises – the grunts, the groans, the screams, the deep, baleful snarls.

John, too, felt the demon’s powerful resistance, felt his own physical strength diminishing as the intense, malevolent cold seeped into his bones. But he continued to command the demon to depart, holding the crucifix over the young man and focusing the power of Jesus into the words. As Sheila began to carry out the baptism upstairs,

John sensed a sudden weakening in the adversary, and a surge of outraged frustration, as the demon shot out of the young man with the force of a bullet. John could "… feel the hair standing on my head as it flew past me."

At the moment of the second demon's departure, Raymond struggled upright in the chair, normal again but very shaken. "That was a terrible battle," he said, his voice little more than a whisper. "I could feel forces raging and churning inside me. They didn't want to come out. Dear God, I didn't think they would. John, I can't thank you enough."

John returned his thanks with his customary grin and his stock response at these times. "Don't thank me. I didn't do anything. Thank Jesus. He did it."

Raymond's mood swings left him. He returned to his placid and cheerful self, and his life returned to a peaceful, if mundane, normality. Sadly, his wife was to disappear from his life but his mother returned his two children to his care. He is now a protective and loving father to them. John told him that the demons had gained access to him in two ways, partly though the sinfulness of his own earlier life and partly because of the evil in the bloodline. At John's request, he arranged to have Masses said for his great-great-great-aunt, the prostitute on the ship, along with other prayers for her forgiveness and for the cleansing of his bloodline.

Commenting later on this episode, John was to say, "Those two devils were hard work. They took a lot out of me. There are times when I'd be taking out demons and I wouldn't even know I was doing it. But those two were tough. I suppose the effect on me all depends on the strength of the demon."

***

A television comedian once said, "If you believe in God, He exists; if you don't, He doesn't." Glib, trite, perhaps even a clever epigram, this comment offers an interesting insight into the nature of faith and certainty. He is saying that the essence of belief in God stems from a predisposition to believe, usually an element of one's nurture. But faith, for Christians, is impossible without grace from God. By the same token, without faith, belief in the devil or demons is equally impossible.

There are many sceptics who would offer a host of rational explanations for what happened in the story related above, who would claim that John was deluded and fantasising when he carried out that deliverance. A commonly held argument, particularly by non-Catholic psychologists, is that the mind and the body will respond to belief in demons as if they are real, so long as a person believes they are real. It is the same argument that is generally used to reject Christian faith in the supernatural. An intense belief creates its own reality.

Such scepticism credits Christian faith as being little more than superstition. Faith, and certainty in faith, depends to a degree on reason. What we believe needs to make sense. The issue of possession, or partial possession, is something that needs to be rationally examined to justify belief in it.

Deliverance is a job that many priests do not like. As John once said, "You have to roll up your sleeves and get your hands dirty." Tracey Wilkinson (2007)_quotes Fr. Francois-Marie Dermaine, a Dominican priest and exorcist in the Italian Port City of Ancona, "Priests don't want to do this. You have to sweat a lot. It's not easy. You have to learn alone. You have to gain experience alone." (p.67) Whatever the reason for disliking the task, any statement of scepticism from priests runs dangerously close to heresy. Fortea (2006) states bluntly, "To deny the reality of exorcism and to hold that it is merely a symbol of deliverance is a heresy."

It is probably safe to assume that when all the stories are told, when all the arguments have been rehearsed, the sceptics will remain sceptical and the believers will remain convinced. There is, however, that category of reader who has approached these pages with little more than curiosity, whose faith has, perhaps, grown weak, whose knowledge of this spiritual warfare is limited, but who yet might find something in what is written here that will give them pause for reflection.

Belief in a personal devil was discussed in Chapter 17 above but the question of whether a devil can actually possess a person's body remains. Arguments against the possibility of demonic possession, or of demonic oppression, generally tend to stem from two separate thrusts. One set of arguments derive from the assumption that the devil does not exist. If the devil is a myth, so too is demonic possession. The other thrust, more forceful and scientific, is the assumption that all forms of possession are explainable as malfunctions of the brain.

In either of these two thrusts, the search for truth will always be in the rational and observable world. Explanations for anything that appears to be strange or preternatural will never be sought in the spiritual realm. The strangeness in such events will simply be seen as a manifestation of something not yet understood.

There is no doubting the fact that many people who claim to be demonically possessed are delusional, are simply psychologically disturbed. Many of the indicators of demonic possession are similar to those of mental illness. But just because that is true, it cannot be assumed that the converse is true. It is feasible that people who appear to be psychologically disturbed may well be the victim of demonic possession. And if this is the case, what help would there be for the victim if the Church can no longer bring the remedies of Jesus? MacNutt (2003) says, "If people are suffering from psychological problems, fine; they can receive help through counselling and_prayer for healing. But if the source of the problem is demonic, they will not be noticeably helped through ordinary psychological intervention." (p.22)_

The fact is that for Christians the question is moot. Christians cannot deny the possibility of possession because such denial rejects scripture. To say that Jesus did not really cast out demons but simply healed mental illness is contrary to the Church's teaching. The reality is made very clear in the scriptures. Jesus spent His life doing three things, and in the gospels they are almost equal in terms of the amount of time given to them. He spent His life preaching the word, healing the sick, and casting out demons. These are the three things he instructed His Church and His disciples to do, and, as can be seen in the Acts of the Apostles, he had clearly trained them to carry out His instructions. The healings and the exorcisms of the apostles' ministry were complementary elements. Jesus made no distinction between them. Neither did the apostles.

Perhaps for Christians, a more significant question arises: Who can exorcise? There does not seem to be any apparent agreement in the literature about an answer to this question. Derek Prince (1998) is sure he knows the answer. "The basic requirement for ministering deliverance is stated by Jesus in Mark 16:17 '*And these signs will follow those who believe: In my name they will cast out demons ...'* Jesus required only one thing: simple faith in His name and in His word." (p.85) The conclusion must be that any believing Christian can exorcise.

The Catholic Church, however, is rather more specific. It is generally held that according to the present discipline of the Church, solemn exorcism is reserved to priests who have received permission from the bishop for this ministry. From this it would seem that not even all priests are allowed to carry out a solemn exorcism.

The word "solemn", however, gives pause. Are there different levels of exorcism? The word 'deliverance' has been substituted for the word 'exorcism' in modern times. Are the words truly synonymous? Why does Ken Olsen prefer the word 'expel'?

While for many Christian denominations the word 'deliverance' is now used to cover all forms of prayer in the casting out of demons, there is, in the Catholic Church's eyes, a significant difference between 'exorcism' and 'deliverance'. Fortea offers clear definitions of the two words: "An exorcism is a liturgical rite that is carried out [by a priest with permission from a bishop] over people who are [fully] possessed … that the possessed person may be freed from the devil. Deliverance is a series of private prayers prayed over people who suffer from some type of demonic influence." (pp.94/95) Deliverance does not require a priest or a bishop's permission.

To gain further insight into the issue, it might be useful to glance briefly at the history of the 'casting out of demons'. Jesus was Christianity's first exorcist. He was followed shortly afterwards by the apostles and the disciples. MacNutt tells us that after the deaths of the apostles "… exorcisms were carried out with no mention of any special class of Christians to whom the ministry of deliverance was restricted."(p.131) Nonetheless, such activity is dangerous and was generally seen as the province of gifted people, those who had been given the specific gifts of the Holy Spirit. Many writings of the early Church make frequent allusion to the special inspiration of the Holy Spirit as an essential element in the ministry of exorcism. Because of this, restrictions on who might perform exorcisms began to appear, and by the Middle Ages the priest was seen as the normal source for exorcism. This restriction was made official by Pius XI, who finally limited the deliverance ministry to priests. In 1972, Pope Paul VI dropped four of the minor orders, including exorcism, paving the way for the need for training and permission from the bishop before even a priest could perform a solemn exorcism.

Again that word 'solemn.' A solemn exorcism is carried out when a person is believed to be fully possessed by a demon. Complete possession of this nature is extremely rare. Sadly, given the anti-Christian values that prevail in modern liberal society, there exists a climate that somehow encourages, more than ever before, the occurrence of demonic possession. It is becoming so common in America, in fact, that Malachi Martin (1992) makes the point that "Possession among the general population is so clear that it is attested to daily by competent social and psychological experts who, for the most part, appear to have no 'religious bias'." (p. xiii)

Nonetheless, far more common is the problem of demonic 'oppression', which John says, "is rife in Ireland today. It has become almost a plague because of the occult having infiltrated people's lives so much." Sr. Briege makes the same point. "Look at TV and magazines. They are full of advertisements for psychics and psychic help of all kinds … all possible doorways into demonic presences."

Demonic oppression can mean that the person is accompanied by a demon who has attached himself to that person, the kind that are often referred to as 'clinging demons'. They can affect people's moods, the luck in their lives, their health and mental state. Oppression can also mean that some aspect of their personality has been taken over by a demon and, while they remain normal in all other parts of their lives, one element can be subject to serious sin (e.g, promiscuity, drunkenness, drug-addiction, dishonesty, etc.) or subject to a specific form of ill-health, or to mental illnesses such as depression or schizophrenia. To lift oppression, it is first necessary to identify the type of demon involved and this can be done by any Christian with the Spirit's gift of discernment. A priest is not necessary for this form of deliverance. Some fairly straightforward prayers and resolutions will do the rest.

Is this, then, the kind of deliverance ministry that John has been called to? Two factors would seem to negate that. Firstly, the deliverance in Raymond's story would seem to imply a much more deeply-seated demonic incursion than oppression. Secondly, Fr. Ronnie was specific during his prophecy that the healing ministry being given to John would additionally require him to "cast out demons".

How is it possible, then, that John, a layman, can perform exorcisms within the Catholic Church? Fr. Amorth (1994), Vatican exorcist, offers the answer. "The Holy Spirit," he tells us, "with divine freedom, gives His charisms however and to whomever He pleases…Among these charisms is the power to liberate from evil spirits and to heal from illnesses … God normally grants these gifts to righteous people of proven humility who pray frequently and live an exemplary Christian life." (p.155) Since John has been given all nine gifts of the Holy Spirit (see Part One), it is clear that he has the calling of the Spirit to carry out his deliverance ministry.

Vatican II affirms that any individual who has been given these gifts of the Spirit, even a lay person, has the right to exercise them. It is on that basis that John is fully entitled, within his ministry of healing, to exercise a ministry of deliverance. He does this, however, with the guidance, support and discernment of his bishop.

John has seen many demonically infected people. He has seen the ruin possession can bring to lives and, if unchecked, to souls. Only the body is capable of being possessed, of course; the soul continues to be free. But too long an exposure to the vile machinations of the devil can weaken the will and thus the soul becomes endangered. John warns that we must always pray for protection against any form of demonic incursion, to avoid practices that might allow the devil in, and to make regular use of the sacraments of reconciliation and the Eucharist. Given the excessive licentiousness of modern Western life, the extraordinary viciousness of its criminals, the aggressive atheism that seeks ever more limitation on the rights of Christians, the moral aboulia that is found in parts of the very Church itself, it is a warning that is more important today than ever. Such an incursion of evil into modern society clearly signals the guidance of a dark, manipulative hand.

***

When diagnosing illnesses, whether of the mind or of the body, doctors invariably seek natural explanations for the malady. They will never search for solutions in the supernatural realm. John has discovered that, because of this, many patients are left to suffer with physical symptoms that baffle the best diagnostic minds, while others, suspected of suffering from psychiatric disorders, are left to languish, on heavy medication, in mental hospitals. Terry Carlin might well be resident in a mental hospital today had not two of his friends suspected that his was a case for John Gillespie rather than a psychiatrist.

***

Terry's Story: Saved From a Life in Psychiatric Care

It was Easter Saturday afternoon and John was working in a local chapel, helping the sacristan to prepare the chapel for vigil services that evening. There was quite a bit to do and John had deliberately left his calendar free for that work. While he was decorating the altar, the sacristan answered a phone call which came from two young men who were anxious to speak to John. The sacristan told them that John was busy and that they should call back in a couple of hours.

When John came back into the sacristy, the sacristan told him about the call.

"What was their problem?" John asked.

"Well ... they were a bit incoherent but, as far as I can gather they have a friend whom they believe is in need of deliverance. I'm not sure if it's a prank, but the fellow on the phone said that their friend was in a terrible state. I told them to phone back in a couple of hours. If the problem is serious, they will."

"Call me if they do," John said. "I might need to talk to them."

The two young men did not, in fact, ring back. They came in person to the chapel and approached John, asking if they could talk to him. John did not know them personally but he had seen them at Mass from time to time and knew they were locals. They introduced themselves as Michael and Tony. They told John that their friend was hearing voices in his head. "They're driving him insane," Michael said. "The voices are telling him to kill somebody and he's demented with them."

"It's true, John," Tony nodded seriously. "They're telling him to commit murder. And other voices are telling him that he's no good, that nobody loves him and nobody could love him. They're filling him with self-loathing. He's in serious need of help, John."

John was very busy working in the chapel and felt that he could not leave the sacristan to do the work on his own but the sacristan told him not to be worrying about that and to go with the two young men. "You go with the lads," he urged. "It sounds as if you're needed. You can come back here when you're finished."

"All right," John said. "I'll go and meet him."

The two men had a car outside and as they were driving him to meet their friend, Terry, they told John something of his story. Terry had a good job that carried considerable responsibility but because of increasing concern about the voices in his head he went to see a psychiatrist. He was diagnosed with a severe psychosis and was admitted for psychiatric tests. He had been prescribed shock-treatment and had received some psychiatric counselling after which he had been released from hospital and was now back home.

"But he's no better, John," Tony said. "We got priests to pray for him and to pray with him but, if anything, he's worse. The hospital and the doctors, even the priests, are convinced that he's suffering from some psychiatric disorder. He's honestly at the stage now where he's going to be locked up in a mental home again or be on medical treatment and heavy drugs for the rest of his life."

"A neighbour of mine knows you and suggested we should see you," Michael added. "He thought maybe you could …" His voice trailed away as if what he wanted to say did not make sense.

Tony was less inhibited. "We think that Terry might be suffering from some kind of demonic attack, maybe some form of oppression."

"How do you know about that?" John asked.

"Ah, well, Michael's neighbour told us about the kind of things you've been doing and we figured it could do no harm to talk to you. But you have to see him today. He has to go into hospital again tomorrow. If they get him in there in this state, he might never get out." The young man's voice was filled with concern.

"Where is he now?" John asked.

"He's at home with his family," Don told him, "but I'm not sure if that's the best place to meet him."

John nodded. "We can't use the chapel either. There are too many people coming in and out this evening."

Don said, "I have a friend who has a flat. We'll borrow his key and take Terry there."

It took only twenty minutes to get the key and collect Terry. When they got to the apartment, John's first approach was to take Terry to a quiet room, talk to him, and form his own conclusions. He wanted first to ascertain if there was, in fact, some demonic base to Terry's problems and, if so, precisely what kind of demon or demons were involved. As he conversed with Terry, he learned that there was a background of hurt and rejection in Terry's family and that Terry, in particular, had suffered a great deal of emotional stress and pain as a child. John prayed over the young man for a while and began to learn that there were several demons oppressing Terry, six of which had a very strong hold over him. Two of them John quickly discerned were ancestral, but the other four were contemporary. Of these, the most powerful was a demon of rejection which, John knew, would always bring several other demons with it.

John immediately began to pray deliverance prayers, telling the demons sharply that they had no right to occupy Terry's body or mind, and commanded them, in Jesus' name, to leave. As he prayed, he became aware that the Lord was instructing him to cast out the two ancestral demons first and deal with the other four separately. As he performed the deliverance rite John told Terry that they would later have to resolve the ancestral problem or he would always be vulnerable to the demons' return. For the moment, however, he began to pray the forgiveness prayer, asking Terry to repeat the words after him and earnestly beg forgiveness for the ancestors in order to break the ancestral hold.

He also prayed for Terry, praying that he would be given the grace to forgive those who had brought so much hurt and rejection into his life. Then he asked Terry to repeat prayers asking for forgiveness for those who had emotionally abused him during his childhood, telling him that it was crucial that this be done with a genuine heart in order to break the demonic hold. Faced with the commands uttered in the name of Jesus, the prayers of forgiveness and Terry's own sincere response to John's instructions, the two ancestral demons slunk away with little fuss.

There was still the matter, however, of the other four much stronger demons, powerful demons of rejection, bitterness, contempt, and self-loathing, who were invariably accompanied by several minor demons. John prayed strenuously, commanding them sternly in Jesus' name to depart from Terry. He continued to pray unceasingly for about forty-five minutes, identifying the demons one by one and praying deliverance prayers against each one in turn. He frequently used the name of Jesus, spiritually washed Terry in the Lord's precious blood, sternly rebuked the demons, and commanded them to be gone from Terry and go to face Jesus.

After a few more minutes had elapsed, John began to believe that Terry was now delivered from the demons. He said some final prayers to bind all evil from Terry, to reclaim his mind and his psyche and place it under the protection of Jesus Christ. But although John had had a definite consciousness of the demons leaving Terry and was now convinced that Terry had been delivered, he could see that Terry's face was vacant and expressionless. He seemed to be in a trance-like state. John was puzzled.

"How are you now?" he asked Terry.

Terry just stared at him and made no response. John studied the young man and suddenly sensed that there was still one demon lurking in the depths of Terry's psyche, a powerful demon still clinging to his 'territory'. John asked Terry again, "How are you now?"

This time Terry responded in a flat gruff voice, "Who are you?"

John knew instantly that it was not Terry but the demon who had asked the question. In that same moment

John received a message from the Lord that he should respond to the query with the words, "I am the Son of the Living Jesus Christ, the King." It was not something that John himself would have said. Indeed, he felt a little strange claiming to be the Son of Jesus but he obeyed the Lord's instructions and answered the question as directed.

Terry's expression remained vacant and unmoving. Again John asked, "How are you now?"

And again the demon said, "Who are you?"

John repeated, "I am the Son of the Living Jesus Christ, the King."

At this, the demon became more aggressive. His eyes began to glare and his face took on an expression of hatred. He began to chant with increasing ferocity in a growling voice, "Who are you? Who are you?"

John heard the Lord instructing him to keep repeating, "I am the Son of the Living Jesus Christ, the King." He shouted the words strongly over the increasingly loud and harsh snarling of the demon, staring into the hate-filled eyes, showing the demon no fear. Then he received a further Word of Knowledge from the Lord to add, "I command you, foul evil spirit, to detach yourself from this man and to depart in Jesus' name." The demon recoiled and John repeated, "Depart foul evil spirit in Jesus' name."

John sensed the entity's frustrated anger as it suddenly departed. Terry shook his head, and his eyes and facial expression returned to normal. He looked at John and said, in a mystified voice, "Where am I?"

"You're okay, Terry," John told him. 'You're in a flat here with me and two of your friends. They're in the next room. They brought me here to pray with you. You don't have to worry about the voices any more. They're gone."

Terry continued to stare at John, around the walls of the unfamiliar room, and back again at John. John called to the other two to come in to allow Terry to connect with something familiar. He gave him a couple of minutes to process what had happened and asked him again, "How are you now?"

Terry's face was filled with wonder. "I feel brilliant. For the first time in I don't know how long, I feel at peace."

John said, "Are the voices in your head now?"

"No, they're gone. My head is completely clear."

Michael, standing beside Terry, gave a little fist pump, turned his face sideways, and hissed "Yes!!"

Terry went on speaking, looking directly at John. "I know you were praying with me and I was saying the words after you. And while I was doing that I could feel things …leaving me, and others struggling to hold on. But they are all gone now. For the first time in years I feel totally at peace."

Michael, wearing a wide grin, slapped Terry's back and shook his hand vigorously. Then he shook hands with John and said, "We can't thank you enough, John. This is brilliant."

Before John left, he instructed Terry to pray for his family members and to arrange for Masses for forgiveness of his errant ancestors. They left John back to the chapel, still thanking him profusely for what he had done.

"Thank Jesus," John told them, laughing. "I had nothing to do with it."

Terry no longer needed any medical treatment. John revisited him a few times over the following weeks to ensure that he was strong enough to prevent any further oppression. The young man was never to suffer from voices or any form of psychosis again. He returned to his job, and is today happily married and living a completely normal life.

For John, however, the incident was not closed. Satan is furious when John brings about the defeat of his minions and often, in his frustration, he seeks reprisals by targeting that which his enemy loves most, usually his family. John has been victim of such revenge tactics on a number of occasions, suffering fear for his children when Satan sent demons to attack them. Accounts of two such episodes have been related earlier in these pages. As a result of his involvement in Terry's deliverance, John was yet again to experience the venom of Satan's wrath.

Late that Easter Saturday evening, after the children had gone to bed, John and Christina were chatting in the kitchen. Suddenly they heard panicked screaming, coming from the attic room where Siobhan and Clare slept. They had learned over the years to distinguish between normal children's night cries and cries that denote spiritual attack. Christina paled and said immediately, "There's something wrong up there, John."

John was already up out of his chair when he heard Siobhan screaming down the stairs, "Something's happening to Claire."

"Get her out the room immediately," John shouted back, as he ran up the stairs to meet them. The two girls, aged seven and nine, were running down the stairs when he met them. He swept them both into his arms and carried them down to the kitchen.

Christina took Clare on to her knee and said, "What happened?"

Siobhan, the younger child, said in a rush, "Claire says that she felt something climbing into the bed beside

her. It was lying beside her and she thought it was Gra[illegible]
…"

Claire took up the story with trembling lips, "And I was nearly asleep and I turned round and said, 'Granny, why are you here?' and … and it wasn't Granny." Tears threatened as the child said tremulously, "It was an ugly face …" Then she threw her arms around her mother's neck and buried her face in her shoulder.

Siobhan added, in the same hushed tones as before, "She screamed and I said, "What's wrong?" and she said, 'Look at that ugly face,' but I couldn't see anything."

John knew immediately that this was Satan's petulant response to the deliverance that he had carried out earlier that day. He told his daughters not to be worried about what had happened and he prayed a prayer with them, commanding the presence, in Jesus' name, to leave the house, rebuking it sternly and informing the unseen force that it had no power or authority over this house or anyone in it. Again, in Jesus' name, he commanded it to depart.

After he was sure that the demon had gone, he took the children back up to the attic and blessed it. "You'll be all right, now," he told them. There's nothing more to worry about."

Once the room was blessed, Siobhan, despite her young age, jumped back into bed, put her head on the pillow, pulled up the clothes and said, "Claire, come on in here beside me. Daddy's here and he has blessed us. Nothing can touch us now."

No mention was made of the incident the following morning. The children were familiar with these kinds of spiritual attacks and since their Dad always chased the evil spirits, they had acquired a great faith in him. John says, "The children are used to this kind of thing. They take it have great faith now. Yet when I tell full-grown and mature adults, it frightens them.”

***

John never fails to stress the importance of protecting oneself from the devil and his influence. In particular, he urges us to remember that “… it is very important when you’re praying for protection that Jesus’ Name is invoked. When we seek deliverance from demons or their influence, no other name will work. They will only leave in Jesus’ Name.” He offers the following prayer for the protection of those who have put themselves at risk or who sense or learn that some demonic influence has attached itself to them.

Prayer for Protection from the Evil One

Lord Jesus Christ, I place myself at the foot of Your Cross and ask You to cover me with Your Precious Blood that pours forth from Your Most Sacred Heart and Your Most Holy Wounds. Cleanse me, my Jesus, in the living water that flows from Your Heart. I ask You to surround me, Lord Jesus, with Your Holy Light.

Lord Jesus, in Your Holy Name, I bind all evil spirits of the air, water, ground, underground, and netherworld. I further bind, in Jesus' Name, any and all emissaries of the satanic headquarters and claim the Precious Blood of Jesus on the air, atmosphere, water, ground and their fruits around us, the underground and the netherworld below.

Heavenly Father, allow Your Son, Jesus, to come now with the Holy Spirit, the Blessed Virgin Mary, the holy angels and the saints, to protect me from all harm and to keep all evil spirits from taking revenge on me in any way.

Holy Spirit, please reveal to me, through the Word of Knowledge, any evil spirits that have attached themselves to me in any way. [Pause and wait for words to come to you such as: anger, arrogance, bitterness, brutality, confusion, cruelty, deception, depression, envy, fear, hatred, insecurity, jealousy, lust, pride, resentment or terror…etc. Pray the following for each of the spirits revealed.]

In the Name of Jesus, I rebuke you spirit of ________________ .I command you to go directly to Jesus, without manifestation or without harm to me or anyone, so that He can dispose of you according to His Holy Will.

I thank You, Heavenly Father, for Your love. I thank You, Holy Spirit, for empowering me to be aggressive against Satan and his evil spirits. I thank You, Jesus, for setting me free. I thank you, Holy Mother Mary, for interceding for me with the holy angels and the saints.

"God indeed is my Saviour; I am confident and unafraid. My strength and courage is the Lord and He has been my Saviour." (Isaiah 12.2) Amen.

PART FOUR: PREACH THE GOSPEL

Chapter Twenty-One

"My teaching is not mine, but it comes from the One who sent me." [John 7:16]

John Preaches the Word

St. Francis of Assisi often encouraged his brothers to '*... preach the gospel and, if you have to, use words.*' Teaching by example is invaluable but there are, inevitably, times when the Christian who aspires to improve his life, who seeks to strengthen his relationship with the divine, who feels the need to understand his spirituality, must hear the Word of God. The Word is "something alive and active" that works in our hearts and in our minds. We are vulnerable without it. Our souls need the nourishment the Word brings. So those who would teach the Word must, perforce, occasionally speak it.

For the first several years of his ministry, John was satisfied that his purpose was to bring God's miracles to His people, to heal the sick and to cast out demons. He was happy to enlighten those individuals or small groups who sought his help about the spirituality that underpinned his healings - the nature of forgiveness, the importance of prayer, the spiritual lacks that were hampering their healing - but he did not consider the possibility of preaching this knowledge to large gatherings. He had left school at fourteen; he had never trained in oratory; he had no experience of public speaking. A priest had once told him that, properly delivered, a good homily should have three elements: first, a divine spark, second, good intellectual preparation by the speaker, especially in a search for the heart of the gospel message, and third, the attention of the people. John understood and approved the priest's comment but it never occurred to him that it was something he himself should do or could do.

Several years into his ministry, however, John had begun to experience soft promptings from the Lord. Different small events would nudge his thoughts to something beyond the individual healings and deliverances that were occupying the greater part of his life. He worked occasionally as a sacristan in St. Agnes Church, and more and more, as he would set the lectionaries on the altar and pulpit in preparation for Mass, he would sense that the Lord was saying to him, "You're setting these books up for priests but one day you're going to have to come up and talk from here yourself. And you're going to have to tell people about your experiences, about the things you have learned from me and about things that you have dealt with. You will have to explain to people how they are to live and what they have to believe."

And on occasion, there would be direct requests from people that he preach the Word. John explains it in his forthright way. "I get called all over Ireland to do healing prayers and that involves a lot of explaining and teaching to the people that I pray with and for. Over the last couple of years lots of people have come to me talking about others they have heard speaking, maybe even priests, but complaining that these people are not talking about the stuff that I talk about. And they'd get annoyed. 'Why don't you tell the Church,' they would say to me, 'about what you're dealing with behind the scenes? Why don't you let them know about New Age and curses and ancestral bloodlines and all that? Nobody in the pulpits is touching this stuff. You have the knowledge and the experience. You're going to have to say something.' But I would tell them that I didn't think that I could go public like that.

"But I knew then that God was saying to me more and more, 'You are going to have to go out and you're going to have to go public.' And I was thinking to myself, 'I'd far rather be doing the exorcisms and such behind closed doors. Get me more into that side of it, Lord.' But that wasn't God's will. I was dealing with that anyway but God wanted me to do more. His instructions to His disciples were to heal and cast out demons but He also told them to preach the Word. And I was starting to feel that He was saying that to me, too.

"It had to come anyway. I was going into houses dealing with one petitioner at a time and I'd be sitting there for five or six hours repeating the same prayers over and over again. I was constantly doing this and the Lord was hinting to me that I could do far more healings with the one prayer if I would do it with a large group and pray over all of them at the one time."

The years passed and the promptings became stronger but John still did not know quite what he should do about them. By now he was extremely busy. He no longer worked part-time in the chapel. The calls on his time were incessant and his hours helping petitioners - praying for healings and miracles, casting out demons - demanded not only full days from him but many long evening hours as well.

It was sometime during 2009 that Sr. Briege suggested to John that he should consider adding a preaching element in his ministry. Her timing was opportune because by that time God's promptings were loud in John's ears. He was having difficulty now in coping with all the requests for healing that were coming to the monastery and to his other diaries as well. He was beginning to sense that he would have to work with larger groups if he was to have any hope of responding to the demands that were now being made of him. "The need out there is just so great," he told Sister Briege when they talked about this.

After some discussion with her about how he might begin a preaching ministry, John agreed to try an experimental prayer service at the monastery, one that would include some prayers, hymn singing, a brief talk by John and, to finish, a healing service during which John would pray over each individual present. And so his preaching ministry began.

A few months later, John's preaching expanded to include talks at a rehabilitation centre outside Newry called Chuain Mhuire (the Harbour of Mary). He now speaks regularly there and carries out group and individual healings. "Given the way that this part of my ministry is developing," he says, "I know that this is only the start. This thing is going to grow and grow … I don't exactly know how, but the Lord will decide where and when in His own good time."

***

Only someone who lives in Christ, as we read so frequently in St. John's Letters, only someone who lives in the Word and knows Jesus, can truly preach the Word of God, can lead others to the truth. When Jesus spoke, He always accompanied His preaching with 'works'. He would say, "If you do not believe me because of what I say, then believe me because of what I do." His 'works' were His healings, intended to be a sign that said, "What I am preaching to you is true because you can see how God is working miracles through me." Much of John Gillespie's ministry reflects this, yet, as he himself so often points out, "I am only a builder's labourer." The questions that Jesus' own people asked of Him are often asked of John. *"Where did this man get all this? What is this wisdom that has been granted Him and these miracles that are worked through Him? This is a carpenter, surely?"* [Mark 6:2]

John's friend, Sr. Briege, has immense faith in him both as a healer and as a preacher. She is convinced of the necessity of his role as a disciple who heals, who delivers people from evil spirits and who preaches the Word of God. In the verbatim account below, she talks a little about John and how she was instrumental in helping him into the preaching part of his ministry.

Sr. Briege says: *One of the problems in the Church today is that priests and other Christian ministers can be great at preaching but they do not, as a rule, accompany their preaching with the signs of God's presence and God's power. When Jesus preached, everything He preached was backed up by the power of God through healings and deliverances. These wonders have always been understood to be direct signs of God's power in the Word and signs, too, that the Word is true. And the gospels make it abundantly clear that Jesus made no distinction between preaching the Word, healing, and deliverance. For him, all three were interdependent, but today's Church seems to have made clear distinctions between them. If I remember correctly, Derek Prince was very emphatic about that. He talked about New Testament evangelism and said that it is unscriptural to pray for the sick if one is not prepared to cast out demons.*

Often you can get a preacher who is a very fine orator, who is very persuasive and charismatic, and that's good. We need speakers like that in the Church. A true preacher, however, even if he lacks these oratorical skills, will have a profound effect on his listeners because the Holy Spirit moves in. Hearts are changed and transformed. Something deep happens. The need for people who can make this happen is greater today than ever it has been, so God is moving. There is today a great movement of the Holy Spirit and God is using the laity, and that is why you have men like John Gillespie and Joe Dalton and Eddie Stone and many others. They are the people that God is raising up because they are obedient to the Holy Spirit. They do what the Spirit tells them to do and say what they are told to say. They don't care about being condemned or criticised; they just do it. And there are now many people like this in Ireland, very holy men of deep faith who are capable of bringing about extraordinary examples of healing.

I was speaking to John about this one evening as he was leaving the monastery. 'You should be preaching the Word,' I told him.

He seemed taken aback although he was to confess to me later that this was something he had been thinking about for some time. 'But sure how could I do that?' he said. 'I've no schooling and no training. I wouldn't know where to start.'

'John,' I told him, 'you have been talking for years about the Word of Knowledge, about how the Lord always ensures that you will know what you need to know to find the root cause of problems, about the instructions you'll need to give to those seeking healing. With tutoring from the Lord himself, I'd say that very few people are better qualified to preach the Word than you are.'

John then told me that he had been thinking along these lines for the past year or so but that he did not know how he could go about it. So I said to him, 'Why don't you try to speak to a group here at the monastery? You can use our Conference Room and I'll get the word out about it.' He agreed to give it a try.

The first couple of sessions were held in our large Conference Room. This was a new development for John and initially he was quite nervous and clearly uncomfortable. There were times when he might not have spoken as loudly as he should have; there were times when he spoke rather too quickly. But I sat there and I watched him and I watched the people. He had them totally in his hand. They loved him. He seemed to touch on subtleties that made contact with the people and reached their hearts. There was something genuine and powerful infused in what he was saying. They fully believed what he said because at the end of each session, when he prayed over each one individually, they could see that his talk was backed up by God at work in them and they could experience the powerful effect his preaching was having upon them.

It very quickly became clear that the Conference Room was altogether too small a venue for these sessions. On the second night, many people had to stand outside because the hall was packed to capacity. I could see then that this would become a significant and important sphere of John's ministry. After the second session, I spoke to John about the crowds and told him that the Conference Room was no longer going to work, that we were going to have to get a larger venue. 'I'll talk to the Parish Priest here,' I told him, 'and see if I can get permission for you to use the chapel down at St. Brigid's Shrine.'

I got the permission without any trouble and his monthly talks at the Shrine have now become an established pattern. Yet even this chapel is proving to be too small and some members from our local support group have had to set up a loud-speaker system outside the building to relay what John was saying to those unable to get in.

It was all new for John at first but he is becoming increasingly comfortable with his new role and he tackles an important new topic each time, offering new and perceptive insights even to those of us who are well-versed in theology and spirituality. And it is noticeable now that something significant is emerging in his preaching. It's the same thing they said about Jesus, the one thing that made Him different from the other preachers of His time: 'He speaks with authority.' They said that about Jesus and you feel that with John. When he says something, it rings so true ... especially when he backs up his points with stories of healings and deliverances that had occurred elsewhere as a result of his prayers.

Something else amazing has also started to happen. At the end of each of these services, John prays individually over each person present and already stories are beginning to emerge about healings that have taken place as a result of these prayers, healings that John himself would not have been aware of at the time. Sometimes, too, during the end part of his talk, John stands at the altar with his eyes closed, listening for the Word of Knowledge. Then, all the time whispering prayers and with his head down and his eyes closed, he would point vaguely at different parts of the room identifying people with problems and assuring them of God's help. About a month ago he did this and said, 'There's a lady over there who's been blind in one eye for seventeen years ... you're not to worry. God is going to give you your sight back.' We didn't know it at the time but there was indeed a blind lady there who was instantly healed.

Then there was a little child, only a year or so old, that was brought to one of the meetings at the Shrine. There were eight holes in its heart and the consultant had told the mother that there was nothing that could be done, that the little baby had not much longer to live. I was there that night and the poor wee mite couldn't stop crying. I felt so sorry for it. It was crying and crying and crying. Then John went over and prayed for it ... only a quick laying on of hands. But the child ceased crying. We heard nothing more about it that night but a few days ago the mother got in touch with us to tell us that all the holes in the child's heart are closing up and her baby is well on the road to recovery.

There are many other amazing stories like that but we don't get to hear about most of them. Usually it is John or the women who organise his diaries who get the feedback. Now and again I'd get a brief word with John as he would be going in to see suppliants in the monastery but he'd never have much time for talk. All he usually says, with a quick nod of his head and a grin as he is passing, is 'There was a lot of healing last week,' or something like that. That's all he tells us.

But yesterday a man came to see Sister Margaret. He is one of the men who organises and prepares the Shrine chapel for John's services. He was telling Margaret about his niece who had been given only three months to live. She had three kinds of cancer that were beyond treatment. She had gone to hear John preaching and had been so impressed that she requested a one-to-one appointment with him. She came to meet him at the monastery a few days later and he prayed over her. Her uncle told Margaret yesterday that at the last clinic appointment his niece went to, she was told that two of the cancers had disappeared completely and that the other one had shrunk to such an extent that it was now easily treatable with chemotherapy. She's going to live. It's amazing what is happening at these talks.

John is becoming more at ease with this part of his ministry and he is beginning to see value in it. He feels so passionate about what he has to say and now he really wants to spread the message. I think it will not be long before he will be doing these services at other venues and, indeed, I was told the other day that he had been invited to address a group of people next week at the Chuain Mhuire Centre outside Newry. So it's starting for him now, and it will grow. I think that's inevitable. But he'll be so much in demand that I don't know how he's going to be able to find the time to cope with everything.

Chapter Twenty-Two

"Let your words strengthen sound doctrine."
[Letter to Titus, 2:1]

Aspects of the Word

St. Brigid's Shrine is located in the country area of Faughart, in County Louth. It is set upon a hill overlooking Dundalk Bay and in the summer time, the views there are magnificent, the long sweep on the valley on one side and the Cooley Hills on the other. The saint was born at Faughart around 452 A.D. and spent her childhood there. She moved around Ireland after she was professed as a nun and settled eventually in Kildare to govern the Church there along with St. Conleth. She was to found two monastic institutions, one for men and one for women, in 468. St. Brigid's small oratory at Cill-Dara (Kildare) was to become the centre of religion and learning in Ireland. Her role here was important. At that time the Abbess of Kildare was regarded as the Superior General of the convents in Ireland.

Within very few years of her death, St.Brigid was venerated as patron of Faughart and the surrounding district. Faughart Church was founded in honour of St. Brigid by St. Morienna (often known as St. Moninna) and the old well of St. Brigid's, adjoining the now-ruined church, is of time-honoured age. For centuries it has attracted pilgrims and continues to do so to the present day. After more than fifteen hundred years, the memory of "the Mary of the Gael", St. Brigid, remains dear to the Irish heart and her name continues to be used as a Christian name of choice for many female Irish babies.

The actual 'well', with countless stories of healings attributed to it, is small and disappointingly uninspiring. It is little more than a depression in the ground, perhaps a foot or so deep and about two feet square. The well, however, with the little rivulet that has always washed through it, remains much as it has been down through the centuries. The grounds around it, however, have changed. Near the well is a large stone sculpture of the crucified Jesus with some kneeling figures around it. Just outside the well area there is a large, substantial car-park and, on a hill above, a new modern chapel, dome-shaped and circular, with walls mostly made of glass. There is a short, steep climb to the chapel from the well, and here and there on the route are fixed the fourteen Stations of the Cross. Thus the area is hallowed. It has a history of healings and cures which lends an additional aura of probity to the services John conducts at the shrine chapel on the first Tuesday of every month.

These services are scheduled to begin at seven-thirty in the evening but the crowd starts gathering about seven o'clock, anxious not only to get a space in the car park but to get a seat in the chapel as well. The congregation is eclectic – business people, professionals, housewives and their husbands, working people, retired people, members of the travelling community. All are quiet and respectful. While they wait for the service to begin, they listen attentively to the melodious singing of Olive Keyes who invariably accompanies John on these evenings. She sings hymns from her CD during the quiet period before the service begins, and again during the period at the end of the service when John prays over the petitioners who wait patiently for the laying on of hands and the whispered prayer. He passes along the front of the congregation and each row moves forward as the preceding row disperses.

The service usually begins with one of the lay-associates of the nearby Poor Clare Monastery going to the dais in front of the altar. She explains briefly what is going to happen – that John will speak for a while and that everyone would have an opportunity for a blessing at the end of the service. “Bring your prayers to the Lord as John blesses you,” she says, “because it is the Lord who does the healing. John is only a vessel.”

She then makes some brief references to healings that have occurred at earlier services. One evening she spoke about a lady who had attended the service the previous month with her husband. She had a blocked artery in her leg that had been keeping her awake at night for years and she had suffered terribly with it. Her husband, too, had a poisoned arm which had been causing him a great deal of pain for a long time. They came to John after the service, got blessed, and neither of them has had a moment of discomfort since.

After two or three of such stories, she introduces John.

***

When John preaches the Word, he does so with a direct and uncluttered frankness. Not for him the niceties of diplomacy; not for him concern with circumspection. “Worrying about people’s feelings,” John says, “is watering down God's word. I preach the Word the way the Lord tells me to. Sometimes when I give a talk, I get people coming up to me afterwards so angry they're almost spitting. But I say to them, 'Is it God's Word you've come to hear or do you just want to hear something comfortable that'll allow you to feel good when you go on doing the wrong thing? Why are you getting angry with me? If what I'm saying is making you angry, then it's into your own hearts you should be looking, not mine.' That makes them stop and think. There was no compromise with Jesus when He was preaching … and look how angry the Pharisees and some of the Jews were with Him! But everybody knows now that He was speaking the truth.

"A few weeks ago I was giving a talk at Faughart. It was just before

Hallowe'en and I was talking about all those demons and monsters that people were decorating their homes with. There were mothers who came up to me afterwards very angry and wanting to know what I was playing at. 'We spent a fortune on those decorations for our children,' they told me. 'They're only a bit of fun.'

"But I said to them, 'Hallowe'en is a totally pagan feast. And Hallowe'en is a night for witchcraft. Read any book on Satanism and you'll learn about the demonic nature of these things and of this night. So, how is celebrating Satan and his demons only a bit of fun? You dress up your home like that; you have those things hanging there in your house like holy pictures. Those things represent evil and there's enough evil about the place without bringing in any more. You show tolerance for Satan like that and he'll take full advantage of it, don't doubt that for a minute.'

"That kinda stopped them in their tracks. 'Well, what do you want us to do?' they asked me. 'Get rid of the stuff,' I told them. 'What else do you want me to say? Stuff like that should be in no Christian home. These things are sinful. I mean, you're praying and going to Mass to get to Heaven but you think more about Satan on Hallowe'en than you do about God. How is that Christian? These things are only an insult to God.'

"Then I get the same cry, 'Well, why are the priests not telling us this?' But I can't answer that. Maybe the priests are telling them about these things and they simply don't hear them."

John is nothing if not kind, yet on paper his words sometimes sound uncompromising, almost harsh. The fact is, however, that what he says is spoken with such evident faith and with such concern for the individual's spiritual welfare that even his strictest words do not offend. Even those who might normally take offence at criticism are somehow disarmed by the clear ring of truth in John's words.

And John now has a pressing sense of obligation to speak the Lord's Word. Much of what he has been doing in his earlier ministry has been for him a series of learning experiences. Almost every healing he prayed for necessitated that God give him 'the Word of Knowledge' so that he would know what to do. He has been made aware of the importance of several kinds of prayer, different forms of spirituality. He has a fervent belief in the necessity for forgiveness. He has come to a deep consciousness of the dangers inherent in modern forms of idolatry, in false holiness, in what he terms 'faithless faith'. His confrontations with the devil and his minions have opened his eyes to the occult in the world and to the harm people can do to themselves and their families, sometimes innocently, sometimes with sinful hearts. All these John sees with tutored eyes, eyes opened by God, eyes that see to the heart of things and to the truth of things. And he burns now with the desire to spread this knowledge, to remind people so blinded by modern values, so confused by today's liberalism and secularisation, so caught up in an era of self-gratification and self-centredness, that they have lost sight of the gospel's essential message of love and forgiveness and faith.

For John, preaching the Word means bringing people to a knowledge of what they must do and how they must think in order to become truly Christian. And if he feels occasionally dismayed by the irregularities he finds in the lives of so many Christians today, irregularities that stem as much from ignorance and weak spirituality as from sinfulness, he feels equally an intense need to teach them where unhappiness and hurt reside in their lives and what must be done to find peace and healing.

Many in today's modern Church are seeking spirituality in a vague and ill-defined religious mysticism. There may be something sincere in this but, lacking true knowledge, confused by a distorted understanding of human rights, confused by the false assumptions in today's secular psychology, they find themselves on a path that can lead to a renunciation of the truth and of the Church's clear creed. Yet John sees that people remain hungry for the Word, for the supernatural, for the spiritual, even if they are searching for it in the wrong places. He tries to harness this yearning by his healings and his deliverances and takes the opportunity always to speak the truth that Jesus has taught him.

***

Something of what John seeks to teach is recorded in the paragraphs that follow, much of it verbatim. Only a single subject constitutes a theme for a particular service but often what John says about it can be new to his listeners and occasionally disturbing. It is disturbing because it has the ring of truth, because it challenges erroneous beliefs. The following are but a brief selection of the many themes that he preaches on.

***

i. Faithless Faith

When John discusses the Word of God, he is at pains to stress that there are always conditions attached to it. Jesus frequently made the point in the New Testament that if we want anything, all we have to do is to ask for it in His name. But He never failed to add that, if the request is to be granted, the suppliant must believe in Him and believe in His Word and live by His commandments. John states that it is a never-ending source of dismay for him to encounter so many petitioners who have failed to grasp this essential truth. "You have to tell people that they have got to meet the conditions if they want to be truly healed," he says. "A lot of people know about God's promises and God's provision in the Word but when they pray, they don't believe that they will get what they are asking for in spite of God's promises and what God can do. It's amazing the number of people that fail in that. So they are praying with a faithless faith which becomes unbelief; it becomes a whole ritual with a whole lot of words repeated over and over again with no real belief."

John delivers his teaching around specific issues that the Lord has asked him to talk about. He says modestly that he knows nothing about public speaking but that he feels supported by the fact that God is urging him on. Essentially he selects a topic prompted by the Lord and simply talks about it in a general way, drawing on the knowledge that he has gleaned from his experiences in ministry. Then he will use a case that he has worked on to illustrate the point he is making. "Once people see how it worked for this person or that person," he says, "they will understand better how they should pray themselves, or how they should relate with others, especially in terms of hurt and unforgiveness.

"Sometimes I'll talk about faith. Sometimes the story I'll tell shows that God does the opposite of what people expect. There are plenty of stories about people who thought they were doing everything right but don't get healing; and others about people who just pray in belief, not sure about what they are doing, but who do get healing.

"You see, the ones who don't get healed, there is lurking around in the back of their heads the thought, 'Ah, I know that this will never work out because the doctor says this and the doctor says that.' So the doctor, then, or the consultant, or somebody else, becomes bigger than God. If the consultant says there is no hope, then they believe there's nothing God can do about it. They couldn't be more wrong. But that kind of attitude really blocks an answer to their prayers. God does not work all that well through those sorts of circumstances. You see, they are not really drawing God's power. You can't expect an answer to your prayers if they are not spoken in faith and hope. For me the letters of the word 'faith' clearly spell out the message: Faith Asks In The Hope. That's how it has to be. The New Testament is full of that. 'Thy faith has made thee whole.' 'Do you believe?' and so on.

"The talks I do at Faughart and Chuain Mhuire are always based on a teaching. Faith is obviously one of them. I speak about the 'faithless faith'. The Church says, 'Pray more. Pray more.' There are a lot of people who pray more, but words and words coming out of their lips are useless if they are not accompanied by faith. Look, if you were in serious need of fifty pounds to pay a telephone bill or something and had no way of getting it and you say to the Lord, 'Lord, I need fifty quid to pay this telephone bill and my only hope of getting it is you. And since you love me Lord, I believe that it is now on its way, and I thank you Lord for that.' And you start walking about for the next couple of days, saying every now and again, 'Thank you, Jesus! That money is on its way. Thank you.' There's no need to get down on your knees and pray any more. You can say it walking about, lying in bed, making a cup of tea. That prayer has far more effect, it is far more beneficial, than hundreds of rosaries said by someone who continues to panic with thoughts, 'I'll never get this bill paid.' They are putting a block on any chance they have of allowing God to do His work. Only faith allows God to work.

"It's like a farmer who plants a field of potato seeds. He's not out on the field the next morning tearing his hair out because there's no sign of the potatoes. He knows they're coming; he knows he has to be patient. But he has no doubt that they'll come. The prayer of faith is something like that. It has to be steadfast. And it has to be patient. Patience is part of the deal, like the farmer waiting for the spuds. The petitioner has to believe that the favour asked for is on its way. He has to claim the favour. [illegible] has to be no doubt that it will be granted. I prayed [illegible] years for a miracle, for my hip to be healed. I used to go to bed in agony but I always believed I would wake up healed the next morning. And when I wasn't, I'd be angry and demand my healing all the harder. I suppose I was a bit short on patience at that time, but I claimed it. I claimed it. But now I know how much patience is necessary."

When John speaks to the large groups that come to hear him, it is words such as these that he speaks. They are not words laced with literary allusions; they are not words that reflect any of the rules or mores of oratory. They are simple, direct, and they come from the heart. They come, too, from the knowledge that the Lord Himself has given to him over the years and they carry with them the power of that knowledge.

ii. The Power of Words

When John speaks of the power of words, he occasionally does so in a context somewhat different from the meaning normally applied to the phrase. He believes that words have a force beyond their surface meaning. Words have the power to influence the mind and the psyche, even when they seem to be little more than a casual comment. Thus words with a negative connotation must be avoided at all costs. Someone might say, 'There's a possibility I might get this disease or that ailment. Will you pray for me?' The words seem innocuous in their tone, almost conversational, even though their import is obviously serious. "But by stating the fact that such an eventuality is possible," John claims, "we greatly increase wing the malady to ourselves." He urges negative fears or concerns to diminish d's power, "... because God can do we stop believing that, we block His ver say words like that, negative words. Words like that open the door to the illness.

"One night I talked about the healing power of God and talked also about the healing power of your own words. The number of people who came up to me after that talk you wouldn't believe. I told them that sometimes a prayer for healing is working, but if they suddenly speak their own words and they are the wrong words, then the whole effect of the prayer is wasted. If your own words are negative, that means they contain doubt and disbelief. There's no chance of healing with that. Your words are supposed to become enjoined with scripture, not with what some doctor or consultant says. It's the promises of God that you need to believe. For example, if you have some sort of disease and you go to the doctor and he tells you that you have six months to live ... like a young girl in America I once prayed over. If you take it for granted that what the consultant says is true, then that's what'll happen. But the wee girl in America and her folks didn't accept that consultant's word and began praying and taking authority and claiming that no sickness and no disease was going to come against her, that Jesus was Lord over her body. They didn't start saying, 'There's nothing can be done,' because they believed that God could do anything. And that wee girl was healed.

"Another thing we do is that we start to accept as final everything that the consultant or the doctor says. Then we pray away to God, begging and begging Him to heal us. But all the time, in our minds, is the belief that nothing can be done because the surgeon says it's final. What we're actually saying to God is, 'You can't do anything about this.' So, the way we pray, the things we say, can limit what God can do. Very often it is our own words that determine the outcome of situations like this. It's like a cheque you prayed for has arrived and you suddenly say, 'I am not worthy of this,' and rip it up. Often God is on the way to heal us and we say something negative. It's like ripping up the cheque and it stops God in His tracks.

"There's a story, it was one time the Lord was telling me that I would have to speak about people presenting a false image to Him, being hypocritical about themselves. This was something he wanted me to talk about at one of my services. It hurt Him that people were dishonest with Him and with themselves. Always when He talks to me like that, something directly connected with it comes up in a day or two. And then I was called to a house and I knew before I got there exactly what the outcome was going to be. I'll tell you the whole story.

"There was a woman made an appointment with me. I knew her. I used to see her an odd time at Mass on Sundays. I don't know whether she went to Mass during the week. If she did, she didn't go in our church. But she came to me and said, 'John, I've terrible pains in my back and hip with sciatica. I can hardly bend and it's terrible when I try to get out of bed in the morning. A friend of mine told me to come and see you.'

"'That's all right,' I told her. 'I'll pray over you and see what the Lord will do for you.' I could sense immediately that her hip and the problem she had with her sciatic nerve was severe and that her movement was indeed severely hampered. 'I haven't been able to walk easily this past while,' she told me.

"I prayed for a few minutes and the next thing she started to feel a tingling in her back and she started moving her right knee up and down. She was doing this with a great deal of freedom and had a surprised look on her face. 'My goodness, that's wonderful,' she said to me. And I said, 'Well, you keep thanking God now for the healing. Your hip will even be freer tomorrow and the next day. So just keep saying *Thank you, Jesus, for healing me*. Don't speak about sciatica any more or say things like *I have sciatica in my hip or a problem with my back*. Don't call it back in after me praying for it to go.' So she said that she would never mention sciatica again. And as she was leaving, I called after her, 'Don't forget now. Keep thanking God. You can do it washing the dishes, lying in bed, watching TV, every time you think about it, just thank him.' And I knew that woman was healed, and she was healed.

"But here's the interesting thing, and I knew as sure as anything that it was going to happen. Within a week, another woman called me to her house and she had exactly the same symptoms as the woman who went to Mass once a week. This second woman was extremely well-dressed and always had on plenty of make-up. She had no connection with the first woman other than her symptoms were more or less the same, she had sciatica in her right hip, but somehow I sensed that there was going to be a lesson for me in this case. She told me she was a Eucharistic minister in a parish some miles away, that she went to Mass every day and was out every day giving Holy Communion to the sick. But she was coming to me now because she was having terrible trouble getting in and out of the car with the sciatica, and walking up and down the altar steps.

"I prayed over her back and her hip and the problem with her sciatic nerve. And as soon as I had finished praying for her, I said to her, 'It's very important that you thank God for your healing. Regardless of how you feel, believe you are healed. And if you need more prayer, we can do it, but you must thank God right now and during the next weeks for your healing.'

"'Oh,' she says to me, 'I love God, and I love the Mass. Where would you be without the Mass? And sure I go round the sick every day with Holy Communion.' But then she said, 'I'm very fortunate. My consultant is one of the top men in the field of sciatica, and I know his mother very well. And he is wonderful, and so skilled at what he does.'

"Well, she went on praising that doctor up to the skies and talked about how well she knew him and what he was doing for her. And the more that woman praised her doctor, I felt the Lord saying to me, 'This woman is wearing high heels and she's trampling me into the ground with them. Those heels are sticking in my face.' My stomach was turning with anger. I could not help feeling that the Lord was being dreadfully insulted. I had terrible trouble containing myself while she went on and on, promoting the consultant, making him out to be the be-all and the end-all of everything.

"And I felt the Lord saying to me, 'It's time for you to get out.' And as I was leaving, which I did very quickly, the Lord said, 'This will be a test case for you to tell other people. This woman will not allow herself to be healed by me and you will see this. She has put all her faith in her doctor. While she was with you she was glorifying him and humiliating me.'

"That woman was never healed and she now gets expensive, and to me useless, injections into her back, whereas the other woman who prayed and thanked God in simple faith is jumping around and in great health. She might only go to Mass once a week but her prayers are simple, private and earnest. The other woman that's trying to be holy, she can go to Mass every day and give out Communion as much as she likes, and she might feel that she is impressing a lot of people. But I know from the Lord's own mouth that He is not impressed, because much of what she is doing is for her own glory. But He is impressed with the ordinary wee woman with the genuine heart who thanked Him wholeheartedly. She is healed. And that is the way that this story has ended up … and that's the way it will stay. The difference is simple and God needs me to get this message out - one promoted God and His power; the other promoted her consultant.

"A great number of people would say that the holy one is the woman that should have been healed because she was the one who was doing the most. But she wasn't doing the most, at least, not for God. She was doing it for herself. There was no genuine humility in her attitude. Even when talking about the great consultant, she was promoting herself by talking about how well she knew such an important person. Well, the other wee woman knew a far more important person, and she's healed.

"The thing is, people think we need to get holy to get healed. But it's not our holiness that heals us; it's God's loving mercy. Our Lord was the one who died on the cross. He's the one who heals. Faith is what you believe in. The self-important woman believed in herself and in her doctor. She had no real faith in God at all.

"So I used that story at a service as the Lord told me to and it was amazing the feedback I got about it, from young and old. There was a woman who came to me and said, 'I'm exactly like that woman. I go to Mass every day and give out Communion, and I don't believe that my attitudes are right. That talk you have just given has taught me a terrible lesson. I have to go home now and have a long think about my life.' Others were saying much the same thing. Their humility, at least, their humility that night, was extraordinary. It shows the power of God's word. He was the one who made me tell that story."

iii. The Importance of Praise

Anyone familiar with the psalms will know that many of them are paeans of praise to the Lord. Their language tends to sit uncomfortably in the mouths of this generation, except, perhaps, for charismatics and fundamentalists. Yet, those who consistently read the divine office learn to love the psalms - the psalms of praise, the psalms of sorrow and lamentation, the psalms of thanksgiving. They become increasingly meaningful with familiarity and help give word to thoughts and feelings that might otherwise remain unexpressed. John is particularly emphatic that we owe constant praise and thanksgiving to God and that praise should always be on our lips.

"I was speaking once at a group service about the first commandment: *I am the Lord thy God, thou shalt not have strange gods before me. You should love the Lord with all thy heart and with thy whole mind*. I have spoken about this in connection with New Age and other things, for example, about how putting material things before God is a form of idolatry. But on this particular occasion I spoke about how we pray, how we are always asking but how we are guilty of not praising God and not thanking God. The thing is, if you truly loved God as you say you do, you would be always thanking Him if He does something for you, just as you would thank a child who showed good behaviour in the house and did some chores for you. But a lot of the time we do not thank God and praise God for what He does for us.

"And we should, because praise exalts God. If you go to any charismatic meeting, they praise God all the time and thank Him with hymns of praise, waving their hands in the air. So when we pray, we should throw the word 'praise' in every now and again. It is important that we do that. It significantly helps our relationship with God to grow.

"I told this group a story about two angels sent down from heaven. They have two baskets. One of them is full of petitions and requests, overflowing. The other one contains thanksgivings but there is hardly enough to cover the bottom of the basket. The people knew immediately what I was getting at and I went on to tell them that as soon as they ask God for something, they should start thanking Him and praising Him right away in relation to whatever the petition is. Thanking God in advance and praising Him releases a supernatural power."

This may have sounded somewhat far-fetched to John's listeners but John invariably bases his teaching on experiences that prove the truth of what he says. Not long before that evening, a very specific event had occurred that reminded John very forcibly of the power that resides in words of praise.

Many children are brought to the Royal Infirmary in Belfast with various illnesses, usually serious. On one evening, a young child, only a few months old, was admitted to the children's ward. The worried mother called John and pleaded with him to come and pray for it. The child was very severely ill and was eventually diagnosed as having meningitis.

When John arrived he was met by the parents. The mother was clearly upset and told him that the child was close to death. She was crying, not only because the child was ill but also because was not allowed to be with the child. Doctors were working furiously, trying to stabilise the child, and visitors were not allowed at that time.

The mother knew, however, that she would be allowed in eventually and said to John, “The first opportunity we get to go in, you come in with me. Only two members of the family are allowed in at any one time, but you come in with me.” Her husband nodded agreement. He had not been allowed in either but he was happy to wait until John prayed over the child.

Eventually a doctor came to the mother and told her she could go in to see her child for a little while. The doctor was a very pleasant and sympathetic woman in her thirties. They followed her to the child’s bedside as she explained to the mother that the child was very seriously ill but that the medication was now sorted and there would be two nurses there all the time. She also assured the mother that she herself would be close by if her help should be needed. “The next twenty-four hours will be very critical,” she added. “but I, and these two nurses, will do everything in our power to save your child.”

She then turned to John who was standing slightly behind her, “I’m very sorry,” she said. “I’m doing all the talking and I have my back to you. Sometimes we forget how strongly the father feels as well as the mother.”

John said, “Don’t worry about that. No need to apologise. And just to put you right, I’m not the father. I’m not even part of the family.”

The doctor appeared somewhat nonplussed and said, puzzled, “How did you get in here if you’re not part of the family? It is only family who are allowed in at critical times like this."

John said, "I know the regulations but it was the mother who consulted me and asked me to come in because I pray for the sick and I was asked to bless this child with holy oil."

"Oh," she said, "so that's why you're here. Well, can I apologise to you again now because I am talking about all we are going to do for this child, and the importance of what we're doing. But what you're here to do now, and what God is here for, is far more important than anything I can do or the hospital can do. So, please, you go and bless the child and I'll stay out of your way."

"There's no need for you to leave the room," John said. "Two minutes will do me here, and I can pray longer for the child at home."

"No, no," she said. "You stay here and take whatever time you need because what you're here for is very important. I am a great believer in the power of prayer."

As she spoke these words John experienced a surge of power entering the room. "It was strong," he told his listeners one night at a service. "I could feel it going round that room, really strong. And I felt every bit of it. And I knew that that doctor, by the words she had spoken about the importance of prayer and how much less significant than prayer were the efforts of the hospital and the consultants, had called in healing on that child by glorifying God. And I knew that God's healing had already started before ever I myself said a word of prayer or even got to blessing the child. I knew it. And to this day I can still feel the power that surged through that room. It was amazing. You could have touched it. And when I stepped forward to bless that child, I could feel the power

going through her as well. That child was out
a few hours and it was sent home from hospital i
days, totally healed. And I heard God saying to me
'That doctor's faith really touched me and glorified m
Sadly I never got to see her again but I can say here and now that that healing came through her words. She released God's power by giving Him unstinting glory. She gave Him His place."

iv. Attachments

One of the themes that cause a number of John's listeners to question him assiduously after a service is the issue of 'attachments'. John defines 'attachments' as spiritual influences, usually demonic, that attach themselves to things that people have been given 'for good luck' or as a little ornament or blessing for the house. He explained that he has come across hundreds of people who have suffered inexplicable illnesses, misfortune of various kinds, depression or chronic uneasiness. All are in near despair wondering what can be the cause of their problem and when they contact John and he prays to the Lord for guidance, he invariably finds that there is something pagan in their house or about their person that is the root cause of their state.

"I remember one morning after eight o'clock Mass," he told his audience at a service towards the end of 2009. "I was working at St. Agnes Church and a woman came into the sacristy to me afterwards. She was in a bad state, very nervous, very agitated. She told me that she wasn't able to sleep at night and that she felt no peace at all in her home, even after Mass or when she prayed. She said that

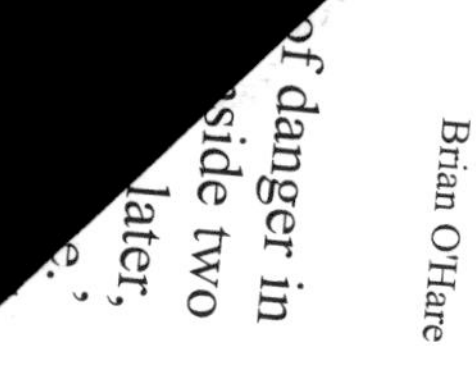

g that God wasn't in her house and g wrong with it.

I am listening to people explaining s already asking God to give me oot cause of the woman's problem. o talk, I felt the Lord telling me that something had been brought into her house and that there was demonic activity there. And the woman was suffering from the effects of it, even though she was going to Mass every day.

"I asked her if there was anything in her house that was not of God but she told me that she was sure there wasn't, that she would never have anything like that in her house. So I said, 'Maybe you have something in the house that you think is of God but is not of God.'

"She said, 'Well, if there is something like that in my house I don't know about it, but I would like to know about it.'

"Now, before I go on to tell you the story about what it was, I have to mention that during our talk she told me about something that she had found strange. There had been a leak in the bathroom a while back and they had to get a plumber in to fix it. He did what he could but he said he could not find what was causing the leak. So they got a second plumber to see if he could solve the problem. He was upstairs in the bathroom for the best part of two hours and when he came down, the sweat was running off him. 'Your tap's fixed now,' he told them. But then he said, sort of laughing but not laughing, 'Every time I tried to fix something, it kept going wrong. I could swear that I was wrestling with a demon up there.'

"The lady told me that she thought that was a very strange thing for a plumber to be talking about, a demon up in her bathroom. 'It's not normally something you hear from a plumber when he's having trouble fixing your taps,' she said.

"Three days later, when she was in the house on her own, she heard a loud crash upstairs. She ran up to the bathroom and found that one of the tiles had fallen off the wall into the bath. Now, if a tile fell into a bath like that, it might break into two or three large pieces. I would know that myself from my days in the building trade. But this tile was smashed into smithereens, hundreds of little bits scattered all over the bath. And she also said, 'You wouldn't believe the noise it had made.' So she was wondering if there was anything significant in this.

"When she told me this, I was given a vision from the Lord about two objects that had been given to the woman. And these two things were like a channel or an antenna, something that would pick up radio signals, except that in this case the signals were demonic.

"And I could see exactly what they were. One was a small figurine in the bathroom, a little statue of a faceless angel, and there was another one in a room downstairs. They were angels which the Lord had warned me about several times before. He has told me that there are satanic chants done over many of these faceless angels to bring harm to the Christians who buy them and He was telling me again that it was through these wee statues that the demonic force was getting into the house and disturbing the woman's peace.

"I asked her about the faceless angels in her house. She was surprised that I knew about them and told me that she had been given them as a present and that she had one up in the bathroom and another one down in the living room. She was shocked when I explained to her that they were the channel through which a demonic force was able to operate in her house. 'But I got them blessed by a priest,' she said. 'How could they be demonic?'

"I told her that there were evil chants done over them three times by Satanists and that if a priest blesses them only once, it doesn't do any good. 'You might as well throw jelly beans or confetti at them,' I said. 'Undoing the evil from these things takes special prayers and blessings and it is not until you get to the fourth blessing that the prayers can have any effect. Each special blessing is needed to get rid of each of the evil chants. It's only with the fourth prayer that the priest can do an effective blessing.'

"And there are hundreds of these things in Christian houses all over the country. They're everywhere and they're very dangerous. Some houses are full of them. I came across a woman in Belfast who had about five hundred pounds' worth of them in her house. That woman told me that her mother wasn't well. How could she be with all that stuff in her house?

"There is a huge spiritual battle going on all around us and every one of us is involved in it in some way and these things are part of the huge arsenal of weapons that Satan uses against us. And through them, we can leave ourselves open to demonic influences. When we buy them or accept them as gifts and take them into our homes, the spiritual forces start working against us. The woman who had the problem in her house threw out the angels that evening when she got home and I called later to bless the house. That woman hasn't had a problem since and she's sleeping great. But if those things had been left there, God knows where she'd be today or what other terrible things would be happening to her. Because these things escalate; they gain momentum. As their influence grows, they can bring all sorts of evil into a place. And here was this, all caused by Christian friends who gave the women these wee presents by way of a blessing for her house. But they were no blessing.

"And that is only one example. I could tell you about hundreds of cases that I've had to deal with. That's why I know about them and worry about them and why I am so emphatic that you should not have them in your house or about your person.

"There was another case I had recently. A woman came to me who had developed severe breathing problems. This was a problem that was completely new to her. She did tell me that she had slight asthma when she was young but that it had all been healed up years ago. She had been to the doctor about this new complaint and had been given medication that had no effect. In fact, she went on to have a severe chest infection for which she had been given antibiotics. They had no effect either. By this time, her breathing problems were getting more and more severe and she was now very concerned. She had made an appointment to come and see me at a house where I prayed regularly over suppliants.

"Now, when you go into a doctor's surgery with a problem like that, he'll examine you and tell you the problem is physical. But when people like me are approached, we first have to distinguish, through asking God for the Word of Knowledge and the power to discern, whether the illness is, in fact, a physical one, or if there is a spiritual force behind it. That's something we always have to discern.

"So, when I asked the Lord to help me discern the root cause of what was troubling this lady, I knew immediately that it was not a physical condition and that there was a spiritual force working against her. And she was a woman who prayed a lot. But the thing is, when

Satan has some sort of access to you and you pray a lot, he gets more and more annoyed and keeps upping the ante. So, the more you pray, the worse things he'll throw at you.

"In the case of this woman, when I prayed for the discernment to find the root cause of her illness, the Lord showed me a vision of scented candles. Remember, she came to me. I had never met her before and I had never been to her house but I knew, almost immediately, that she had a number of scented candles in her house. Now, the same thing goes on with scented candles as with faceless angels. Satanists chant over some types of candles these but of course, the retailers who sell them to the public know nothing about this. But the Satanists, or their supporters, send them out to shops with nice little messages on them so that Christians will buy them. And it doesn't matter what picture you have on the wall, be it Our Lady or a crucifix, and it doesn't matter how many rosaries you say, if you light that candle, you are making an offering to Satan, and you don't even know you are doing it.

"So I asked her if she had any scented candles in the house. She was very surprised. 'Oh, how did you know that?' she said. 'Yes, I have the house full of them. I love them.'

"'And how do you find them?' I asked her. 'I think they're brilliant,' she said.

"'Well,' I said. 'I need to tell you that those candles are the root cause of your problem. You are being subjected to spiritual attack and the demonic forces are getting at you through these candles.'

"She was horrified and, at first, she didn't believe me, although she was amazed that I knew about the candles. I told her a bit more about the Satanists and the chants they

do and she got frightened and aske
do. I told her she would have to thr
gave her some prayers to say for h
blessing to pray over her house. Sh
what I told her and she was able to pl
later to tell me that she was completel

"But what if she had not come to me? She was attached to those candles and evil was attached to them. Without the Lord's Word she never would have got rid of them and she could have ended up with something very serious indeed. What she was suffering from was a spiritual attack. It need not have been a breathing problem. It could just as easily have been something psychological like depression, or a haunting feeling of unease, or discouragement about her life. It could have been anything. And if you have those things in your house bringing in the occult force, praying your heart out is not going to bring healing. You have to deal with those things first and that means getting rid of them. It's like having a flat tyre. Pumping it up all the time will keep you going but it doesn't fix it. It has to be properly repaired.

"Satan is always finding loopholes to get into places, whether through the man of the house or the woman of the house. People are always giving each other wee objects and they say something like, 'This is to bring you good luck.' or 'This is to bring you a wee blessing on your journey.' And many of them are fine. But if I was to show you the things I have found in houses, things that were supposed to be religious objects, yet when I examine them, I know immediately that they're not right, hundreds of them. And I tell the people to throw them out. I don't care what they might have cost. They're not worth the damage they can do to your health, spiritual or physical or mental or all three.

e was a lady came to me feeling very tired, very lways exhausted. All the energy was drained out of body. She told me she had to go to bed every fternoon, something she never had to do in her life before. On top of that, her eyes were all red and swollen and one of them was all bloodshot and nearly closed. She was having a lot of pain with it and told me it felt as if something was stabbing it all the time. She had been to see a couple of doctors. She had various tests and examinations, had blood work done, but neither of the doctors could give her any idea what was wrong. They gave her some medication but it was useless. She was feeling desperate and when one of her friends mentioned me, she arranged an appointment immediately.

"As soon as I met her, I knew that here was a woman under spiritual attack. I prayed to the Lord for help to discern the root cause of her ailments and talked to her a while, asking her the kinds of questions that experience has taught me to ask. I asked her if she had any wee ornaments about the house that might be sort of odd but she said she couldn't think of anything like that. But then the Lord gave me the Word of Knowledge and I felt that someone had given her a lucky charm of some sort a little while back and that she was carrying it about with her. I put the question to her again, asking her if she had any wee good luck charms or something unusual that she had been given and that she carried about with her. She suddenly remembered that her son had come home from a holiday in Lanzarote a few weeks before and he had brought her home a wee present for good luck. She said that it was lying somewhere in the bottom of her handbag which was out in the car. She never looked at it much because she had never really liked it but only carried it about because her son had given it to her. It was a wee figurine and she had forgotten all about it.

"I asked her to describe it to me and she told me it was a wee 'Tasmanian devil', a sort of bright red wee thing that carried a three-pronged fork. And when she was describing it she sort of looked thoughtful and told me that every time she got the stabbing pain in her eye it was as if it was in three different places at the same time. When she started telling me this, I could see that she had more or less figured out for herself what was wrong. I told her that all her fatigue and her physical weariness and the pains in her eyes were all demonic attacks, focused on her through this 'Tasmanian devil' she was carrying about. And that was why the doctors couldn't help her. Spiritual problems can only be dealt with spiritually.

"I prayed with her and gave her some other prayers to say at home and told her to get rid of the thing. She threw it in the bin as soon as she got home and she was totally healed from that night.

"So you can see that many of these ornaments are very dangerous. Chinese Buddhas, all sorts of wee Eastern ornaments, all that Hallowe'en stuff, you never know what you're bringing into your house. You can't be too careful. And if you have a suspicion about something but you don't whether it is bad or good, throw it out. It might not be bad, but it also might be. Better safe than sorry. The least wee thing can become an antenna for the dev
some of his demons to zone in on.

"People talk about being frighter
things. No need to be frightened; i
and you'll be free of them. The
ignorance because that leaves you

v. False Guilt

John frequently speaks about forgiveness. It is probably the element of his preaching that he emphasises most. The Lord is love, he will say, total love. And what can love do but love? And love means forgiving all those who hurt you. In forgiving, we honour God and we become like God. But when we nurse a grievance, when we cannot let go of hurt, we are refusing to acknowledge the fact that God has forgiven us of everything and expects nothing less from us in return.

There is a parable in the New Testament about a servant who owed a king, his master, a large sum of money but could not pay. He pleaded with such heartfelt anguish to be given time to pay that the master remitted all his debt. As he left the king's palace, however, the official met someone who owed him a fraction of what he had owed the king. But instead of listening to the debtor's pleas for time to pay, he had him thrown into jail.

When the king heard of this, he recalled the ungrateful official, and said,

"Wicked servant, I forgave you all that you owed when you begged me to do so. Weren't you bound to have pity on your companion as I had pity on you?" The Lord was now angry and he handed the servant over to be punished until he paid his whole debt.

And Jesus added, "So will my heavenly Father do with you unless each of you sincerely forgive your brother or sister." [Matthew 18: 32-35]

[illegible]n remembers the first time he attempted to preach. [illegible]eek, he chose forgiveness as his theme:

"The first week I spoke about forgiveness and its importance. There were people there who reported various miraculous healings the very next week as a result of my praying over the congregation in accordance with the Word of Knowledge at the end of the service. What I was trying to do that night was to teach them about God's Law and the importance of forgiveness. I told them that we can pray and pray ... but so often we pray only with our lips. Very few people have problems saying prayers and rosaries but a lot of people have problems with God's conditions, and that is where we fail. St. John makes it very clear. He says, "Anyone who claims to be in the light but hates his brother is still in the dark." [John 2:9] It is easy to pray to a God who hasn't hurt you but to pray to God for forgiveness for someone who has hurt you, especially if they have hurt you very badly, is a different thing. But it is God's commandment that we forgive. Sometimes I would tell people that it is their own interest to forgive, that by forgiving they can lift a heavy psychological burden from themselves. And that is true. But there is a far purer motivation which is God's way, to forgive without hope of return or of any benefit to oneself. That's the difficult thing to do but it was always Jesus' way. 'Father, forgive them for they know not what they do.'

"But what sometimes happens is that people can forgive others but cannot forgive themselves. That is false guilt and there are so many good Christians who fall victim to it. But it is wrong. Carrying the guilt of something beyond a certain point, especially if you have been forgiven, becomes eventually a tool for the devil. He can use it to worm his way into our minds and challenge our hope. When you go on feeling guilty like that, you are rejecting what Jesus did on the Cross. When you make a decision not to forgive yourself, you are going up to Jesus on the Cross and slapping Him on the face as He hangs on the Cross and you're saying, 'You died for the sins of the world but you never died for me.' That's exactly what you are saying. And there is only one type of person that would ever encourage you to do that and that is a demon. What has happened is that you have become convinced by the demon. You are listening to the demon and not to God. God does not talk to us at any great length. He gives us a short word here and there for us to think about. But Satan will talk to you twenty-four hours a day if you let him.

"We're all told to examine our consciences but you can take it too far. You start analysing everything you do through and through, and of course you are going to find all sorts of faults. And the devil loves that and he'll be in there accusing you and accusing you. That's what the canticle was talking about: "For our brothers' accuser has been cast out, who accuses them night and day before our God." [Rev. 12:10] When you feel the weight of this accusation and the inner guilt that goes with it, fend it off. Just say plainly to God that you tried but failed and that you are sorry for that. Then tell Him you'll make it up to Him some other time. Christians are supposed to be joyous and at peace. But if you get too caught up in self-blame, you open the door for the devil and you end up depressed and discouraged. And where's the joy in that? Just say this wee prayer: "Lord Jesus, I forgive me because you forgive me. You died on the Cross for me. Thank you Lord for your forgiveness and now I forgive myself."

vi. The Effects of Past Hurts

Many of John's themes stem from the line in the Our Father – 'forgive us our trespasses as we forgive those who trespass against us.' He seems to find many insights into the concepts of forgiveness and trespasses that allow him to speak to the line from many different points of view. Very often his insights are tinged with significant psychological sense as well as moral guidance. One evening he went to speak at Chuain Mhuire. He introduced his talk with that line from the Lord's Prayer, talking about the trespasses that people have experienced against them.

"Why does our Lord tell us to forgive others who have hurt us? Because it is actually a condition of the Lord's Word that we forgive others. And there are psychological as well as moral reasons for obeying this command. If we don't forgive hurts that we have experienced in the past, the past still affects us and we have never been released. We are handcuffed to memories and to emotions and anger, whatever feelings we go on having. God has told us to forgive so as to break that hold over us. Somebody's got to open the handcuffs. And a lot of the time, the people who have caused you the hurt just carry on with their lives and they are not even aware of what they have done to you. But you are the one who carries the effect of it and you are the one who continues to feel the upset. Harbouring unforgiveness doesn't hurt the other person; it only hurts you. It's like a person who stabs you with a knife. They don't feel the pain. You do.

"There was a man called to see me one time, a joiner, a young man, probably in his thirties. And the minute he came through the door, I could see he was depressed because he had his head looking down at the ground, bowed over, and there was no joy about him. He just looked really sad. So I asked him what he wanted me to do for him. He said he wanted me to pray for him because he was very depressed, that he had been depressed for a long time and now he was on medication for it.

"I asked him if he had been to the doctor and he said that he had and that he had also gone for counselling as well. So I asked him if he had ever realised that there might be a root cause for this that would need to be sorted out and he told me he was aware of that but neither he nor the doctors were able to figure out what it was.

"He also told me that he had a girlfriend whom he loved but that he was afraid to consider marriage because he knew that he was often very temperamental and angry and could not find peace. He wanted to get married but he couldn't risk it with all this pain and rage that he sometimes felt … emotions that he could not explain. He didn't know where they coming from.

"So I told him that I would pray over him and try to find out about it. 'God will show me where it is coming from,' I told him. 'There's definitely a root cause for this. It didn't fall from the sky.' And I did pray for him. And as I prayed, I could see him growing up, going up through his life, especially from the seventh year on. I saw him working with his father, doing different things with him around the farm. I could see that the father was a very gruff man and he never praised the boy or showed him any affection … and he was always putting him down when he tried to do things. And I could see it in the seventh and the eighth, ninth and tenth years, and the eleventh and the twelfth. And it was all through those years that the boy did what he could to please his father but all he experienced was hurt and rejection. And he now felt in his own mind that he was no good, that he couldn't do anything right. He was carrying a deep anger and resentment and it was that anger that would boil up between himself and his girlfriend at times. It was caused by the father but the young man didn't know that.

"When God showed me this vision, I knew to ask the young man how he got on with his father because I wanted to hear how he still felt. And he said, 'I hate my father's guts. I would like to kill my father.' And I asked him if he knew why but all he could say was that he had always felt like that. So I told him that his father had never shown him any affection from when he was seven years of age, that he had always put him down, and that it didn't matter what he did for his father, it was never right. He was nodding with a serious face when I told him that and then I said, 'You have to forgive your father.' But he said, 'How can I do that? All I want to do is kill him.' So I said, 'Would you like to be healed of your depression?' And he told me that he would. 'Well,' I said, 'you will never be healed of your depression. You can pray novenas, go to shrines all over the place, but you will never be healed of this depression if you don't forgive you father because you are handcuffed now to the hurt and the pain and the emotions he has caused in you. Until you make the decision to forgive your father, you will always suffer from this depression.' And he said to me, 'I would find it very hard to forgive that man.' But I told him that he could make a start right away, that I would lead him in a forgiveness prayer that very minute. 'All you need to do is speak the words after me,' I said. 'You don't need to feel anything. Just saying the words is the start of making the decision.'

"I prayed the prayer and he said the words after me. I gave him a copy of the prayer and told him to keep praying it at home and to try also to pray for his father's soul. He said that he would do that. And he came back to see me a few times for further prayer, assuring me that he was still saying the forgiveness prayer and praying for his father. And that young man was healed, totally healed. And a few months later he was married and I am told they are very happy."

John went on to explain to his audience the importance of self-forgiveness. Some of them he knew to be people with addictions but he wanted to keep his remarks general. He also knew that many addictions stem from great hurts and he had hopes that what he said would affect some of them.

"Sometimes," he told them, "you feel victim of hurt and injustice. But it is important that we also look into our own lives. It could well be that we have done things ourselves that have hurt others. You can ask God to forgive you but perhaps your family or friends won't forgive what you've done. But the important thing is that once you repent of what you have done, God forgives you. If your family does not forgive you, that is their problem and they have a problem with God because of that. But ultimately it is not man's forgiveness that you need, it is important to get it, of course, if that is possible, but the real forgiveness you need is the forgiveness of God, because God's forgiveness will set you free, in ways you can't even imagine.

"And it is also very important that you forgive yourself because, if you don't, you are rejecting the sacrifice that Jesus made on the Cross to take on to Himself all the pain of our sins. If you don't forgive yourselves, you are rejecting God's forgiveness. Always remember that. God has forgiven many terrible sinners. John Newton was a slave trader who used to throw slaves overboard if they got sick on the ship on the way to England from Africa. He did terrible things. If there was any attempt at a mutiny, he would immediately kill the ringleaders. But his ship was saved in a storm once and he knew that a supernatural event had taken place. He studied about God and became a man of prayer and gave up slave trading and fought against it … and became a preacher along with John Wesley. And he was the man who wrote the words of the hymn 'Amazing Grace'.

"So, if God can forgive him and all the killing he did, and then he can go on to save thousands of souls, then surely He can forgive you." Then John laughed and said with a grin, "So there's hope yet for some of you down there."

John said later that a lot of the residents took his words to heart and remembered them. "There was great good will after that from everybody," he recalls. "And there were a whole lot of them came up to talk to me. And when I went back a few days later, I was approached by a young man from Tyrone who wanted to speak to me privately. He said to me, 'You spoke about forgiveness the other night and the importance of forgiving others and forgiving ourselves. I have never heard anything like that in my life. It didn't matter what I did, I always knew that I could never forgive myself. But I know now that I have to do it.' And then he said, tears in his eyes, 'As a result of your talk the other night, my mother is coming up to see me on Saturday. I haven't seen her in six years because I wouldn't talk to her. But after your talk, I thought about what you said and I phoned her and now she's coming to see me.'"

John goes on to say, "Addictions and hurts are often very close together. Very often the root cause of addictions comes from past hurts. There was a desperate case a while back of a young woman who came to me. She wasn't well at all. She was attending doctors but she was losing weight at an awful rate. The food she took was running through her. She was not all that heavy to start with but she was down now to fewer than six stones. It wasn't anorexia, but she had diverticulitis. She was having all these painful cramps and nausea and vomiting and was having an awful time with it.

"Also the ducts in her eyes had dried up so there was no fluid in her eyes. They were very painful. She told me that if felt like there was sand in them all the time.

"She had been suffering from this for months before she came to me and the doctors could do nothing for her. When I prayed for the root cause of this, I felt God saying to me that her problems were linked to her partner, that she was suffering a lot of stress and worry over her partner. And I was also led to know that the partner was drinking a lot but that he, too, was suffering very severe hurt from his own family and that was the cause of his drinking problem. And because of his drinking problem, his wife was suffering the side effects in her own home of the hurt that her partner had experienced from his own family.

"So I spoke to her about what the Lord had shown me and said, 'I think you're very worried about your husband. And you're keeping it all to yourself. And I believe alcohol is involved in it. But I also believe that your partner, too, is carrying a great hurt, something to do with his own family. And all these things are linked together, your partner's hurt, his drinking, your own ailments – the diverticulitis and the dry ducts in your eyes, your weight loss. I believe it's all the worry and stress and your organs can't cope with this going on all the time.'

"The girl looked at me and said quietly, 'I know exactly what you're talking about. My partner did suffer a great hurt and he's just admitted a few weeks ago that he has a drink problem.' I asked her if he always had that but she told me he didn't. She said, 'My partner comes from a very strong religious family, one of those Protestant groups but I'm not sure which one. But my partner stopped practising his faith some years ago. Initially the family did all they could to bring him back but he just wasn't interested. The father then cut him off from the family and they haven't spoken to him since.'

"And I said, 'Your partner is not drinking because he wants alcohol. He's drinking because of the hurt his father and mother have caused him.' Then I told her, 'You'll have to convince your partner to start praying and he'll have to pray for them and to forgive them, no matter how they act towards him. He has to get rid of that bitterness in his system or he'll never get better. And you won't either. And you yourself have to pray for them, too, because you're suffering the effects of that hurt as well.'"

John recounts how he explained the importance of forgiveness to her, how he gave her copies of the prayers she and her partner would have to say, and how he told her how to make the act of will and the decision to forgive. She agreed to do as he instructed her and John reports, "And she went on to be completely healed. The condition of her eyes, the diverticulitis, all totally cleared. Her partner stopped drinking and she put all her weight back on and suddenly their lives were happy again. I never heard whether his family was speaking to them yet but given the way they're praying, I'm sure the Lord won't let that sit."

Chapter Twenty - Three

"For I am not ashamed at all of this Good News;
it is God's power saving those who believe."
Romans 1:16]

At One with the Word

Much can be gleaned about John Gillespie and about the way he thinks, simply by reading the stories he tells, or by pondering the comments he makes about the spirituality that underpins the various situations he has to deal with. But there is still much we can learn about him and, more specifically, about the Word of God, by listening to his spontaneous but sharply perceptive comments in the interview recorded below. Once an uneducated builder's labourer, now a deep and articulate thinker, John is linked to the mind of God in such total surrender and with such boundless confidence, that his will seems no longer to be his own. And that is exactly how he wants it.

***

An Interview with John

Question: How long have you been engaged in the ministry of healing?

John: *I started in a sort of a way in 1995 but I suppose I was settled in the ministry about 1996.*

Question: Initially you were reluctant to undertake this ministry. How do you feel about it now?

John: *Oh, well, I suppose you could say that I enjoy doing it. What I particularly delight in is seeing people released from pain and being released from the power of evil. There's so much of the power of evil about, far more than many people realise. I'm very grateful to God for giving me this gift and this opportunity. I always enjoyed helping people. That was always something I wanted to do. Perhaps this ministry is in an area that can be very difficult at times but there is nothing I have to do in it that God hasn't given me the weapons to fight with. I am not unduly anxious about it the way I was at first. I know the battle can be tough but* [laughs] *I have a great Defender.*

Question: Most people have a one-way line to God but you seem to have a two-way line. That must be an extraordinary feeling?

John: *Well, I take it in my stride. People say to me, "How come you can experience this connection? You see someone throw away crutches because you say a prayer or two; are you not sort of jumping up and down about this?" But no, it is something I now accept as normal in* *my life. It's just a job, I suppose, like any other job. I just do it for God. I don't get all hyped up with emotions about it. You couldn't live your life like that for days never mind years. But I love it, I have to say. To see people healed ... and delivered from the evil one. And the connection with God, of course, that's the great bonus in the work. I strive to help people as hard as I can. I always go to God and I say, Show me ... show me ... show me ... what's behind all of this, so that I can get at it. I don't really go on praying and praying and praying, although I would sometimes have to do that at home about some cases, and fasting as well, but I keep demanding from God to give me the keys I need to get in here or in there.*

Question: Yes indeed! You often say, in your stories of healing, "The Lord told me," or "The Lord showed me." How exactly does He do this?

John: *Different ways. A lot of the time through a vision, or through the spoken word, the word of Knowledge, a voice within your head. You sort of hear it in your head.*

I'll give you an example. I prayed for a travelling woman a day or two ago who has been in and out of hospital with severe pains in her head. They scanned her and they did this and that. She had severe headaches, they were driving her crazy and painkillers were not fit to ease the pain at all ... even morphine. And she rang me, and over the phone she told me she'd been in hospital and they couldn't figure out what was wrong with her. She was scared there'd be a brain tumour and other stuff but nothing was showing up. So I prayed with her over the phone, and as I prayed I was asking the Lord what I should be praying for. And I felt the Lord saying to me,

"Ask her if her neck is sore, and ask her if she has pains in her shoulders." So I asked her and she told me that her neck was sore, that she could hardly move it and that she had pains in her shoulders, too. As soon as she said that, I felt the Lord saying to me, "Her spine is twisted. There is a part just below her neck where the spine is twisted that causing pressure up through her head." So, when I heard that, I started praying for her over the phone and, in Jesus' name, I commanded the spine to straighten. And in less than two minutes she started telling me that the pain had left her and that she could move her neck every which way. She was delighted..

Question: You say you 'felt' the Lord speaking to you. What exactly does that mean?

John: *Well, you hear words ... and they're very clear. You don't actually hear the voice of God but you know it's God that's speaking to you. It's like a little voice. It's not loud, it's sort of gentle. In fact, it's not actually a sound, but I can hear it so clearly. Maybe it is telepathic, you could say.*

Question: You say you sometimes get information from the bible. How does that work?

John: *Sometimes when I'm working in a difficult area and I'm not getting any answers through the voice of the Lord, it might be an ancestral thing where I have already got the vision but don't really understand what I'm seeing. I would sometimes pray for answers through the bible. Now, I wouldn't have the bible open; it would always be closed. But I would ask the Lord to give me the numbers of three pages, any three pages. The numbers of three pages will then come up in my head and I would* *write them down before I would open the bible. I would already have in my head what the Lord has already shown me or told me, say a vision, for example. Now, when I read these three pages, there must be something there to back up the vision I've seen because what God will show me somewhere in these pages will be the root cause of the problem I'm dealing with and He'll be telling me there what I need to do to sort the problem out. So basically, I get directions from that. And if what I need is not in those three pages, then I can't work on that problem. The anointing of God is not on it. God hasn't backed it up, so to speak. I might go back and pray some more, but the answer has got to be crystal clear. If it's not clear, then there is nothing I can do about that particular situation.*

Question: How does it work exactly, I mean, what do you see?

John: *Normally there will be words on the pages that will stand out to me immediately. It's like some lines are blacker than others, and when I study them I usually know exactly what I'm supposed to think about or do after that.*

Question: Do you ever fail to bring healing to a petitioner?

John: *Well, I'm not sure "fail" is the right word. Sometimes a petitioner isn't healed but is that God's fault? If God doesn't get the co-operation of the petitioner, it is unlikely that any healing will take place. I find that I've studied this stuff so much that I am always teaching the petitioner how to pray for healing. This last year, I hear God saying to me all the time, "Teach them. Teach them what they need to know, that they must have faith in me, how to pray, what to do, what not to do." I* *have seen many people cured of arthritis or spinal ailments within minutes and after a few weeks the pains come back. But what people have to learn is that they forget what they were told to do. They are not claiming their healing. They have stopped believing. They say, "Ah, well, that didn't work. I'll go to a surgeon or some other avenue." But, you see, they are not standing steadfast with the prayer words that they have been given. They seem to lose their faith and their understanding of what they were told to do. And you see, and here's something they don't know, very often Satan will attack the place that has been healed and bring pain to it. It might not be the arthritis back again, or whatever, but the petitioner feels the pain and thinks it's the original problem. And they start to say, "That's it back." But the minute you say, "That's it back," you show doubt and you've opened the door for Satan. If God comes and knocks at the door and you respond, we say that we're inviting Him in. If Satan knocks at the door and we react like that, we're inviting him in, too. So you've both of them in the house. How do you deal with that, huh? So, it's really the petitioner who fails.*

But there are cases, sometimes, when I just don't get early answers, when God does not reveal to me the knowledge I need to deal with the problem. Sometimes I have to go back to the person, and back a few times more. It's like an onion. You peel one layer off, and then another and then another. You might have to peel six layers off, but you can't get to the layer you're looking for until you peel off the other six. Sometimes I never find what I'm looking for, because God has other plans for that person. There's no way that I or anybody else can control that.

Question: How does that make you feel?

John: *Well, it's ... the way I see it is that God's trying to bring healing to*

everyone. It's how I exercise my ministry and how people want to receive it. I know full well that no matter how much I pray or how much I fast, God is not going to give me control over all healing. I know that. I might want control and want everybody I meet to be healed, indeed, that's what I pray for. I keep praying and striving for it. It's a bit like those great sportsmen who are never happy with their last victory but are out looking to win again. That's what they strive for, and I feel a bit that way too. I strive for that in healing, to learn more. I try to learn different things from different avenues. I keep praying the Lord, "Show me more. Show me more." I'm not happy just to sit still and do the same thing over and over again. I want to keep learning, getting greater and greater insights into the healing process.

Question: So you would never fall into the fallacy of assuming that, if there is a failure of healing, it is your fault?

John: *Well, there might have been cases away at the beginning where I might have thought, "Yes, I've lapsed here," or "I could have prayed harder over that one" and you'd feel hurt after you'd lost a few people, especially that young woman with cancer. She had three young children. We did everything around that healing, I prayed and fasted. Eddie Stone and Joe Dalton were praying for her, too, and there was a nun praying for her as well. All of us were praying for her healing, praying for an anointment. But she died. We thought we had failed. We all thought she was going to be healed. Everyone had the* *word that she was going to be healed. But the healing was that God had prepared a wonderful place for her in Heaven. But I was a bit hurt by that at the time.*

Question: You spend much of your life praying for others. Do you have much time in your life for personal prayer?

John: *Well, my life is so linked with God at the moment that I'm never*

sure when I'm praying and when I'm not, or maybe it's all one constant prayer. He's always in my head, even if I'm not saying words. Now and again I would say a wee prayer for my own needs. I would ask God for something that's necessary for me and then, knowing I have it, I would start to make claims for it, short wee prayers quite frequently, until I get what I need. I mean, this job I'm doing, there are plenty of difficulties that come with it. And there are times when I need a lot of help. I would pray for that help. And now that the ministry has expanded this year, with me having started going out and preaching the Word, there are even more problems to contend with. A lot of difficulties have come with that. There's a lot of hidden stuff behind all that, stuff that people don't even realise or don't understand what you're going through. You've all these forces lined up against you but you have to battle through all this stuff. You've got to carry on. It's at times like this that I would be more aware of my need for personal prayer.

Question: I'm not sure that I'm following you. What kind of difficulties?

John: *Well, don't forget that people in my line of work are on the front line of a huge spiritual battle. We're* *very vulnerable out there. We're sort of the main contenders and we're targets for Satan. I'm in his sights all the time just as he is in mine. But that's part of the deal. You accept that. But from time to time he has a real go at you and you need to turn to the Lord for extra help. But that's not something I talk much about.*

Question: Okay! I'll move on. Do you ever do "group" healings?

John: *Well, there are those healing services that I do every now and then at different places. So many people are coming for help that I had to do something to be able to heal with the one prayer instead of repeating myself over and over again.*

Question: How do they work? Have any successful healings that you know about taken place in a group situation?

John: *All sorts, and a whole lot that I wouldn't know about if the people didn't get back to me or to some of the people who help with my appointments. There was one woman last week who was blind in one eye for seventeen years. I had my head down up at the top of the room and I was simply saying what the Lord was telling me to say. I repeated what I heard in my head, "There's a woman over on the left side of the room who has been blind in one eye for seventeen years. The Lord is going to heal you." I didn't feel anything but after the meeting was over and everyone was leaving, a woman came up and told me that she was the one with the blind eye and that as soon as I spoke the words, her eye began to burn and before the meeting was over, she was able to see perfectly out of it.*

Question: That must have been an extraordinary moment?

John: *Well, yes, of course. But I'm sort of used to it. It's happening all the time.*

Question: At one of these meetings you spoke about New Age therapies. What are your views on these?

John: *With any therapy or any healing, you must find the root source of where the illness is coming from. Any praying I do, even when I'm doing it at those public occasions, you can listen to the words that I speak. You can actually record them. And every time I speak, even before I start to pray for any healings anywhere, in private or in public, I always start with a forgiveness prayer, for ourselves, for our ancestors, for those who sinned against them. I always pray for forgiveness first. God has stipulations. You just don't go looking for healing without forgiveness and you certainly don't go opening yourself up to other avenues like New Age therapies. Most of those New Age therapies are rooted in false gods and false religions from the Far East and elsewhere. They're all false gods. None of those gods have ever died on the cross for us. You, as a Christian, cannot adapt your healing or prayers for healing to include these false gods. If you do that, you're moving into the demonic. It depends what you are into with your New Age ideas. But you can be sure that any therapy that takes its power from a source that's not coming directly from Our Lord Jesus Christ has to be avoided. As I've told you before there's the white, and then there's the light grey and the grey and the black. If you move out of the white at all, even if it's only into the light grey, you are already* *moving into the devil's territory, because the Lord's territory is only the white.*

Question: So your advice is to avoid all New Age therapies no matter how innocent they appear?

John: *Well, if these therapies are so good, the way they are presented to be, then I don't know why I have people coming to me that have spent hundreds, maybe thousands, of pounds on these New Age therapies and have not been healed, and yet they can come to me with the same problem and a prayer to Jesus has them healed within minutes. If it's so good, why is that the case? The fact is that some of the people promoting it are making a lot of money out of it, and that's just the ordinary worldly disadvantage with it. What about the effect on the immortal soul when you stray too far into a false religion as so many of the practitioners innocently do?*

Question: Often when you talk about New Age, you express concern about faceless angels and scented candles. Where does this concern originate?

John: *I don't believe Our Lord ever had faceless angels. I don't think he has faceless angels up in Heaven. The thing is, when Satan was kicked out of Heaven after the battles there, he was accompanied by the angels that supported him. They're all angels, but Satan's crowd are now known as demons. So you have all these faceless angels that have come on the market now, and Satan's angels that are plundering on this earth are also faceless. They sneak around in the shadows and in the dark and they won't show their faces. So these faceless angels* *represent what Satan represents. And to my mind it is well known now that there are Satanic chants done over a lot of these things before they are ever released on the market. It's the same with the candles. The Church has already spoken about them. Father Rupert Pererez from India has found out that there are Satanic chants said over a whole lot of those scented candles, not them all, but a lot of them. Christians are buying them, especially Catholics who have a tradition of lighting candles, and they burn the candles. If a Satanic chant has been said over a candle and you burn it in your house ... it doesn't matter if the bible is in your house or there's a holy picture up on the wall or the priest has blessed the house, you are doing an offering to Satan unknown to yourself.*

Question: Are these Satanic chants done deliberately?

John: *Yes. It's known by Satanists that Christians will buy these candles and this is one of the hundreds of ways that Satan tries to undermine Christianity. He's got millions of helpers everywhere, on the earth as well.*

Question: What advice would you give to people who believe New Age healing is harmless?

John: *That's simple. If you think it's harmless you're deluded and you're asking for trouble. Stay away from New Age. If you want to be healed, what's wrong with going to Jesus? And the side-effects of Jesus' healing are all wonderful and positive. The side-effects of New Age healing ... you're talking about misery and disaster.*

Question: Does the devil ever attempt to inhibit your ministry?

John: *Of course he does. That's his job all the time. If you have a major healing success, or the word spreads about what you're doing in Jesus' name, Satan hates that. You can rest assured that he'll be raging. He'll have all guns trained on you to try to stop you. He really hates any success God might have no matter what it is. And healing especially. When a healing takes place as a result of my prayers to Jesus, I don't ask or want any thanks for it. I tell the petitioner to give thanks and glory to God. That drives Satan mad altogether. When those who are healed go about spreading the word about what has happened and giving glory to God and thanking him, Satan can't stand that. He does not want to see or hear God gloried in any way. He hates it with a vengeance and because I'm the one put there picked by our Lord to do this, he's out to get me twenty-four seven. The result is that there are all sorts of annoying wee things happening in my life, that's an on-going thing, from small things like the car not starting or being crashed into, to the sort of things I told you about that have happened to my family.*

Question: Talking about the devil, how difficult is it for you to deliver people from demonic oppression?

John: *Some of the deliverances are very straightforward. Some minor demons can be chased in a few minutes. Over the past while I have got stronger and have more confidence about this part of my ministry. But some deliverance events can be problematic. If in my prayers I am warned that the case coming up is a difficult one, I will sit and pray with the Lord before I go to the* *victim and I ask God which demons I am going to be dealing with. After that, when I go to the house or meet the individual, I'll come with all the knowledge with me. I'll go to the person knowing that there are four or five or six demons to be dealt with and I'll know who they are and the order of their strength and the order in which to start getting them out. Because the Lord has already informed me, I don't need to get into a big debate with the individual about all this. I don't need to spend hours with the person trying to figure out who's possessing him or oppressing him. I already know before I even get there. I know the five or six demons and I know the rotation and all I'll need to find out from the person is how the demons got in. Once I know that, I'll get the person to start praying for forgiveness for whoever brought him hurt or to repent from the past behaviour that brought him this oppression and then I start casting the demons out, one after the other.*

Question: Is it easy, or difficult, for the person under demonic influence to say the prayers of forgiveness or repentance that you need them to say?

John: *This is the area where I have to take authority because the Lord's not going to come down to do it. I have to be very authoritative with what I do. I stress to the person and insist that they have got to repeat the words of forgiveness or repentance after me, just repeat them. That's all they need to do at this point. But you'll find that when the person is speaking the words, the demon will try to interfere, to invalidate what I'm doing. They're quite clever at that. They will stutter up the victim's voice so that the words are not clear. Then at some point, they'll* *change the words. It might even be only one word. For example, I will have told the victim to say "I repent" but what will come out in a slurred way is "I resent", and if I let that go and continue the prayer for even another twenty seconds, I will have lost that whole deliverance before I have even started, because the forgiveness is not done. Satan is so cunning. Even one word, only slightly twisted, is enough to wreck the deliverance. So what I do is, I stop everything immediately and go back and start again and ensure that the petitioner says the prayer perfectly with me. And when I'm doing that I am also binding the demon because I'm taking authority and letting the demon know he has absolutely no right or control here. I would tell him, "You're not having any authority here ever this person, over his speech, over his mind. I am the one who has authority here in Jesus' name ... and you are leaving this person now."*

Question: How often are you called upon to bring this kind of healing?

John: *Deliverance is as much a part of my ministry now as is praying for healing or forgiveness, because when you are dealing with someone who is suffering deep hurt or trauma, for example from sex abuse or something like that, there are always demons behind that, all the time You've got demons of lust, of pain, of anger, of hurt ... you'd be amazed at the millions of them that are out there. But I don't let the person know that. I pray to take those forces away. I know how those forces work and how keen they are to get at this body and this mind. So I just pray through these situations. Once I can get the person to forgive or repent and start repeating prayers after me, I can take authority over these forces in Jesus' name and cast them out of there. People need to realise that when* *they go out to do evil, like those young thugs you read about who kick people in the head and kill them, that's demonic. They are under demonic influence. That does not mean the demon is actually in them, he might be, but he can also be influencing them without being in them. That's called oppression.*

Question: How much of the evil we do is a result of our fallen nature as opposed to demonic influence?

John: *Our fallen nature is a result of the sin of Adam and Eve. And why did they sin? Because they were under the influence of Satan. Anybody who would try to minimise the effect of the devil's influence on the evil we do is almost trying to deny the devil, to deny his strength and his power. And he has great influence over those who reject and refuse God's grace. If you allow sin to rule your life, you are opening yourself up to demonic influence.*

Question: Thank you. Let's move on to something more mundane. You have a wife and children. How do you provide for them?

John: *When I'm travelling here and there, people give me offerings and donations to pay my expenses. If I get more than I need for a bit of food for the family and to pay a few bills, I will hand the rest to charity or give it to someone who needs it. Sometimes people will offer me money and God will say to me, "You're not to take that money." Other times He might say to me, "Take it but pass it on ... to whoever ... somebody in need." I don't live any sort of extravagant life and I don't need any money and I know I'm not going to take anything with me* *when I go and if I'm called tonight* [John laughs] *there'll be no money left for people to be fighting over. And if I'm called in twenty years' time, it will be the same way. Christina and I live from day to day. In Father Ronnie's prophecy, Christina was called to be my partner and support in this ministry, so we always live from day to day. It doesn't bother us. We know that God will always see to it that we'll have as much as we need.*

Question: There can be no doubt that you are in a position to make more money than that. Why don't you?

John: *It's not about making money. You have to survive, and that's all I do. Money is useful, but as far as I'm concerned it's for passing around to help everybody. I don't charge anybody anything. Many people give me some small amounts, some a bit larger which I usually don't take, and some nothing at all. But that's all right. I know that Lord will always ensure that I can pay my bills and feed my family. It's a long way from what I might earn if I had a secular job but I need no more than that. God gives me the breath to breathe and the power to walk. I'll always have enough.*

Question: Do you ever get people accusing you of fakery or, perhaps, mind-games of some sort?

John: *Lots of people don't believe in what I do and, yes, I suppose some of them think I'm spoofing, or something. But the strange thing is that a lot of people who don't believe and who haven't been to church for years and years but come to me anyway because they were recommended to come by somebody else, they walk away healed, totally healed. There was one man, he was a* *mechanic, you might want to put this in a story, but he was a Protestant and he wasn't even going to Protestant church. But because he had spent so much of his life bending over bonnets and peering into engines, he was now hardly fit to move or bend. He went to see consultants in hospitals who found all sorts of problems, pains in his hands, some kind of bone disease. His spine was twisted and he couldn't stand up straight. But he was a great mechanic, and, on top of that, very honest and very reliable. But there was another Protestant, a woman, who had come to me and got healed of many things, who asked this man to come and see me. But he said, 'No, I don't believe in that sort of stuff. There'd be no point in me going to somebody like that, I wouldn't believe a word he was saying.' But the woman told him that he was still a young man, far too young to be so crippled that he couldn't work. 'You need to get healed,' she told him. 'You're helping other people all the time. It's time now for you to accept a wee bit of help for yourself.' But he wouldn't go. 'I read about those guys,' he told her. 'It's all hypnotism or something.'*

But his health got worse and worse, particularly his bones and his back, and he had to give up his job as a mechanic. This Protestant woman got to hear about that and she went back to see him. 'Right,' she told him. 'I'm having no more nonsense out of you. I'll be here in the car for you at two o'clock on Wednesday and you're coming with me. You might say "No" to everyone else, but I'm not taking "No" any more. You're going to see John.'

And right enough, when she arrived there on Wednesday, he was ready. She had great difficulty getting him into the car because he was hardly fit to walk or bend and he was in awful pain, even on the journey down. When she got him to the house, we brought him in and we had trouble even getting him down on to a chair because he was almost crying with the pain. So I prayed and I prayed, and I felt that his spine was all twisted and out of alignment, working at cars all the time. I couldn't touch the legs at all; they were causing him such pain. So I prayed over the legs and one leg, you always find this in people with back problems, one leg was shorter than the other. I prayed for it to lengthen, for the pain to leave the leg. I prayed for his spine and for it to straighten. And now he's up walking about, cured. That was about six or seven years ago and that man is still working on cars all the time. He has never come back himself but he has sent plenty of other people. [John laughs aloud] *He's doing the work of God. He thought at the start that I was a fake, but he doesn't think that now. Every time he meets somebody that's sick, he sends them to me.*

The thing about that is ... it's very strange. I prayed over a woman the other week and she was completely healed. It was a real miracle. She had a friend who had the same problem and came to me for healing. But she didn't believe. She reads the Word in chapel occasionally but she's only doing it with her lips. She has no faith. And she wasn't healed. And it's not me that she needs to have faith in. She or anyone else can call me what they like. It's nothing to do with me. Jesus does all the miracles. And I do not have to defend myself, and I do not have to defend God, but some people can't even believe what they see with their own eyes. And yet there are thousands of God's miracles all around us every day. I will go on doing what the disciples did, praying to Jesus for people who come to me for help. But I can't make people come to me or believe in my prayers or in Jesus' power if they don't want to. That's their problem.

Question: For many Catholics, priests are the natural successors of Jesus' disciples. Why do you think the priests of today do not seem to have healing powers or the skill to cast out demons?

John: *Well, there's probably something in the old saying, 'You do not have because you do not ask.' A lot of the time, when you're called into a ministry like this and you feel the call, you still have to pray for it and you fast for it. The Lord gives you something to do and, if you're good enough at that, He enhances it and He brings on your ministry. But you do not jump out of bed one morning and say, 'Lord, I'm going to become a healer,' and expect that to be that. It doesn't work like that. You must surrender to God. It's all about surrendering to God, because every time I go out, it's total surrender. There's no knock on effect. Past successes are just that, past. It doesn't matter how many times I have prayed for healings, how many people have already been cured of cancer or whatever, I don't know how many crutches have been thrown away this past while, maybe six. I couldn't tell you how many spines have been straightened this year alone ... hundreds. And all sorts of cancers and other ailments healed, I see that all the time. But when I start to pray for somebody new, it starts all over again. It's fresh, it's different, it's particular to this person. You don't know what's going to happen. You're walking off a plank every time into shark-infested waters. You're stepping out in faith into a total unknown. People talk about the comfort zone of God. But there's no comfort zone when you stand up waiting for the Word of Knowledge in front of a big hall full of people who are expecting you to pray for healing, people that God is telling you to pray for and you standing there with absolutely no idea what God's going to do on this occasion. It's total trust, total surrender.*

There's no comfort zone there. You're totally out on a limb.

And it's great talking in church about God's work and doing the readings and all that, but stepping out to do God's work is a different thing. You have nobody behind you, nobody with you. You're like a boxer in a ring. It doesn't matter how good your trainer is or how many fans you have or how many are against you, in the ring you're on your own.

Question: I think there are two issues here. I mean , you're in the boxing ring alone … are you saying that the enemy, the devil, is singling you out, or are you saying that you have to depend on God not to leave you out on that limb to face criticism or blame if healing does not take place?

John: *Basically what I am saying is that many people, I'm sure, would love to have the gift of healing but how many would be willing to pay the price? There is a price to be paid. That price is endurance. It's spiritual warfare. It's coming under severe criticism from people, even from the Church. And it's coming from the attacks you have to face from the devil. It's all there. And a lot of people don't want to get into this ministry because they'll say "What if somebody's not healed? What if somebody dies?" I'm sure when Our Lord was about, there were people who died. Many looked at Him as simply a person, not as the Son of God with the power of God, and so they had no faith. And where there was no faith, Jesus' hands were tied. He went back to His own town, we're told in the New Testament, and He could work hardly any miracles there because He found so little faith.*

Question: So priests, if they want to get into the healing ministry, to be genuine inheritors of the disciples' ministry, they would have to open themselves up more to God, to pray for the gifts of the Holy Spirit? Would this have been taught in the seminary?

John: *They would have to open themselves, but they would hardly have come across that in the seminary. The healing ministry comes from the nine gifts of the Holy Spirit and the priest who seeks those would have to open himself up to the Holy Spirit. It is very different from formation. The ministry of the priest, that's about being out and talking about God and looking after your parish. But surrendering to God is something else. They're two totally different things.*

Question: But even holy priests, and I know many very genuinely spiritual priests, would have a problem with that, surely?

John: *True, not everybody gets the gifts. The gifts ... you sort of sense that something special might happen and the way to respond is to pray and pray for the gift or gifts and then you might one day get a sensation that something has happened to your mind, or maybe a sensation going through your body, that gives you the power to do things. But then you've got to step out. And every time you pray over someone, you know ... I know ... that every time I pray over a sick person there's absolutely nothing I can do for the person. Only God can help them. I have to rely completely on the power of God. I take as much authority and as much faith as I can over that situation, and that is important, it's part of the gift. But the Lord does the healing.*

Question: So where does that leave the ordinary priest, if I could call him that, in terms of discipleship?

John: *Well, one priest told me that he fully approves of what I do, a good, holy man that I know well. But he also said to me, "Your ministry is a very specialised one and priests like me have so much parish work to do - Masses, confessions, visits, committees, and loads of other stuff that might seem in comparison to what you're doing to be very mundane - but it's got to be done. It's very important. If we got into healing and deliverance we would have no time for the ordinary work." So, yes, priests have to do Church work, but healing and deliverance is all about the gifts of the Holy Spirit. You see things differently; you see scripture differently. I can lift a bible and I can see one line and adapt it to a whole lot of situations that only I can see. I suppose if most priests started going on like that, they would maybe end up neglecting some of the very important work they do.*

Question: Yes, I believe that is a very important point. But back to your own ministry, what is the hardest part of it?

John: *What is most difficult about this kind of ministry is trying to take it in your stride, and not get caught up in all the hurt and the pain that people are suffering. You'd wear yourself out very quickly if you gave way to that. You have to keep trying to remember that you're a human being and that you're very limited in what you can do. I mean, in my fifteen years or so I have seen thousands of miracles Jesus performed in answer to my prayers, but the need out there is so great that I feel that I am just a very small fish in a massive lake. And then you* *feel for ... em ... sometimes your prayers don't work all the time. Some cases, even really serious ones, you can sometimes get them healed in a couple of minutes. Other times you pray and pray, and you have to go back and back, and it's a long time before your prayer is answered. But a lot of that has to do with the people themselves. If they were to get an instant healing, they would never change. Part of the healing is a spiritual awakening, and some people need time to come to that. You nearly need to grind them down and down to get them to go the Lord's way. And that applies to me too. I'm going to have to make changes next year in the way I think and work. But I have always to be aware not to take the thing too seriously to heart. If I were to really take this to heart, I don't think I could go out through the door. The enormity of what goes on around me, it's way beyond anything I ever could have imagined. But it's not me that's responsible. I'm only an instrument, and that's the level I have to keep my thinking at. I can't be breaking my heart every time a healing turns out differently from what the suppliant hoped for. In the end, what I have to do is to take the Lord's instructions, do what He tells me to do, do the praying, and then I have to walk away saying, "Now, Lord, I've done my bit. The rest is up to you. I can't do it." [John laughs] Because I have to let Him know, too, that this is His ministry as well.*

Question: So, it's very important that you avoid the pronoun "I" when you talk about what is being done. You would never say, "I did this healing, or I did that healing"?

John: *Oh, Lord, no. Once the 'I' comes in, Satan is right in behind it, straight away.*

Question: What is the best part of your ministry?

John: *Ah, that's easy. The greatest part of what I do is watching God's power at work, over and over and over again. When you see consultants and doctors baffled or giving up because nothing can be done, and then you say a wee prayer and you see tumours vanishing and spines straightening, or you pray for people down over the phone and they're healed. It's extraordinary. I mean, imagine if there was a surgeon in the hospital and people were saying that he can heal your bad back or your cancer over the phone. He wouldn't get a minute. And yet I'm praying over the phone regularly and God does the healing. There's no greater feeling. God is wonderful.*

Question: How do you see your life in, let's say, twenty years from now?

John: [Laughs] *I don't even see midnight tonight. I never plan ahead. I live from day to day. I drift in the Lord's wind. I have no plans for this ministry. I just do what the Lord wants done. I have had so many offers to do this and to do that but if God doesn't want me to do it, I won't look at it. And I always know when the Lord doesn't want me to do something.* [Laughs] *I don't need plans. God takes care of all of that.*

***

John Gillespie continues to help God's people. The cries for help grow louder and come from many different sources and many different directions. He feels their need and, while he wants to refuse no one, there are many whom he cannot reach. He wishes he could do more but, as he says himself, "... the need out there is great and I feel that I am only a very small fish in a very big ocean. I'm just not able to get to everybody." How he can respond to all of the calls he does not know. Already he has to work many nights to try to keep abreast of the demands for help that reach him. What he can do or where he goes from here, he does not know. Larger venues? Bigger crowds? He doesn't know. He waits in faith and in patience for the Lord to make whatever changes are necessary in his life to enable him to deal with greater numbers of petitioners in the finite amount of time available to him.

But still he tries. January 2010 has seen Ireland hit with one of the worst winters in over thirty years. The roads were treacherous and the frost and snow so widespread that the Roads Services were scarcely able to grit the principal highways. Minor roads were left untouched and many were covered with hard ice and packed snow. Despite this, John phoned Sister Briege on the first Tuesday of the month, as usual, to tell her that he was preparing the make the fifty mile drive to the Shrine for his monthly service. Sr. Briege told him that the roads around Faughart were very dangerous and that they would be even worse when he had to drive the fifty miles aback to Belfast after nine o'clock that night.

But John was not to be dissuaded. All he said was, "I have to be there, Sister. Someone might need me."

Someone will, John. Someone will.

ENDPIECE

[by Sr. Briege O'Hare]

A few years ago Francis McNutt published his book "The Nearly Perfect Crime". He added a subtitle: How the Church Almost Killed the Ministry of Healing. In his introduction he makes it clear that his desire is to help the Church return to an essential part of the life that Jesus Christ came to give us. It is a sad fact that the ministry of healing, which the Spirit poured out on the Church at Pentecost, and which was vibrantly operative in the early life of the Church, gradually declined and, indeed, was almost totally lost to us. In fact, over the centuries, were it not for the belief among the common people and their faith in God's love for them, this wonderful ministry of healing would indeed have been lost. Even to this day, within many circles in the established churches, the term faith healer is a term of reproach and those who believe in the desire of God to heal through prayer and who exercise their faith by praying for the sick are often at best dismissed as somewhat naïve, or even ridiculed.

Thankfully God, who is always faithful, is restoring this wonderful gift of healing to churches across all the religious denominations. John Gillespie is but one of the many people called by God to restore this ministry which is so central to the Gospel life. There are now many books available on the healing ministry but The Miracle Ship is unique in the way the author brings the reader into the mind and experience of John in the exercise of his ministry. John is passionate in his belief that

Jesus came to bring us healing and deliverance at every level of our being and that even today Jesus desires to continue to do this for His people. It is obvious that John has spent many years in a search to understand how to bring the healing of Jesus to the people who come to him and in this book he generously shares with his readers the insights that he has received through his prayer and experience. Sometimes it can be disheartening for people in ministry, who sincerely try to answer the call of Jesus, to pray for the sick only to find their prayers do not seem to be answered. This book is a great encouragement to such people not to lose heart but to learn the ways of this wonderful ministry so that, through the Holy Spirit, God's afflicted people can again experience the healing power of Jesus.

Here in Dundalk at the Poor Clare Monastery of the Light of Christ, John has become a regular part of the ministry of the Sisters and the Lay Associates. He brings a special giftedness, not only in his ministry of healing but also in his person. His unpretentious manner and good humour are well suited to the spirit of joy and simplicity which our founders St. Francis and St. Clare so valued as true signs of the Gospel. St. Francis frequently sent the sick and oppressed to St. Clare's monastery where she and her sisters were renowned for their powerful healing and deliverance ministry. Today, at our monastery in Dundalk, we like to think that Francis and Clare recognised in John a true brother and have led him to our monastery to be a brother to us. I thank God for this book and pray that those who read it will find courage and faith to follow the command of Jesus, "Go out to the whole world; proclaim the Good News to all creation." [Mk 16:16]

Briege O'Hare osc

Poor Clare Monastery of the Light of Christ

Faughart,

Dundalk,

Ireland

APPENDICES

APPENDIX 1

Personal Testimonies

(written by the suppliants in their own words)

Josephine's Story: You Don't Call Illness on Yourself

[Reproduced verbatim from a recorded conversation with Josephine Clerkin, (real name)]

I live in a beautiful coastal village in County Down in Northern Ireland. I am married, with three children, and I was thirty-six years of age when I first heard of John Gillespie. That was sometime in May, 2000. At that time a number of people in my family were suffering from various illnesses, some of them very serious. There was psoriasis, arthritis, osteoporosis, asthma, even heart disease. I was talking about this to a friend one day and she told me about this great man, John Gillespie, who lived in Belfast and who had a great reputation as a healer. She gave me John's number and I phoned him.

I asked him if he was a faith healer and he laughed and said, "No, I'm not." So I said, "I'm sorry. I must have the wrong number. Sorry about that."

But before I could hang up, he laughed again and said, “I don’t do anything but I have a gift from God and He does healings when I pray for people.”

That’s John. He never wants people to think that he does the healing. After a short conversation, we made an arrangement that he would come to my house the following Tuesday evening. When I finally met him, I must say I was very surprised. I was expecting an old man but when I was welcoming him into my house, my immediate thought was, “Good heavens! What a young man to have such a great gift.” I suppose he was around his mid-forties at that time.

All my aunts and uncles and other relations were there and it was arranged that John would stay in a separate room and the people would go in to him one by one. And as I sat there, this was going on for a long time, I saw people coming out of the room very emotional, some of them in tears, some of them very quiet and prayerful, some very delighted and relieved. And as I saw these different things happening I said to myself, “This is unbelievable.”

As the night went on, the phone started ringing and more and more people were asking if they could call in to see John. What was happening was that as each of my relatives went home after their prayers, they began telling other people about the great man down at Josephine’s house and that they should go down for a prayer. I was getting a bit worried about this and I knocked the door and said to John, “I’m sorry, John, but I’m getting all these phone calls. There are more and more people wanting to come.”

John just said, “That’s OK. Tell them to come on ahead.”

So that prayer session went on until half-past one in the morning. When it was all over and everyone had gone, I said to John. "I feel that there is a great peace in my house now. I believe that something good has happened here tonight."

The thing is that after John left and I went into the sitting room, there was a lovely smell of roses and I said to myself, "Well, really that is God's work."

The next day I talked about all of this with my husband and we agreed that for as long as John was needed by sick people we would let him use our house. I set up a time with John for the following Wednesday night and said to the Lord, "Well, really God, if this is from you the phone will ring."

And indeed, it kept ringing, and it has been ringing now for almost thirteen years. We had to change the time to afternoons on Wednesdays because the evening sessions were running far too late into the night. Every week since, to this day, people are phoning in for appointments with John on the Wednesday with all sorts of different things wrong with them. And all word of mouth, no advertising. People come in and get a great healing and great comfort from John and they go out and tell others. Just word of mouth. And that has been going on all these years, and it is still going on. And every week I saw his work. I saw the way he was working with the people, and I saw and heard about some amazing healings and miracles.

But then, about seven years after John started using my house for healings, it was March 2007, I decided to go to the doctor. I did not have any reason to go but I thought I would go for a check-up. The doctor asked me if I was feeling unwell but I told him that I wasn't, that I was feeling good. So I got some tests done and some days later

I went to Daisy Hill hospital in Newry for the results. That was when I was told that I had cancer of the cervix. When you get told you have cancer, it's an awful shock. I could feel my whole body sinking into the chair. I was just drained. I didn't know what to think and I said to the doctor, "How bad is this?"

She said, "I don't really know how bad it is or how bad it will be but at this point I do know that you will have to have a hysterectomy as soon as possible. There will be more tests to be done and different other procedures but the operation is necessary."

All I could say was, "That's fine."

At that time, I suppose I could have said to myself, "Why me?" I mean, I had opened my house to God's work and all these wonderful healings were going on and then suddenly, there I am with cancer of the cervix. But I didn't think that at all. John told me later that it was precisely because I was doing God's work, or helping with God's work in a special way, that I was under attack from Satan. And indeed, I would hear this nasty wee voice in my ear plenty of times after that, "Look at you now. You're the girl that opened your house to John Gillespie and what have you to show for it? Cancer. And all that work you're doing for others. What good has it done you? And what are you going to tell everybody? You have cancer. John Gillespie was no good to you. That's what they're going to think." Things like that were forcing themselves into my ear from this voice.

I was told to go home and tell my parents, my family, my children that I had this cancer. But I said that I couldn't tell my father and mother. They had just lost a son, my brother, four years before that. There had only been the two of us so I couldn't go home and put all this worry on my daddy and mammy, making them think they were going to lose their only remaining child.

The first person I told was John. I was still in Daisy Hill at this stage but I phoned him from there. And he said to me, "You're under demonic attack, Josephine, for doing God's work. You're going to have to be strong now." And he prayed for me over the phone. And suddenly I could feel my spirit lifting and all the fear that was beginning to fill me after the doctor had spoken to me began to leave me. And I said, "John, I'm not going to tell my mammy and daddy anything."

And John said, "That's up to you. Whatever you think yourself." He went on praying with me and told me to repeat over and over again a wee prayer: 'Jesus you bear my sickness, you carry my pain and any other disease in my body …'

As I was driving back home I kept repeating this wee prayer over and over again in my mind. And when I got home my parents were there. They didn't know what was wrong with me but they did know that I had been going for tests. They weren't sure why so when they asked me how I had got on in the hospital, I said. "I got on very well."

My mother said, "Do you have to go back?"

"Well, yes," I told her, "they want to do some more tests. Maybe it's just to make sure everything is all right."

And my daddy turned round to me and said, "Well, thank God it's not cancer."

I just smiled at him and said, "Thank God it's not." That was partly because John would always tell you not to call any disease upon yourself by saying it's there or by giving it any kind of hold over you.

Anyway, they went off home. My boys, who were fifteen, nineteen and twenty at that time, were out working or doing their own thing so I was able to talk to my husband alone. He started crying and saying, "How am I going to live without you. How am I going to cope with the boys without you?" Then after a while he began to say, "You're going to have to tell your mammy and daddy. They're going to figure out that there's something wrong."

But I said, "There's nothing wrong. You have often heard John say that you claim God's healing, the healing He promised us. You don't speak about the thing or call it on yourself. So we won't be speaking about this thing again and we won't be telling anybody about it. We've seen God's miracles many times in this house and surely He has one for us, for me. And he's going to give you the strength as well to keep going on living our lives normally and doing what we're doing." So my husband accepted that.

John phoned shortly after that to see how I was doing. I told him that I was doing well, that I was saying his prayer over and over and that I was getting a lot of strength from it

Some weeks went past and we went on with our lives. There was no mention of cancer. We never talked about it to anybody or even between ourselves. People kept coming to the house for prayer as always, my house was still open for people, and I talked to many of them about their problems. But I never said anything to anybody about my own illness or hinted that there might be something wrong with me. I just kept praying. And always I kept up the prayer of faith, even when John was in the house praying for the healing of other people. I would pray for them too, even as I was praying for myself. In fact, at those times, I was probably praying more for other people because I knew they needed the help as well.

And that is how we lived our lives, just as normal. I was feeling great spiritual and mental strength from the prayer and I continued on praying it until I got the phone call to go to Belfast City Hospital. When I spoke to the consultant he confirmed that the womb would definitely have to be removed. But he also said, "There's one thing you need to know. This cancer is serious and you'll have to have a lot of further treatment, probably chemotherapy, after the operation, to kill of any remaining cancer cells. That is one thing we will definitely have to do."

I just said "Let's get the hysterectomy over and we can discuss afterwards what needs to happen."

I was then given the date when I had to go into hospital. That was on the twenty-first of April, 2008. I was put in a ward and that evening, when the doctors and the consultant were doing their rounds, they stopped at my bed and again explained the situation to me, telling me what was going to happen afterwards. But I wasn't even listening to them. I just nodded here and there and let them get on with it. I knew I had to have the hysterectomy, I knew that. But all this stuff about there still being cancer afterwards and lots of treatment. Somehow I knew that that had nothing to do with me. That was why I said to do the operation first and talk about the post-operative treatment later. When they asked me if I understood what they were saying, I simply replied, "Yes, I understand." But I did not give it a thought. That is the gospel truth. Somehow I knew that when the operation was over, God's healing would happen.

When they went away my husband, who had been there with me, turned to me and said, "Do you really understand?"

And I said, "Yes, I do, Willie, but I'm not listening to them. I put far more trust in God's word than in any of those doctors who were around my bed. So I am not paying them any heed."

John came to visit that evening. He prayed with me for a while and then said, "How do you feel?"

I said, "John, I feel good. I am not nervous. There's no fear there. There's nothing. I'm just praying God's Word and I know and I believe that I am coming out of this with nothing to worry about."

The next morning at seven o'clock I was taken down to the theatre. Just before I left the ward I checked my mobile phone and there was a text on it from John: 'Jesus is with you.' And I knew that was true. The whole time I sensed that God was with me … I just had a very strong feeling about that. I had the presence of God there.

And as they were taking me down I got into a conversation with one of the nurses, a woman I didn't even know. She was talking about Newcastle and other meaningless things. I never spoke for a second about why I was there or what was going to be done. That wasn't mentioned at all.

It wasn't long before I was under the anaesthetic and I came back to consciousness later on that afternoon. And as soon as I awoke I began thanking God. There was a bit of a problem with my blood pressure just then … it was dropping but no one was quite sure why. Was it fear setting in? But I remembered John telling me to ignore all that and simply to claim, over and over, that my blood pressure was 120 over 80. He had told me to be very specific about it and claim it. So that's what I did. I kept claiming in Jesus' name that my blood pressure was120 over 80 and very shortly my blood pressure was back up to normal again.

I know that if I told this to a stranger or someone who knew nothing about John … well, you know the way they would look at you. But what I'm saying is true and that did happen exactly as I said. I did feel tired, of course, because of the anaesthetic and the operation.

I knew John was due to pray in my house again the next day. He phoned and asked if we should put the people off but I said, "No, John. God's Word has to go on. I have opened my house to people who are sicker than me. Those people will be coming to my house looking for healing and you will need to be there."

And there was no problem. Even though my husband was down at the hospital visiting me, I had a friend who was organising the visits, looking after the house, making sure the people were going to the room in the right order, making tea and generally helping with God's work. I knew there'd be no difficulty at all but of course I still phoned home to make sure that everything was all right. I had a wee word with John and he assured me all was fine although he did say that they missed me there. And I told him that next week I'd be fine and everything would be back to normal.

The next evening John called in to see me and pray with me. He asked me how I felt and I said, "John, I feel brilliant. And I just thank you and I thank God for helping me with what I have come through. Now it's just a case of waiting three weeks for the recovery and the results of the latest tests. But I'm going to fight this, John, because I don't want this cancer treatment they're saying I need."

But John said, "Whatever God's plan is for you, Josephine, you're going to have to accept it."

And I said, "Of course, John. God has plans for us all and we're going to have to accept them. But I believe He has one for me that doesn't include chemotherapy or anything like that."

So I continued to pray the short prayers John taught me. Over and over I would say, "By your stripes, Lord Jesus, I am healed." I kept doing that. But a new problem entered my body shortly after my operation and I had the grave suspicion that it was yet another attack from the Evil One. I began to experience severe pain coming into my hips and down my two legs. I kept sensing a voice in my head saying things like, "You think you're healed, do you? You're not. Look at the pain you have now." But I ignored the voice and kept praying the prayers even though I was still experiencing this burning down through my legs.

Then on the 16th May, I think it was Wednesday, I went down for my results. The waiting room was filled with people, probably people waiting for results as I was. Eventually I was called in to the office. My husband was with me and we both went in. The consultant asked me how I had been feeling after the operation and during the previous few weeks. I told him that I felt very well but mentioned that I was experiencing some pains in my legs.

He nodded and went on looking at the results in his hand. Then he said, "I have to tell you that you are one of the few lucky people here today. I have really good news for you. All of the cancer has disappeared …" He was sort of shaking his head, almost as if he didn't believe what he was saying. "… and there is no further treatment required. This is really excellent news for you."

I said, "Thank God!"

And he said, "Well, whatever." That's the way he answered me. But he was definitely a bit puzzled by the absence of any cancer. The scans I had before the operation had very strongly indicated that post-operative treatment would definitely be needed. Yet now no further treatment was required.

Then I asked, "What about the pain in my legs?"

Again he was puzzled. "All the indications that the cancer is gone are very clear. This pain is hard to explain. All I can suggest is another MRI scan and see what shows up."

With God on my side, I had to wait only three weeks for the scan and a while longer for the results. What the scan showed was two prolapsed discs in my back and some nerve damage to the lymph nodes. This nerve damage had come after the operation. When I got my next appointment to discuss this new situation, I was told that they could do nothing for me in terms of treatment apart from painkillers, sometimes in the form of injections.

I have to say that by now the pain was very severe, in my back and right down the sides of my legs. Both legs felt very numb and I did not feel that I would be able to go back to work. So, of course, I went back to John and he prayed with me and over me. And I could hear him asking the Lord to heal my joints and my bones and to make all ligaments and nerves and muscles to be like new, and to restore the discs in my back. He kept praying like that in Jesus' name asking for all this healing for me. And then he told me to keep on praying the way I had been. And I said, "John, when you tell me to do something, I'll do it."

And it was no surprise to me that all the pains left me shortly after that and in less than eight weeks from I first went to the hospital I was back at work, fully cured. No cancer. No nerve damage. No disc damage. I was strong and healthy, doing all my usual housework, going to my job and looking after my daddy and mammy. And I know I never could have done this without John and his prayers.

I still have John to my house one day a week where he continues to help the sick. We don't advertise it or attempt in any way to make it known that we do this but the phone always rings and John is busier there than ever, even after thirteen years. And for me, I never cease to feel that it is an honour for me to do something like that for John … and for God.

And great things continued to happen, even for members of my own family. My father had trouble with his arteries and was to have a triple by-pass but he was healed and the by-pass was never necessary. My mother was crippled and in terrible pain with osteoporosis and now she has no pain and her bones are perfectly healthy. And my youngest son, at thirteen, had severe asthma and was on a nebuliser four times a day. Because he was so young I had to do the praying for him after John prayed over him. He, too, was healed and has not had to touch an inhaler or a nebuliser since.

Thank God … and thanks, John.

Josephine Clerkin,

12th April, 2013

Majella's Story (not her real name): Demonic Abuse

(Majella lives in a seaside town in Northern Ireland. What follows is a transcript from a cassette that was sent to me through the post. These words, calm, low-key even,

are Majella's own but unfortunately I am unable to reproduce the intense emotion that was in Majella's voice as she told her story.)

My name is Majella and this is my testimony about things that happened to me, coming from a past generation. I first noticed things were wrong in my life when I was suffering from an internal itch that nobody could find a diagnosis for. I was at every doctor but nothing would ever show up in tests. I became extremely tired, tired to the point that if I even brushed the floor I would have to go and lie down for maybe three or four hours.

Then came a time when my husband and I would be in bed at night and the mattress would start popping and thumping as if something was underneath the mattress pushing and punching at it. One night I was in bed alone and something jumped on the bed. The force of that was so strong that I was tossed into the centre of the bed.

One day shortly after that I was at adoration and I felt myself suddenly levitating. I knew then that things were very bad and I went to seek help from some priests. One priest told me that it was nothing to worry about, that it couldn't possibly be the devil. So I went to another priest and he wanted to give me the number of a psychiatrist where I could get some help. He thought I was mentally ill. Another priest asked me if I was on medication.

Unhappy with these responses, I started to pray to the Lord, asking him to reveal to me what was going wrong with my life. Not long after that I was given the phone number of John Gillespie. I went to him one Wednesday evening to a house where he regularly came to pray for people.

When I first met John, God started to reveal to him that somewhere in my past ancestry there was witchcraft and Free Masonry and that the effects of these were now coming down on to me. When John revealed this to me, I began to experience a severe burning sensation that I can't even describe. It started in the crown of my head, went down into my forehead and across my eyes, and then on down into my heart, my chest, my stomach, groin, and then into my legs and around the ankles.

John was clear about what was happening. He knew that it was demonically inspired and he told me to start clearing things out of the house, things that I wasn't even aware of. These things were, for example, curtains with dragons on them, faceless ornaments, pictures with hidden eyes. There was even a book I had from my school days, a Spanish book, with demonic figures in it. There were bottles of wine with dragons on them and lots of other stuff as well. My husband had a ring which was in the form of a two-headed snake and there were CDs, music CDs, with witches in the corner of the covers. I even had holy things in the house where serpents and snakes were hidden, for example around the outside of holy pictures. All of these were like magnets to which demonic forces could attach themselves.

As we started clearing out the house, things began to get worse. One evening I was coming down the stairs with things in my hands that were to be thrown in the bin and there was a shadow following me. The electricity started to buzz and flicker, the television turned itself off, doors started banging, and the curtains were being blown up into the air. That was terrifying.

After that the burning increased. It increased so much that I'd have to sit in a bath of cold water maybe three times a day trying to get my body to cool down. This burning was something I can't compare to anything. It was so severe that I was sure that I was suffering the fires of hell.

At night I would go to bed, or try to go to bed because I couldn't sleep. At this point I wasn't eating either and had lost about two stone of weight. I couldn't hold down food. I was vomiting constantly. Even the smell of food was making me vomit.

I also started losing my hair and I could feel this awful presence around me twenty-four hours a day. When I got into bed at night and I could feel this presence all around the crown of my head. I put blessed salt on the pillows and all around the room. I would cover my body with blessed oil just to try and get some peace, to try to make this presence go away. And all the time there was cold air being constantly blown on the centre of my forehead. It was freezing cold.

One night my husband and I were in bed. I had managed to doze off but was awakened again to find my husband's fingers around my throat and with his other hand he was performing some sort of ritual over my body. He was unaware that he was doing this because he was still asleep. Something had taken control over him. I became hysterical and ran down the stairs into the family room and started to pray. But I was so full of fear, fear I thought would never leave me. This fear was so bad that it would keep me in one room. I was too afraid even to move around the house on my own. All the time I was terrified, wondering what was happening.

John would be on the phone to me three times a day and he would have to come down to the house to me maybe twice a week to pray over me. I was surviving on maybe four hours sleep over a period of three days. I was physically, mentally and spiritually exhausted all the time.

And always there was the burning. It never ceased and I suffered greatly with it. I associated it with hellfire and started to feel that I was going to hell, that my soul was lost. I could hear a voice telling me this over and over again in my mind, "You're going to hell. You're going to hell." And I would constantly become hysterical.

On top of this I also had an overwhelming desire to commit suicide. I would find myself in the kitchen with a knife pressed against my heart, and I could feel … a force … telling me to commit suicide, that everything would be better if I was dead. My husband would read the bible to me but all I could hear was the noise of heavy drums playing in my ears. I couldn't bear it and wanted my husband to stop reading, to stop praying. But he kept on reading and praying and that was very, very hard for me. The more he would pray, the worse all these feelings would get and the louder would be the drums in my ears. And the burning, too, got more and more extreme. I tried to put holy water on to cool it but that made the burning even worse. It was a burning that started on the inside of my body and worked its way out. It wasn't from the outside in. I was on fire inside.

I also had ... it was like a tape-recorder … playing twenty-four hours a day in my head, blaspheming God. Out of everything, that was the hardest to cope with. I thought I was going to have a nervous breakdown. My body would also be thrown into violent shaking that I couldn't control. Sometimes the burning inside would change to freezing and though I was freezing on the inside, I would still be sweating on the outside.

John would be in contact with me constantly, constantly praying. He was always there for me. As God showed John how to break this down, piece by piece, the symptoms started to ease off and I started to get some relief. John was told by God that the blasphemy and the drumming, the drumming in my ears, was coming from ancestral witchcraft in my bloodline. The drumming was when they were making human sacrifices, child sacrifices. They would beat the drums so that they wouldn't hear the children screaming.

There were also some forms of extreme Free Mason rituals when, during the initiation services, they would put a hood over the initiate's head and a noose around their neck and if the novice ever tried to leave a curse would be called on them, on their organs and on their heart. These were the kinds of things that I was experiencing in my own organs, and in my heart and my body.

I thank God every day of my life for His love and His mercy for giving me the grace to come through this. I thank God every day that He used John Gillespie to heal me and set me free. This was so traumatic for me that after the healing I had no memories. For six months afterwards I couldn't remember anything of my life. I couldn't remember anything. I couldn't retain any information. I had no memories of my daughter, of being married. I could remember nothing. I could not even remember all of the things that I had gone through.

But six months later I couldn't forget. It all came back and I would go over it and over it in my head. That was terrible … it would bring on panic attacks and great fear. But then I realised that I had to leave the past where it belonged … and that was in the past. When I finally grasped that, I was able to go on with my life.

I am now working full-time, able to do the things everybody else does. I am healed and I'm free and I thank God and I thank John Gillespie for his prayers.

Recorded in April 2013

Ethna's Story: I Thought I Might End My Life

On the 2nd July, 2007, I went to St. Agnes' Chapel on the Andersonstown Road to see John Gillespie. He worked as one of the sacristans there. I had been told by a taxi-driver that John had prayed with people and that he knew people who had received healing through John's prayers.

I was sceptical but I was at the end of the road with my health problems. I had been ill for two years. The illness began suddenly one morning in July 2005. I felt an intense pain in my left leg. I was admitted to hospital after tests showed that a clot had formed in my leg at the back of the knee. The pain was dreadful.

Weeks went by, then months, and the pain would not subside. I was distraught. Seeing me in so much pain was having a terrible effect on my family. The simple tasks of housework became an awful ordeal as I had to use 'crutches' to get around the house. Getting upstairs was particularly painful and distressing. I lost my job as a special-needs classroom assistant. I was heartbroken.

We have four daughters whose ages at that time were ten, thirteen, twenty and twenty-one. We were a very busy family. Each of my children had exams to sit. I tried so hard to keep going for them. My husband was under terrible strain worrying about me, trying to keep his job going, and now having to do a lot of running after the girls that I used to do.

I had been to see every doctor who we thought might be able to help. I had an MRI scan, a bone-density scan and a CT scan. After the CT scan the doctor told me that I had a large cyst on one of my ovaries. I had an operation to have it removed.

I had hoped that it was the cyst that was causing the pain in my leg, but weeks after the operation, the pain continued in my leg. It was now getting worse and seemed to be travelling up my spine. By now, I had to use a wheelchair to relieve the pain of walking.

I had to move to my mother's bungalow as I couldn't cope at home any more. I was prescribed a huge amount of painkillers, muscle relaxants, morphine patches and anti-depressants. I was also using a 'tens machine' to relieve pain. My body weight had increased from ten stones to fourteen stones. My legs and feet were so swollen I could barely get shoes on.

My doctor didn't know what to suggest at this stage. I wheeled myself in and out of her surgery with no hope of help. I couldn't go on. I thought I might end my life. But I had a family and a husband who loved me. I didn't want to distress them. Going to John Gillespie was my last hope.

When I got to the chapel, my Mum helped to push me in, in my wheel chair. John listened as I told him what had happened. He was very calm. He made a sign of the cross on my head. He said he would pray for healing.

He held his thumb against my forehead, praying out loud to "Our Lord Jesus Christ". He made the sign of the cross on my hip-bone, my spine, and on my knee. He held my swollen feet in his hands and prayed again aloud to "Our Lord Jesus Christ". He put his thumb on my forehead once more and prayed again. During this time I was imploring the Lord to help me.

Suddenly John stopped praying. He stood back and said, "Well, what's the pain like now?"

I suddenly realised that the pain had *stopped*. It was as though it had been turned off. I said, "It's gone. It's gone." I looked down in amazement at my legs.

John calmly said, "There you are. Thank God now."

I was so happy, beaming with joy. John held out his hand and said, "Get up now, and walk." I was nervous at first but did as he asked. I stepped off my wheelchair and walked unaided … by myself. I was overjoyed that the pain had stopped and I kept thanking the Lord out loud.

John told me to sit down again. He said that I was still limping to one side, that my spine was "out of line". He prayed with me again. He held my feet in his hands and said that my left leg was shorter than my right leg. He prayed again, pulling gently as he prayed. *(Ethna does not mention that as John prayed, her legs automatically realigned. John says that this non-alignment is a common problem in people with bad backs and spinal problems and that, through him, Jesus has realigned thousands of legs in this way. John also says that Ethna misunderstood what was happening at that point. He did not "pull gently as he prayed." He does not pull or adjust the legs in any way; he simply allows the person's heels to rest on his palms and waits for the Lord to do His work.)* The pain was gone. I was elated. I walked around the room several times while John thanked God for the healing. I walked into the adjoining room where my mum was waiting with the other sacristan. She was amazed to see me smiling and walking unaided, while John came behind pushing my wheelchair. I told my mother that I was healed, that the pain was gone. I was overjoyed. I showed her how I could bend right down and touch my toes, then stretch my arms up high above my head

Mum and I went into the chapel. We were so full of joy. I had been healed through prayer by Our Lord Jesus

Christ. For the first time in two years I was able to kneel down to pray. We praised God for taking the pain away, for healing me. We told some other women who were in the chapel praying. One woman had a little child with her. I was so happy that I picked the child up and swung her around. I was ecstatic with joy. I wanted to tell everyone that God really does hear our prayers, that He is real.

I then phoned my husband who was at home having lunch with the children. I told them I was healed, to come to the chapel quickly. They could hardly believe what I was saying. When they came I showed them how I could walk, how I could bend down and stretch up. They were all so happy. We had been through such a dreadful time and now it was over.

That night my youngest daughter, Francesca, wrote an account in her own words about what had happened. It was given to John Gillespie. Everyone who knew me was astonished at my healing. It renewed their faith.

I went off all my medication. I had very bad withdrawals for several months. Even though today, two years later, I still take some painkillers for a pain in my knee, I feel a million times better and I know that my healing is still continuing. I have been back to work and feel great.

John Gillespie asked for nothing other than that I continue to praise God and to thank God for my healing.

I know that I have been healed through Jesus Christ.
Ethna O'Connor (real name),

Sr. Elizabeth's Story: A Long-Distance Healing

When Sr. Elizabeth delivered this oral testimony at one of John's services in the Shrine chapel at Faughart, she spoke with such smiling animation and with such joyous delight in God's goodness that, when she had finished speaking, the congregation broke into spontaneous and sustained applause.

My name is Sister Elizabeth Ng (real name). I was born and lived in Singapore. I studied and trained to be an accountant but after some years I felt a calling to serve God in the religious life. I joined the Poor Clares and spent my novice year at the Poor Clare convent in Sydney. Then I came to the Irish house, the Monastery of the Light of Christ, at Faughart, to finish my formation. I live there now and I think of it as my home.

I would like to tell the story of how I asked for one favour and two special favours were granted at the same time. Just before I came to Ireland in July 2009, a relative was diagnosed as having cancer. This was the second time he had cancer. Three years ago he had a cancer attack which was one of the very rare types of cancer in the world. All of the skin on his body became lumpy and the doctors in Singapore could not get any proper medication for him.

My relative he is non-Catholic, a pagan. He is in his mid-fifties and he runs a family business, putting down underground pipes, cable pipes, for big companies like Telecom. So he has a construction business and he always has to go on the site to supervise. He is married and has three children, two boys and one girl. This family is very dear to me. When I was a student, this relative helped me a lot to finance my studies and he, too, is very dear to me. So, three years ago he contracted cancer. His whole body was lumpy and the tissue just collapsed, a very rare form of cancer and the doctors did not know how to treat it.

This horrified us all. I was in the convent at the time and when I heard the news I was devastated. Day and night I kept praying to the Lord. I ran to the tabernacle and prayed to the Lord for the right medication. That's what I told the Lord and I said, "Dear Lord, I cannot lose this relative. You just have to heal him. Please help his doctors to find the right medication." And true enough, not long later they found the right medication. He suffered a lot through chemo but after a while he was back to his normal self, healthy and strong.

But now again in 2009, he got another cancer attack in his throat. He had four tumours, three large lumps at the front and one at the back. Here again he lost half of his whole weight. This time I was not so devastated because I know from the last time that I have my Lord here to heal him. So my whole family prayed together in our own space and time. I wondered very much when I might pass through Singapore again but I knew that I could not minister unto him because first of all he was a pagan and second, my faith is not strong enough to proclaim God's healing touch on him even though I know God can heal. But God did put me into a special faith through a miracle and this is the testimony that I am going to give.

I came to Ireland just at that time and once I arrived at the Monastery of the Light of Christ, I got to know John who has a great gift of healing from God through his strong faith. I contacted the lady who makes his monastery appointments and said, "Marie, could you fit me in to see John sometime because I want to ask him to pray with me, by proxy, for my relative who has cancer."

But John is so busy and there were so many people rushing to see him for God's mercy and I did not see him for two months. I couldn't get an appointment and I was very disappointed but I prayed to God and I said, "If this is your will Lord, then so be it."

I had to go back to Sydney on the eighteenth of September and I still had not seen John. The last Tuesday before I was to leave had come and I still had not seen John. And I prayed that morning, "Dear Lord, John is coming today. Could I please have a chance to see him but, if not, your will be done."

I was praying over some people who had been knocking on the door of the monastery for prayer … I am always happy to pray with people who come like that. They were leaving at five o clock and just at that time the lady who organises John's appointments met me in the corridor and said, "Elizabeth, would you like to have a minute to talk to John? A lady with an appointment at five o'clock has had to rush her babies to hospital and she came at two o'clock instead. John is free for half an hour; would you like to say hello to him?"

And I said, "Why not?" And I said to the Lord, "I am very happy."

So I went into the room and I said, "Hi, John. I need a favour from you to pray over my brother-in-law." And he said, "Okay, sit down." So I sat down and before he began to pray for my relative, he prayed for me first. He kept praying for my body, for my back. And I am thinking, "Oh, my God! How come John knows that I have a bad back?" Then he prayed for my relative's cancer.

So when he had finished praying, he sat down beside me and we had a wee chit-chat. And I said, "John, before we start, how come you know I've got a back pain?" And he said, "Yes, when I prayed over you, I got a vision that your back was crooked." And I said, "Oh, my God! John, God is great. He is very great."

I have been suffering from back pains since I was young. More than twenty years ago, we moved into a new house and the whole family and my brother were washing the floor with towels. I didn't know and I opened my bedroom door and stepped on one of the towels and go backwards and fell and I was in hospital with concussion for three days. And I have had back pains ever since then. I have to go all the time to hospital for physiotherapy and I have to be always very careful with my back. I didn't know it was crooked but it was always sore.

So John asked me to sit up and he showed me my legs, one long and one short. And I was amazed. I didn't know that either. And John healed me by resting my feet on his hands and my legs became the same size. He put his hand under my feet and the feet just moved by themselves. And then I was rejoicing because I saw something happen without any human power.

My back was still a little bit sore and I had mixed feelings, half believing and half doubt. But when I went to evening prayer that night, I was sitting in the chapel when I felt a sudden sharp pain in my back where I always felt pain. But I knew that this was a healing pain, but I still cannot believe. I said to God, "All right. If my back is not healed, that's okay. I can get used to the pain again."

But during the night I always have to lie on my stomach so as to ease the pain in my back. So I did the same thing on this Tuesday night but I don't feel anything and I say, "Oh, my God, where is the pain?" And I felt a great joy coming up from my heart and I just kept praising the Lord with great faith and joy. And my faith had come back and I said to the Lord, "There you are. You really healed me." And I just could not sleep from then. I just kept praising the Lord and singing hymns in the dark, praising Him all the night through.

And I was so excited about my back that I didn't even think of my relative getting healed. You see how unfaithful I am? But next day I remembered and I decided to phone my relative's wife to give her my strength and to tell her that I was supporting her in prayer. So I phoned her. I was not thinking about a miracle but I just told her what I had done for her husband and what I was hoping for. And she said, "All right. You're sure God is so good?" And I said, "Yes. You remember that the last time I prayed for the right medication and, there you are, it came. And here we are again. I have prayed to the Lord for your husband."

This time I said to the Lord, "Dear Lord, please let his heart's desire be fulfilled." Because, you see, Tian Lu does not want to die yet. He wants to see his children grow up and be settled and then he will happily go back to the Lord … but to him it is not to go back to the Lord. It is just to die; to go to the grave. For pagans it is the grave. So I said to his wife, "Just remember that God can heal, that's all." So she said, "All right." And we put down our phones.

So I went to Sydney for a couple of months. And when I was coming back to Ireland, I passed through Singapore. When I got to the airport I called Tian Lu's wife and said, "How are you? How is your husband getting on?"

Well, she just could not wait to tell me the good news. She was shouting into the phone, "I have been wanting for weeks to tell you the miracle …"

And I laughed and I said, "There you are. Miracle." Then I was keen to know and I said, "What miracle?"

And she said, "That time when you called me … two days later Tian Lu felt so weak and fell over. And I got a shock. When he fell over, he uttered a groan and he went unconscious. And I got Adrian," [Adrian is her eldest son] "and I was frightened and I was lost and I didn't know what to do. But Adrian kept patting his dad's face and calling his dad's name and finally he revived him and we called an ambulance. But before the ambulance could reach the house, Tian Lu vomited up all this green stuff up from his throat. And I do not know who prompted me to do this but I got a plastic bag and collected the stuff in the bag. I just knew I had to do this. Then the ambulance arrived and they took Tian Lu to the hospital with this bag of green stuff. And the doctors said that they needed to do tests on this stuff and took it away. The moment when Tian Lu arrived at the hospital, the whole throat had come back down again, no more big swellings on it. The whole throat had been swollen very much. It was stage four of the cancer and it was very serious. He could not eat and it was very difficult to drink.

But then the doctor who tested the green stuff came back and examined Tian Lu. He said that there was no more cancer, that Tian Lu had vomited up all the cancer lumps into the plastic bag and he was discharged to go home, free from cancer."

Isn't that amazing? Isn't God wonderful? Tian Lu's wife was so happy and could not wait to tell me. Normally she didn't call me at the convent. This is how she had been taught when I was in the other convent. So when I contacted her from the airport, she couldn't wait to tell me this good news. And she said, "The Lord really worked miracles for me." She wanted me to continue to pray and asked me to come over and pray for him again. And I laughed and said, "Yes, why not?" And then my faith came and from then on I got the strength and the faith to pray over anybody who comes along to ask for prayers, even my family. God is great. Every time God is great.

And when I got to the house, my relative's wife wanted me to pray again over Tian Lu and even her son. "Come, pray over Adrian," she said. I could see that the Lord is working on them and I asked my relative, "Do you believe?" And he said, "Yes, I do believe in healing."

But God has started on them and I wait. The hospital report shows that he is completely cured of his cancer and he is now back normally at work. Now he believes in healing. One day, I am sure, he will believe in God."

Sr. Elizabeth Ng,

Monastery of the Light of Christ,

Tracey's Story (real name): A Child under Demonic Attack

My dad, John Gillespie, asked me to write a few lines in my own words about how the devil sometimes attacks us, his daughters, when he wants to upset my dad. This has been happening to us all our lives and we are quite accustomed to it. There have been some stories told about this in the book, dramatic stories. But sometimes when the devil tries his nasty tricks on us, they are quite ordinary things and, while they can be upsetting and annoying and, indeed dangerous, it is sometimes difficult to distinguish between the ordinary misfortunes of life and the devil's petty vindictiveness. Some of the things that I am now going to write about may well just seem like normal events but when my father comes into the picture he can always tell whether what has happened is demonic or not.

For example, in December 2004 my sister, Helen, and myself left the family home and bought our own house together. We were barely there a couple of weeks when I awoke one night and went to the bathroom. But when I tried to open the bathroom door, it was jammed shut. I pulled and tugged with all my strength but I could not budge it. I went back to the bedroom and sat there wondering what was happening. About fifteen minutes later I decided to go back and try again but when I got there the door was fully open, right back against the bathroom wall. Helen had been sleeping all this time, so it was not her who had opened the door.

I just let that go, however, and didn't reflect too much on it. But a couple of months later, March 2005, we were a bit unhappy about the house and its general environment, so we decided to put it up for sale. The 'For Sale' notice went up on Good Friday. On Easter Sunday, while my sister Helen was starting to cook our dinner, I decided to have a quick shower. I had scarcely got the water running when I heard the smoke alarm going off. I thought that Helen had probably burnt something but within a few seconds I heard her hammering frantically on the bathroom door, screaming at me that we had to get out of the shower because a fire had broken out in the hall and was rapidly spreading to all parts of the house.

We managed to get out through the back door unharmed just in time to greet the emergency services as they arrived. When they had brought the fire under control and had extinguished the flames, Helen and I were allowed into the house to gather up a few personal belongings. Due to the extent of the smoke damage, however, we were not able to remain there and we were put up over the next few months in various hotels around

Belfast until the house could be brought back into a habitable state.

We did make a few visits to the house to speak to the builders who were carrying out the repairs and we learned that the fire had started in the fuse-box in the hall. Normally, the fact that a fire had started because of some faulty wiring in a fuse-box would never be questioned. But the significant thing was that, while all of our personal belongings, the soft furnishings and the contents of the house, were destroyed, there was a blessed picture of Our Lady on top of a radiator in the hall. This had been given to us by our mother, Christina, who had it in her own house and who asked us to display it in the new house somewhere. I had left it on the radiator because I had not yet got around to having it framed. For all intents and purposes, therefore, it was little more than a piece of paper. Yet, although it had been in the hall right beside the fuse-box where the worst of the flames were, it was the only item in the house that had not been touched by the flames or affected by smoke damage. When we recovered it, it was in exactly the same state that it had been in when our mother gave it to us. Since the fire was unable to affect the blessed picture, we believe that it must have been supernatural in origin.

We were out of the house for four months until all of the repairs were completed. One evening, a few weeks after we had moved back in, I was in the house alone. I began to hear voices speaking to me, although I had no idea where they were coming from. On a few other occasions, when I was in the sitting room, I heard loud footsteps upstairs as if someone was walking about in my bedroom wearing a pair of heavy boots. I was a bit concerned about this and eventually phoned my dad (John) to come over and see what was happening. He called around shortly after that and blessed the house. He prayed a bit and said that since the house had been more or less open for four months with workmen walking in and out as they carried out repairs, there was no knowing who or what might have had access to it. After he blessed the house, however, there were no further sounds of voices or footsteps.

But the attacks did not end. It is possible that we, or the house, had been subject to further curses or demonic influence. In any event, there were two further incidents. My cat, suddenly and quite unusually, was seriously troubled by fleas. But that was only the beginning. We began to find fleas in large quantities in our clothes, in our beds, and all over the upstairs rooms despite the fact that the cat was not allowed upstairs and never went there. We tried several recommended treatments to rid the cat of the fleas but it made no difference to our state. The infestation began to escalate and all of the rooms were now infected. The house was a misery to live in and again we phoned Dad. Again he came over and blessed every room in the house and immediately all of the fleas disappeared.

Not long afterwards, however, we had yet another attack. This one was particularly terrifying for me because all my life I have suffered from an irrational fear of spiders. It's called arachnophobia and even realistic spider toys can bring about panic attacks and fear. No matter how unreasonable the fear might be, it is very real and very hard to cope with. Needless to say, the new attack played upon my fears.

Not long after the incident of the fleas, I began to find spiders in the house. One here, one there, but shortly after that they began to appear in numbers, groups of eight or nine at a time. I found them during the day and during the night. All during this time I was living in terror and dread about when I might find the next one. When they would appear, especially if there were a number of them, I would end up terrified and in tears.

Again my dad came and blessed the house and explained to me how I should pray to God when I was dealing with fear of this sort. And he told me, too, that if I suspected they were demonic, how I was to pray to cast them out. On this occasion, when my dad prayed and blessed the house, the spiders disappeared almost immediately. I found one or two over the next few days but very shortly they were gone altogether.

The events described above might well be described as 'nuisance attacks' and, while the Gillespie children might be accustomed to such demonic attacks on ourselves and our parents, that does not make them any less stressful. The devil never stops trying and we just have to keep fighting him.

Sometimes, however, his attacks escalate into something quite horrifying. Like most young women, there came a time for me when I wanted to settle down and have a family. I gave birth to a baby girl in June 2009 and named her Shona. During my time in the hospital maternity ward, Shona was very settled and content. However, when I brought her home and a few weeks passed, Shona began to become very unsettled indeed. She was crying a lot, refusing to drink her milk and I was finding it very difficult to nurse her to sleep. And even when she did drift off to sleep, she would waken up again in a little while, screaming continuously. It was no better at night. During the night she would be in a deep sleep and suddenly she would be awake, screaming, and nothing I could do appeared to comfort her. Throughout the time she would be screaming, however, I began to sense fear in her cry and I knew that something had been disturbing her sleep.

I made several visits to the doctor and to the midwife in the hospital, explaining what was happening. They both told me that Shona had colic and was being disturbed by acid reflux. They did discover that some of the milk we were feeding her was not suitable and we changed that. They also gave me medication that was supposed to solve my baby's problem but the medicine did not work. Shona remained deeply unsettled and crying and although I kept explaining to the doctor and the midwife what was happening, they refused to accept that it was anything unusual and kept giving me fact-sheets and leaflets showing that such behaviour was normal.

I became very frustrated by this and in constant tears because there was something serious disturbing my child and there seemed to be nothing I could do for her. And I could get no help either from the doctor or the hospital.

Matters came to a head one evening when Shona was at her worst, screaming all day and refusing to eat or drink anything. After two hours during which I tried everything I could to get my baby to go to sleep, she finally drifted off, more because of exhaustion from her screaming than because of anything I was able to do for her. But ten minutes later, she woke up again screaming frantically. Her face turned red and the tears were streaming down her face. I decided to try to record Shona in this state and made a short video of it on my mobile phone so that I could show what was happening to the doctor and the midwife. But first I ran to my mum's house to show it to her and to leave the phone with her for dad to hear. Dad was out but I asked mum to send him over as soon as he got home to pray for Shona.

John takes up the story:

I knew that Shona was in terrible distress at Tracey's apartment but the odd thing was that when Tracey brought her to visit our house, the child seemed to be better. The crying might not have gone away completely but she was definitely more settled in our house. It was something the same when they brought Shona to her other grandparents' house.

But gradually the situation got worse and worse. Tracey was getting no sleep. She was sure that she could see a fear in the child's eyes. She had witnessed enough things in her own home before to know the sort of thing she should look for. It got so bad one evening, that she decided to record the child crying because the screaming was terrifying. I was away that day but Christina told me about the recording as soon as I got home and said, "You need to hear this."

I listened to the recording. It wasn't just an ordinary 'cry' pain. It was a pain of fright, almost of someone being tormented. And I said straight away, "That child is not in pain, screaming like that. That child is under demonic attack."

Christina said, "Will you go up to Tracey's flat?"

I said that I would go, of course, but first I went to look at the scripture. When I opened the page, it was at the episode where the apostles had cried to Jesus to calm the storm. And the line that caught my eye was 'Why are you so frightened?' And I knew then that there was something behind the screaming that was not normal. So I prayed to God asking Him for the root cause of this. But I had already learned enough from the scripture to convince me that the child was definitely under demonic attack and I had to find out what it was that was making her '… so frightened.'

And I went up top Tracey's flat, praying constantly to the Lord to tune me in exactly to what I needed to know in order to be able to help my daughter and my grandchild. When I went into the flat, Tracey was exhausted and the child, too, was worn out from crying and screaming.

Now, Tracey would have known enough to allow nothing into her house that might bring any kind of evil influence in with it and when I asked her if she had brought in anything she assured me she hadn't. But even as we were talking, my focus was drawn to two candles on a window sill. They were a dark reddish colour of a type I had never dealt with before. They did not seem to have much of a scent of them and I didn't think they had anything to do with aromatherapy or anything like that. I asked Tracey if she knew anything about them and she said that they were only ornaments for her window sill and said to me, "Why are you asking me about them?"

And I said, "Well, my attention is being drawn to them. Have they been there long?"

She said that they had been there for a good wee while so I went over to look at them. They seemed ordinary enough. The light wasn't great at that part of the room but as I moved the candles about, I could see wee flecks of what looked like grey wax here and there all over them. And I felt God saying to me, "Take these candles out to the light outside. This is something new you have to see."

I felt that I should be focusing my attention on the grey wax and I went out into the hall where there was far better light and I felt that I should focus on one particular area. God often does that. He'll tune you into an area and you know to examine it very, very closely. So I prayed as I examined the grey area and after a while I could see that it was a tiny imprint of a very ugly face. I took it back into Tracey and asked her to examine it, too.

I didn't tell her what it was but after a couple of minutes she said, "That's a wee face in there."

I said, "Yes, and it's an evil face."

And as we looked, we saw more of them, nearly all the grey bits were evil faces. We got the other candle and found exactly the same thing. They were so well hidden that if the candles were not examined very closely, these faces could never have been seen. And I checked the base of the candles to see where they had come from and I found that they were made in India. And I told Tracey that they must have had some sort of connection with some sort of eastern earth god, or demon, for this sort of power to be working from them.

So immediately we took those two candles and another one that was sitting innocently on a table, we took that one as well, and I blessed the whole lot, prayed some prayers over them to break any curses, and threw them out in the bin.

I also discovered in the room a little angel, or something that was supposed to be an angel, that had been given to the child for baptism. But when I examined it, it had a teddy-bear head, with two little ears standing on the top of its head. It might have looked cute but I said to Tracey, "That's not an angel. That could represent anything."

She said, "I thought that but my friend bought it for Shona."

"Well, that would need to go, too," I said.

Tracey said, "I have no problem with that. If it's affecting Shona, I want it out."

There was a display case with it and a document giving it some sort of meaning but I didn't heed any of that. I blessed it, too, and threw it out as well. Then I went to Shona and prayed with her. I rebuked all evil and any spiritual force that was coming against her and the child was instantly settled. When the candles went out and the prayer was done, you could see an instant change in the child. Her complexion seemed immediately to change; the fear left her eyes; she just totally relaxed. I think she must have actually been seeing something because a child will see a thing quicker than an adult will. And then suddenly she was seeing it no more. Anyway, she slept all that night and was never troubled with that screaming again. She has been a totally different child ever since.

APPENDIX 2

Some Shorter Accounts of Healings Attributed to John

A. The Power of Forgiveness

The Health Professional with Spine Cancer

"Unforgiveness and forgiveness are equally powerful," John says. "One causes great hurt and the other can bring great healing. And the best cure for a malady caused by unforgiveness is forgiveness.

"I remember one time a woman called to see me. She had cancer of the spine and she told me she was very devastated and hurt because she herself had worked as a health professional with cancer patients for over twenty years and now her reward for that life of caring was to be given cancer herself. She was very upset at what she saw as the injustice of that.

"So, I sympathised with her but I told her that I knew that it wasn't the Lord who had given her the cancer. 'I'll pray over you,' I told her, 'and try to find out what has happened.' And I began to pray over her and, at the same time, I was praying to the Lord asking Him if there was a root cause here of something that I would need to be dealing with.

“As soon as I said this, I could see through the Word of Knowledge that I was given that six months before she had been diagnosed with cancer she had suffered a very deep hurt in her life, a hurt that had never been healed and had never been resolved in any way. I felt the Lord telling me that she had never forgiven the person who had hurt her and that every time she would think of the hurt, it was like a knife going through her. I wasn’t told exactly what the problem was but I had the sense that it had been her husband. He had been unfaithful to her and had left her. And she never got over this.

“So I prayed for her and I asked her, ‘When did the cancer start exactly?’ And she said to me, ‘It was diagnosed about two years ago’.

“‘Well,’ I said to her, ‘the Lord’s just after telling me that six months before that you suffered some kind of serious hurt. You know yourself what it was.’ I didn’t speak about it but I was now sure that her husband had committed adultery and had left her for another woman. I just went on to say, ‘You never got over this hurt, and every time you think about it, it’s like a knife going through your heart.’

“And she burst into tears and said, ‘You’re exactly right. My husband was unfaithful to me and left me for another woman. I have never forgiven him.’

“And I then said to her, ‘I’m deeply sorry for that but this is an area we’re going to have to talk about. You cannot go to God for healing with bitterness and unforgiveness in your heart because you’re keeping in your system the very root cause of what is making you ill.’ And I said, ‘I can tell you that is this bitterness in you that is the root cause of your cancer. All that bile and bitterness and negativity, it has had a physical effect on your system.’

"She was shocked by this but as I talked I could see that she understood. She knew enough about illnesses and diseases to be able to talk about psychosomatic causes. So we talked a bit about forgiveness and, although it was a serious struggle for her, she began to see that her unforgiveness was doing a lot more harm to her than it was to her husband. So she decided that she would try to forgive him and asked me to help her. I prayed with her and got her to say the prayers of forgiveness out loud after me and told her to go on praying the forgiveness prayers and to pray for her husband's soul which was in mortal danger. She promised that she would. That woman is now healed. All trace of the cancer in her spine in gone.

B. Ancestral Links

An Inexplicable Malady

Anne is a young woman, no more than a girl really, who developed a most peculiar mark on one of her legs. John describes it as, "… the strangest looking thing. That part of her leg where it was located was hollow with the flesh circled around it. It looked very much like a mushroom turned inside out. It looked like the stem was the piece in the middle of the mark. The skin wasn't broken, but there was a redness all round it, and the flesh had curled up as if something had pierced it. She was able to move around and walk with it but it was very painful."

Anne herself averred that the pain was causing her a great deal of suffering and she felt that sometimes the mark was burning. She went to two or three different doctors but none could diagnose what the mark was, what might have caused it, or what its long-term effects might be.

Anne's mother knew John (he had helped her with a New Age problem) and she brought Anne to him. John told her that he would ask the Lord to show him the root cause of the malady. "No matter what kind of problem it is," he said, "there's always a root cause."

He laid his hand on Anne's head and, as he prayed, he was given a vision of someone using a gun to shoot someone in the leg. He received further knowledge that the victim was a member of the girl's family and that there had never been any repentance for this act. John then told the girl, and her mother who was also present, "Somebody in your family has been shot in the past, maybe in the recent past. It was a punishment shooting and there has been no forgiveness in the family for the person who did the shooting." John went on, "I believe that this thing is appearing in your leg now because God is drawing attention to a situation that needs to be put right. So what both of you need to do now is to pray for the victim and for the shooter as well, to offer up Masses for them and also for the people who weren't able to forgive."

Anne's mother looked very uncomfortable at this. As John looked at her questioningly, she said in a quiet voice, "I remember that incident and I know who you're talking about. We'll pray and get the Masses said. Do we have to do anything else?"

John was guided by the Spirit at that point to prescribe additional special devotions for them, relating particularly to the seeking of forgiveness. The two women left, promising to carry out the instructions John had given them.

A few days later the mother called to tell John that her daughter's mark had disappeared and that she was completely healed. John was pleased but not surprised. "Some of these things medicine can't cure," he said. "Nowadays they've got all sorts of fancy names for medical conditions … some mental conditions, too … and sometimes they're right. But sometimes they're not right. They don't even know what's going on or what they're doing. That's when you need people like me … to diagnose the supernaturally created illnesses and to pray them away."

C. New Age

Burning Palms

Sarah was a young mother with four young children. Her life had never been free of trials and tribulations and when she came to John, she was suffering from pains in her hands, especially in her palms. John prayed over her, asking the young woman to let go of any bitterness or unforgiveness that might still reside in her heart and to pray for anyone who might have hurt her in the past. He continued to pray, asking the Lord to reveal to him the root cause of Sarah's pain, asking if it might be arthritis, something else in the bone, or perhaps nerve damage.

In a short time, John received 'the Word of Knowledge' prompting him to ask Sarah if she had any dealings with fortune tellers. Sarah admitted that she had. "But it was only a half-hearted thing," she said. "My life was falling to bits around me and I wanted to find out if there was anything better in store for me and my family."

John told her that only God is allowed to know the future. In allowing her hands to be used to read her future, actually her 'alleged' future, she had opened herself up to a demonic link. "Fortune-telling," he told her, "is banned under the heading of 'spiritual divination'. We're told that in Deuteronomy. So, if you got any information that seemed to be true and the fortune-teller couldn't have known it, then it could only have come from Satan because, even though he mixes many lies into the 'sooth-saying', Satan still has great knowledge about each of us which he uses in such circumstances."

John was thus able to deduce that the pains Sarah was suffering were the result of a demon attacking her hands. "You'll need to go to confession and communion," he told her, "and repudiate all links with that fortune teller. It's impossible for me to expel a demon out of anyone without this kind of promise." Sarah said that she "definitely would," that she suddenly felt a terrible need for spiritual help and guidance.

"Find a good priest," John advised her, "and you'll be fine."

John met Sarah a few weeks later. She was bright, cheerful and contented. "My palms have completely healed," she told him. "But not only that," she went on. "For some reason my life seems to have changed … it's happy. Nothing's going wrong any more."

John smiled. "You've got God at your side now. What more do you need?"

Appendix 3

List of New Age Practices
[The Examples given below are extracted from a Catholic website: www.unhealthydevotions.com and from the Vatican's Reflection: Jesus Christ: The Bearer of the Water of Life]

***New Age is** a broad movement of spirituality characterised by a group of individual seekers, teachers, healers and other participants. Rather than following the lead of any organised religion, New Age practitioners typically construct their own forms of spirituality using aspects of Eastern religions, Wicca, past-life experiences, spirit guide channelling and other forms of occult practices. Below is a list of some of the more common beliefs and practices.*

Astrology: A belief that the position of celestial bodies is useful for understanding or interpreting information about a person's life.

Acupuncture: An ancient Chinese practice of piercing the body at various key-points with needles for the relief of pain and the healing of ailments. Analysis of its background, however, reveals an occult connection and, in the long-term, leads to various forms of ill-health, depression and other maladies.

Candle magick: A tool used by New Age practitioners to increase the power of spells.

Chain Letters: Letters circulated by mail or email that carry with them a blessing or a curse. If a person fails to forward the letter, the curse can be a threat of bad luck. If a person continues the chain letter, he is promised good luck or other forms of prosperity.

Channelling: A practice used to receive messages from spirit guides, the Ascended Masters, or fallen angels.

Crystals: Glass objects widely used in the New Age movement because they allegedly contain healing powers and cleansing properties.

Cyclomancy: A practice of fortune-telling where a person consults a spinning object like a wheel or a bottle.

Divination: The practice of obtaining information through supernatural sources.

Druids: Members of the Celtic order of wizards who practise witchcraft; also known as magicians or diviners.

Enneagram: The enneagram is a circular diagram with a nine-point star which symbolically describes nine personality types and has been developed by New Age practitioners. It is founded on pagan beliefs and was originally used by Sufi mystics for fortune telling. It has been a fad in various Catholic retreat centres for some years but, because it ignores the primacy of grace in spiritual development and introduces ambiguity into the doctrine and the life of Christian faith, the Vatican is strongly opposed to it.

Homeopathy: Alternative medicine using herbs. (Some New Agers believe that these can be enchanted by invoking magic formulas.)

Incantation: The words spoken during a ritual or when casting a spell.

Initiation: in religious ethnology it is the cognitive and/or experiential journey whereby a person is admitted, either alone or as part of a group, by means of particular rituals to membership of a religious community, a secret society (e.g. Freemasonry) or a mystery association (magical, esoteric-occult, gnostic, theosophical etc.).

Karma: (from the Sanskrit root *Kri* = action, deed) a key notion in Hinduism, Jainism and Buddhism, but one whose meaning has not always been the same. In the ancient Vedic period it referred to the ritual action, especially sacrifice, by means of which a person gained access to the happiness or blessedness of the afterlife. When Jainism and Buddhism appeared (about 6 centuries before Christ), *Karma* lost its salvific meaning: the way to liberation was knowledge of the *Atman* or "self". In the doctrine of *samsara,* it was understood as the incessant cycle of human birth and death (Huinduism) or of rebirth (Buddhism). In *New Age* contexts, the "law of karma" is often seen as the moral equivalent of cosmic evolution. It is no longer to do with evil or suffering – illusions to be experienced as part of a "cosmic game" – but is the universal law of cause and effect, part of the tendency of the interconnected universe towards moral balance.

Monism: the metaphysical belief that differences between beings are illusory. There is only one universal being, of which every thing and every person is a part. Inasmuch as *New Age* monism includes the idea that reality is fundamentally spiritual, it is a contemporary form of pantheism (sometimes explicitly a rejection of materialism, particularly Marxism). Its claim to resolve all dualism leaves no room for a transcendent God, so everything *is* God. A further problem arises for Christianity when the question of the origin of evil is raised. C.G. Jung saw evil as the "shadow side" of the God who, in classical theism, is all goodness.

Mysticism: *New Age* mysticism is turning inwards on oneself rather than communion with God who is "totally other". It is fusion with the universe, an ultimate annihilation of the individual in the unity of the whole. Experience of Self is taken to be experience of divinity, so one looks within to discover authentic wisdom, creativity and power.

Neopaganism: a title often rejected by many to whom it is applied, it refers to a current that runs parallel to *New Age* and often interacts with it. In the great wave of reaction against traditional religions, specifically the Judaeo-Christian heritage of the West, many have revisited ancient indigenous, traditional, *pagan* religions. Whatever preceded Christianity is reckoned to be more genuine to the spirit of the land or the nation, an uncontaminated form of natural religion, in touch with the powers of nature, often matriarchal, magical or Shamanic. Humanity will, it is said, be healthier if it returns to the natural cycle of (agricultural) festivals and to a general affirmation of life. Some "neo-pagan" religions are recent reconstructions whose authentic relationship to original forms can be questioned, particularly in cases where they are dominated by modern ideological components like ecology, feminism or, in a few cases, myths of racial purity.

Lithomancy: A form of divination using crystals

Lucky Charm: An amulet that is worn to bring good luck. Sometimes the charm needs to be placed in a specific location in a person's house to be effective.

Mantra: An incantation of repetitive verses that are recited for the purpose of quieting the mind and contacting the spirit realm.

Numerology: A form of divination in which the value of numbers (or letters from the alphabet) is used to interpret mystical readings for a person's life.

Palmistry: A practice of telling fortunes from the lines, marks and patterns on a person's hand.

Pantheism: (Greek *pan* = everything and *theos* = God) the belief that everything is God or, sometimes, that everything is *in* God and God is in everything (panentheism). Every element of the universe is divine, and the divinity is equally present in everything. There is no space in this view for God as a distinct being in the sense of classical theism.

Psychic Birth: The birth of a person's psychic abilities.

Psychic Healing: An attempt to bring physical healing to a person by invoking supernatural powers from Reiki, hypnotism, or a number of other New Age practices.

Psychometry: A form of divination derived from physical contact with objects.

Reflexology: An ancient Chinese practice where a person's feet are massaged in an attempt to impart spiritual power to heal the body.

Reiki: A form of healing where supernatural powers are imparted into a person's body by using Reiki power symbols or by calling upon the names of the power symbols.

Reincarnation: This belief is prevalent among many involved in the New Age movement, or with Hinduism, Sikhism, and other Eastern religions. In a *New Age* context, reincarnation is linked to the concept of ascendant evolution towards becoming divine. As opposed to Indian religions or those derived from them, *New Age* views reincarnation as progression of the individual soul towards a more perfect state. What is reincarnated is essentially something immaterial or spiritual; more precisely, it is consciousness, that spark of energy in the person that shares in cosmic or "christic" energy. Death is nothing but the passage of the soul from one body to another.

Spell: An incantation accompanied by magical powers used to destroy a person, church or society.

Spirit Guide: A demonic entity that wants to enter a person's life. Once these entities have been granted permission to enter a person's life through the sin of idolatry, divination, sometimes unconsciously through certain New Age practices, or through a number of other occult practices, it is very difficult to get them to leave.

Spiritism: The belief that natural objects have indwelling spirits.

Superstition: An irrational belief or practice that a person feels he needs to embrace or perform in order to bring about good luck.

Tarot: Divination by use of Tarot cards. There are many different sets available like The Witches' Tarot, Celtic

Dragon Tarot, Egyptian Tarot, and even the Catholic Saints' Tarot.

Transcendental Meditation: A technique of meditation derived from Hindu traditions that promotes deep relaxation through the use of a mantra.

Transpersonal Technologies, the Movement for Inner Spiritual Awareness, Organisational Development and Organisational Transformation: are all put forward as non-religious, but in reality company employees can find themselves being submitted to an alien 'spirituality' in a situation which raises questions about personal freedom. There are clear links between Eastern spirituality and psychotherapy, while Jungian psychology and the Human Potential Movement have been very influential on Shamanism and "reconstructed" forms of Paganism like Druidry and Wicca. In a general sense, "personal growth" can be understood as the shape "religious salvation" takes in the *New Age* movement: it is affirmed that deliverance from human suffering and weakness will be reached by developing our human potential, which results in our increasingly getting in touch with our inner divinity.

Transmigration: A New Age belief that a soul can transfer itself into another body after death.

White magick: A form of magic where the participants [mistakenly] believe that they are casting "good spells" on other people, or helping the earth through positive forms of energy.

Wicca: The use of supernatural powers for the purpose of obtaining and exercising control over other people, circumstances or events.

Yoga: A Hindu system of body posture that uses meditation and mantras to help people to achieve spiritual enlightenment, increased flexibility and energy flow.

Zodiac: An ancient system of twelve signs in the sky used by New Agers to denote various eras which change every two thousand and one years. They believe that the year 2000 heralded "the dawning of the Age of Aquarius". The signs are based on the names of star constellations: Aquarius, Pisces, Aries, Taurus, Gemini, Cancer, Leo, Virgo, Libra, Scorpio, Sagittarius and Capricorn.

REFERENCES

Amorth, (Fr.) Gabriele, *An Exorcist Tells His Story*, Ignatius Press, San Francisco, 1994

Cuneo, Michael. W., *American Exorcism*, Random House, New York, 2001

Committee on Doctrine, United States Conference of Catholic Bishops, *Guidelines for Evaluation Reiki as an Alternative Therapy*, March 2009

Fortea, José Antonio: *Interview With An Exorcist*, Ascension Press, Pennsylvania, 2006

Glennon, Jim: *Your Healing is Within You*, Hodder & Stoughton, London, 1998

Heron, Benedict, (OSB): *I Saw Satan Fall,* New Life Publishing, Luton, 1997

Kiely, David M. & McKenna, Christina: *The Dark Sacrament (True Stories of Modern-Day Demon Possession and Exorcism),* Harper One, New York, 2007

MacNutt, Francis: *Deliverance from Evil Spirits*, Chosen Books, Michigan, 1995

McAll, Kenneth (Dr.): *Healing the Family Tree*, Sheldon Press, London, 1984

McCraw, Phillip C: *Self Matters: Creating Your Life from the Inside Out*, Free Press, London, 2001

McManus, Jim: *Healing in the Spirit*, Redemptorist Publications, Hampshire, 2002

Martin, Malachi, *Hostage to the Devil*, Harper One, San Francisco, 1992

Christian Healing Ministries, *Newsletter,* July 2009

O'Brien, (Fr.) Bartholomew, J., *The Curé of Ars*, Tan Books and Publishing, Inc., Illinois, 1957)

Olson, Dr. Ken, *Exorcism: Fact or Fiction?* Thomas Nelson Publishers, Nashville, 1992

Pontifical Council for Interreligious Dialogue, *Jesus Christ: The Bearer of the Water of Life (A Christian Reflection on the New Age),* The Vatican, 2003

Prince, Derek: *They Shall Expel Demons*, Derek Prince Ministries, Hertfordshire, 1998

Seewald, Peter, *Benedict XVI*, Ignatius Press, Fort Collins, Colorado, 2008

Shea, Dr. John B: *The Church and the New Age Movement*, Catholic Insight, Nov. 2005

Thérèse of Lisieux, *The Story of a Soul,* Tan Books and Publishers, Inc., Illinois, 1997

Wilkinson Tracy, *The Vatican's Exorcists*, Warner Books, New York, 2007

Dear Reader,

If you found this book helpful to your spirituality or in any way inspiring, I would really appreciate it if you please take a few moments to write a short review of it on Amazon's website.

Thank you for taking the time to read the book.

Kindest regards,
Brian O'Hare

Other books by Brian O'Hare:

Non-Fiction

A Spiritual Odyssey [*Diary of an Ordinary Catholic*]
Pub: Columba Press, Co. Dublin, 2005
[Now also available on Kindle]

Fiction

Fallen Men [*A Story of Three Priests*]
Soon to be re-issued by Crimson Cloak publishing

The Doom Murders
Soon to be re-issued by Crimson Cloak Publishing